Computer Communications and Networks

The Computer Communications and Networks series is a range of textbooks, monographs and handbooks. It sets out to provide students, researchers and nonspecialists alike with a sure grounding in current knowledge, together with comprehensible access to the latest developments in computer communications and networking.

Emphasis is placed on clear and explanatory styles that support a tutorial approach, so that even the most complex of topics is presented in a lucid and intelligible manner.

Richard Hill • Laurie Hirsch • Peter Lake
Siavash Moshiri

Guide to Cloud Computing

Principles and Practice

 Springer

Richard Hill
School of Computing and Mathematics
University of Derby
Derby, UK

Laurie Hirsch
Arts, Computing, Engineering and Sciences
Sheffield Hallam University
Sheffield, UK

Peter Lake
Arts, Computing, Engineering and Sciences
Sheffield Hallam University
Sheffield, UK

Siavash Moshiri
Metanova and Vistex Inc.
London, UK

Series Editor
A.J. Sammes
Centre for Forensic Computing
Cranfield University
Shrivenham campus
Swindon, UK

TOGAF is a registered trademark of The Open Group.

ISSN 1617-7975
ISBN 978-1-4471-5828-8   ISBN 978-1-4471-4603-2 (eBook)
DOI 10.1007/978-1-4471-4603-2
Springer London Heidelberg New York Dordrecht

To Dad

Richard Hill

To Andy McEwan

Laurie Hirsch

To my Dad and Julia

Peter Lake

To my wonderful family

Siavash Moshiri

Foreword

More so than most IT trends we have seen come and go over the past couple of decades, cloud computing has infiltrated the IT mainstream as a collection of innovations, technology advances and intelligent new applications of not-so-new IT models and technologies. The proliferation of cloud computing is a double-edged sword, readily swung by both professionals and amateurs alike. The broad commercialisation and attractive price points of public cloud computing platforms make cloud-based IT resources accessible to pretty much any organisation with interest and a sufficient credit rating. Methodology, governance and even a project plan are not prerequisites, leaving the door wide open for those who want to create (or recreate) convoluted and ineffective technology architectures that are distinguished from past failed on-premise environments only with the 'cloud' label.

In other words, cloud computing provides us with technology innovation that we must choose to apply based on how and to what extent it helps us fulfil our business requirements. It can improve scalability and reliability and provide cost-effective access to vast pools of resources—but it does not automatically help us improve how we align our business with IT automation, nor does it automatically improve our IT automation (even if it is already aligned). In fact, it can make things significantly worse, especially for those entering the nebulous cloud industry with tunnel vision.

Understanding and making the most of what cloud computing has to offer all comes down to education. This book provides clear guidance in the most essential areas of cloud computing, ranging from its technologies and models to its applications for real-world business. When it comes to considering or planning for cloud adoption, we must make educated decisions or not even attempt that path. Clarity amongst the clouds is critical to determining not just how cloud technologies can solve business problems, but what distinct problems introduced by cloud computing can be addressed and, hopefully, avoided.

Arcitura Education Inc. & CloudSchool.com   Thomas Erl

About Thomas Erl

Thomas Erl is a renown IT author, a speaker of international fame and founder of SOASchool.com® and CloudSchool.com™. Thomas is also the editor of the *SOA Magazine*. With over 140,000 copies in print world-wide, his seven published books in SOA related areas have become international bestsellers. As CEO of Arcitura Education Inc. and SOA Systems Inc. Thomas has led the development of curricula for the internationally recognized SOA Certified Professional (SOACP) and Cloud Certified Professional (CCP) accreditation programs.

Preface

Overview and Goals

Although the term cloud computing is relatively new, some of the concepts that underpin this rapidly expanding area of computing have been with us for a while. IT professionals need to be able to separate the hype from the facts and understand how the new platforms can help organisations become more efficient and more responsive to internal and external systems users.

A Guide to Cloud Computing: Principles and Practice addresses the need for a single text to describe the cloud computing landscape from first principles. It considers both the technologies involved in designing and creating cloud computing platforms and the business models and frameworks that result from the real-world implementation of those platforms.

Key objectives for this book include:
- Present an understanding of the key technologies involved in cloud computing
- Explore the potential use of cloud computing in a business environment
- Demonstrate the technologies and approaches utilised to build cloud computing infrastructure
- Understand the social, economic and political aspects of the ongoing growth in cloud computing use
- Consider the legal and security concerns of cloud computing, which may act as barriers to its success
- Identify areas for further research in a fast-moving domain

Organisation and Features

This book is organised into three parts:
- Part I introduces cloud computing concepts and principles.
- Part II discusses the technological aspects of cloud computing.
- Part III is devoted to issues and challenges with business aspects of cloud computing architecture, both now and in the future.

Target Audiences

A topic as disruptive as cloud computing immediately draws interest from a wide body of individuals. We have written this book to specifically support the following audiences:

Advanced undergraduate students and *postgraduate students* will find the combination of theoretical and practical examples of cloud computing, of particular relevance to a modern computer science, software engineering, computer networking, distributed systems or any course that makes reference to the latest developments in computing as a utility. As such, *university instructors* may adopt this book as a core text. Similarly, *researchers* will find the direct application of theory to practice of use, especially when using clouds for research projects.

Since this book adopts a learning-by-doing approach, the extensive worked examples that explain how to construct a cloud platform will no doubt be relevant to *IT infrastructure technicians*, as well as *application developers* who will also be able to understand the issues faced when developing upon a cloud platform.

Business leaders, IT infrastructure managers and *technical consultants* will have a need to understand how cloud computing can positively affect their organisations and will find the chapters on adoption strategies, financial appraisal, security and governance of particular interest, when they are faced with making critical strategic and operational decisions.

Suggested Uses

Guide to Cloud Computing: Principles and Practice can be used as a solid introduction to the concept of computing resource as a utility, and as such it is suggested that readers acquaint themselves with Part I of this book to start with.

This book is suitable as both a comprehensive introduction to cloud computing, as well as a reference text, as the reader develops their skills and abilities through practical application of the ideas. For *university instructors*, we suggest the following programme of study for a 12-week semester format:

- Weeks 1–2: Part I
- Weeks 3–7: Part II
- Weeks 8–11: Part III
- Week 12: Assessment

Part I defines what cloud computing is and places it in context by comparing it with its underlying technologies. It also examines some of the typical cloud models from a business perspective. Themes such as cloud types, cloud deployment models and sustainability are covered.

Part II elaborates upon cloud technologies, service models and data storage within the cloud environment. It also introduces knowledge discovery through intelligent analysis of structured and unstructured data, a rapidly emerging area of cloud development. It introduces topics such as virtualisation, scaling beyond traditional relational models, collective intelligence and visualisation.

Part III examines the business context of cloud. It addresses the strategic context of the cloud option and the mechanisms used to extract business value from cloud investments. These chapters introduce topics such as cloud economics, investment appraisal for cloud, strategic planning, cloud security and Enterprise Cloud Computing.

Review Questions

Each chapter concludes with a set of review questions that make specific reference to the content presented in the chapter, plus an additional set of further questions that will require further research. The review questions are designed in such a way that the reader will be able to answer them based on the chapter contents. They are followed by discussion questions that often require research, extended reading of other material or discussion and collaboration. These can be used as classroom discussion topics by tutors and prompts for extended self-study research or used as the basis of summative assignments.

Hands-On Exercises

The technology chapters include extended hands-on exercises, commencing with the installation of a virtual machine (VM). Readers will then use the VM to practice cloud environment configuration, before progressively engaging in more complex activities, building skills and knowledge along the way. Such an approach ensures that a solid foundation is built before more advanced topics are undertaken. To facilitate the maximum uptake of this learning experience, only open source technologies that are freely available for download have been utilised.

Chapter Summary

A brief summary of each of the twelve chapters is as follows.

Chapter 1 is an introduction to cloud computing, and we define what is meant by the cloud. The cloud is placed in its historical context and some of the key concepts such as service orientation, virtualisation and utility computing are described.

In Chap. 2, we examine the different approaches that can be taken when implementing cloud-based solutions and discuss how an organisation can begin to evaluate which approach is right for them. We then go on to look at the legal implications of this fundamental shift in business practice.

In Chap. 3, we examine the impact of the cloud on society, economy and politics. We look at how people around the globe are beginning to use cloud as a way to provide them with more influence than traditional decision-making approaches. We go on to critically review the claims that cloud computing offers a 'greener', more sustainable approach to IT.

Chapter 4 reviews the current state of web, virtualisation and distributed computing technology. We examine how the underlying technologies support key cloud features such as elasticity and scalability. At the end of the chapter, you will build a simple system using MapReduce.

Chapter 5 examines the architecture of cloud systems focusing on the layered model often referred to as the 'cloud stack'. In particular we examine infrastructure as a service (IaaS), platform as a service (PaaS) and software as a service (SaaS) using examples. At the end of the chapter, readers build a cloud application using Google App Engine.

In Chap. 6, we begin by examining the myriad types of data that are found in organisations. We then go on to look at different ways of storing that data, many of which have sprung to prominence because of the cloud. We also look at cloud-based solutions to a typical database administrator's tasks, such as backup and disaster recovery.

In Chap. 7, we discuss various approaches to extracting useful information from data stored in the cloud. In particular, we examine approaches to utilising user-generated content in an intelligent way, to produce practical functionality such as recommendation engines.

In Chap. 8, we consider the strategic context of business investment into cloud computing by discussing key economic drivers. Approaches to investment appraisal are also considered, illustrating how common financial techniques can be used to assemble a business case for cloud adoption (or rejection).

Chapter 9 considers the topic of Enterprise Cloud Computing; how can the business potential of cloud computing be utilised to develop enhanced customer-centric systems? This chapter explores cloud services, as a fundamental building block of the service-oriented enterprise, and introduces enterprise architecture as a proactive means of managing emergent IT infrastructure.

Chapter 10 examines the impact of cloud computing upon security and governance, in particular the use of public cloud services. Approaches to mitigate security risks are described in terms of processes, methods and applicable technologies for protection against accidental and malicious threats.

In Chap. 11, we take the reader through the process of developing a strategic roadmap for cloud adoption, including the selection of appropriate tools and techniques to assist strategic decision-making, as well as understanding the importance of demonstrating business and technological alignment.

Finally, in Chap. 12, we note that the future of cloud computing, like much in the IT arena, is unpredictable. We attempt to highlight drivers and barriers that can help anticipate cloud trends, and report what some experts have said, that might help us make sense of the uncertainty.

Contents

Part I

Cloud Computing Fundamentals

Introducing Cloud Computing

1

What the reader will learn:

- That 'cloud computing' is a relatively new term, and it is important to clearly define what we mean
- Cloud computing is a new delivery model for IT but that it uses established IT resources
- That the concept of abstraction is critical to the implementation of cloud architectures
- Businesses will adopt cloud computing because it offers financial benefits and business agility, not because the technology is inherently 'better'

1.1 What Is Cloud Computing?

Everybody seems to be talking about cloud computing. As technology trends go, cloud computing is generating a lot of interest, and along with that interest is a share of hype as well. The aim of this book is to provide you with a sophisticated under-standing of what cloud computing is and where it can offer real business advantage. We shall be examining cloud computing from historical, theoretical and practical perspectives, so that you will know *what* to use, in *which* situation, and *when* it will be most appropriate.

So first of all, just what is cloud computing? This isn't such a silly question. That many things now attract the cloud computing badge, that it is difficult to understand what cloud actually means.

In a nutshell, cloud computing is a means by which computational power, storage, collaboration infrastructure, business processes and applications can be delivered as a utility, that is, a service or collection of services that meet your demands. Since services offered by cloud are akin to a utility, it also means that you only pay for what you use. If you need extra processing power quickly, it is available for use in an instant. When you've finished with the extra power and revert back to your nominal

R. Hill et al., *Guide to Cloud Computing: Principles and Practice*, Computer Communications and Networks, DOI 10.1007/978-1-4471-4603-2_1,
© Springer-Verlag London 2013

usage, you will only be billed for the short time that you needed the extra boost. So you don't need to invest in a lot of hardware to cater for your peak usage, accepting that for most of the time it will be underutilised. This aspect of the cloud is referred to as *elasticity* and is an extremely important concept within cloud computing.

That's the short answer and not necessarily the key to becoming an expert in cloud computing; for some extra information, read on. To understand what makes a cloud different from other established models of computing, we shall need to consider the conceptual basis of computing as a utility and how technology has evolved to date.

1.2   Utility Computing

Utility computing was discussed by John McCarthy in the 1960s whilst working at Massachusetts Institute of Technology (McCarthy 1983), and the concept was thoroughly expanded by Douglas Parkhill in 1966 (The Challenge of the Computing Utility, Parkhill 1966). Parkhill examined the nature of utilities such as water, natural gas and electricity in the way they are provided to create an understanding of the characteristics that computing would require if it was truly a utility. When we consider electricity supply, for example, in the developed world, we tend to take it for granted that the actual electrical power will be available in our dwellings. To access it, we plug our devices into wall sockets and draw the power we need. Every so often we are billed by the electricity supply company, and we pay for what we have used. In the summer time, the daylight hours are longer and we place less demand on devices that provide lighting, hot water or space heating. During the winter months, we use electric lighting and space heating more, and therefore, we expect our bills to reflect the extra usage we make of the utility. Additionally, we do not expect the electricity to 'run out'; unless there is a power cut, there should be a never-ending supply of electricity.

So the same goes for computing resources as a utility. We should expect the resource to be available where we want, by plugging into or by accessing a network. The resource should cater for our needs, as our needs vary, and it should appear to be a limitless supply. Finally, we expect to pay only for what we use. We tend to consider the provision of utilities as services.

1.3   Service Orientation

The term *service orientation* refers to the clear demarcation of a function that operates to satisfy a particular goal. For instance, businesses are composed of many discrete services that should sustainably deliver value to customers now and in the future. Utility companies offer their services in the form of energy supply, billing and perhaps, as energy conservation becomes more widespread, services that support a customer's attempt to reduce their energy consumption. The services that are offered to the consumer are likely to be aggregations of much finer-grained services that operate internally to the business. It is this concept of *abstraction*, combined with object-oriented principles such as *encapsulation* and *cohesion*, that helps define services within an organisation.

Service-oriented architecture (SOA) utilises the principle of service orientation to organise the overall technology architecture of an enterprise. This means that technology is selected, specified and integrated to support an architectural model that is specified as a set of services. Such an approach results in technologically unique architectures for each enterprise, in order to realise the best possible chance of supporting the services that the business requires. However, whilst the overall architecture may appear bespoke, the underlying services are discrete and often reusable and therefore may be shared even between organisations. For instance, the processing of payroll information is common to most enterprises of a certain size and is a common choice for service outsourcing to third-party suppliers.

From an organisation's perspective, SOA has some key advantages:

- The adoption of the principles of service orientation enables commonly utilised functionality to be reused, which significantly simplifies the addition of new functionality, since a large portion of the existing code base is already present. Additionally, the emergence of standard protocols for service description and invocation means that the actual service is abstracted away from the implementation program code, so it doesn't matter if the constituent parts of a newly composed service are implemented in different ways, as long as their specification conforms to a commonly declared interface contract.
- Changes in business demand that require new services to be specified can be accommodated much easier, and it is quicker to react to business market forces. This means that an SOA is much more fleet of foot, enabling new business opportunities to be explored quickly with less cost.
- The abstraction of service also facilitates consideration of the enterprise's performance at the process level; quality of service (QoS), lead times and defect rates become more obvious measures to observe and therefore targets to specify, since the underlying complexity is shrouded behind a service declaration.
- Tighter integration along value chains is enabled, as a particular functionality can be made available as a service between an enterprise and its satellite suppliers. A supplier may deal with several business customers, and it might not be practical to adopt a number of different systems to integrate with. SOA simplifies this by the publication of services that suppliers can 'hook into' with their own systems. This has the added advantage that any changes to a customer's system are encapsulated behind the service description, and therefore, no other modifications will be required from those that consume that service.

Service orientation and its architectural model SOA are key concepts for the realisation of utility computing. Now, we shall consider some technological developments that can support this realisation. Later, in Chap. 5, we shall encounter SOA again, where you will be building a Google App as an exemplar use of web services.

Fig. 1.1 Overview of grid
computing architecture

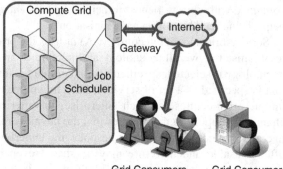

1.4   Grid Computing

Grid computing emerged in the 1990s, as Ian Foster and Carl Kesselman suggested
that access to compute resources should be the same as connecting to a power grid to
obtain electricity (Foster and Kesselman 1999). The need for this was simple:
Supercomputers that could process large data sets were prohibitively expensive for
many areas of research. As an alternative, the connection and coordination of many
separate personal computers (PC) as a grid would facilitate the scaling up of computational resources under the guise of a virtual organisation (VO). Each user of the VO,
by being connected to the grid, had access to computational resources far greater than
they owned, enabling larger scientific experiments to be conducted by spreading
the load across multiple machines. Figure 1.1 gives a brief overview of a grid architecture. A number of separate compute and storage resources are interconnected
and managed by a resource that schedules computational jobs across the grid. The collective compute resource is then connected to the Internet via a gateway. Consumers of
the grid resource then access the grid by connecting to the Internet.

As network speeds and storage space have increased over the years, there has
been a greater amount of redundant computational resource that lays idle. Projects
such as the Search for Extraterrestrial Intelligence (SETI@HOME, http://setiathome.
berkeley.edu/) have made use of this by scavenging processing cycles from PCs that
are either doing nothing or have low demands placed upon them. If we consider how
computer processors have developed in a relatively short time span, and then we
look at the actual utilisation of such computational power, particularly in the office
desktop environment, there are a lot of processor cycles going spare. These machines
are not always used during the night or at lunch breaks, but they are often left
switched on and connected to a network infrastructure. Grid computing can harness
this wastage and put it to some predefined, productive use.

One characteristic of grid computing is that the software that manages a grid
should enable the grid to be formed quickly and be tolerant of individual machines
(or nodes) leaving at will. If you are scavenging processor cycles from someone

else's PC, you have to be prepared for them turning their machine off without prior warning. The rapid setup is required so that a grid can be assembled to solve a particular problem. This has tended to support scientific applications, where some heavy analysis is required for a data set over a short period, and then it is back to normal with the existing resources when the analysis is done. Collaboration and contribution from participants has been generally on a voluntary basis, which is often the basis of shared ventures in a research environment.

Whilst grid computing has started to realise the emergence of computing resources as a utility, two significant challenges have hindered its uptake outside of research. Firstly, the ad hoc, self-governing nature of grids has meant that it is difficult to isolate the effect of poorly performing nodes on the rest of the grid. This might occur if a node cannot process a job at a suitable rate or a node keeps leaving the grid before a batch job is completed. Secondly, the connection of many machines together brings with it a heterogeneous collection of software, operating systems and configurations that cannot realistically be considered by the grid software developer. Thus, grid applications tend to lack portability, since they are written with a specific infrastructure in mind.

1.5　Hardware Virtualisation

Hardware virtualisation is a developing technology that is exploiting the continued increase in processor power, enabling 'virtual' instances of hardware to execute on disparate physical infrastructure. This technology has permitted organisations such as data centres to improve the utilisation and management of their own resources by building virtual layers of hardware across the numerous physical machines that they own. The virtualisation layer allows data centre management to create and instantiate new instances of virtual hardware irrespective of the devices running underneath it. Conversely, new hardware can be added to the pool of resource and commissioned without affecting the virtualised layer, except in terms of the additional computational power/storage/memory capability that is being made available. Figure 1.2 illustrates the key parts of a virtualised architecture. Working from the physical hardware layer upwards, firstly there is a *hypervisor*. The role of the hypervisor is to provide a means by which virtual machines can access and communicate with the hardware layer, without installing an operating system. On top of the hypervisor, *virtual machines* (VM) are installed. Each VM appears to function as a discrete computational resource, even though it does not physically exist. A host *operating system* (OS) is installed upon each VM, thus enabling traditional computing applications to be built on top of the OS.

Virtualisation offers three key advantages for data centre management. Firstly, applications can be confined to a particular virtual machine (VM) appliance, which increases security and isolates any detrimental effect of poor performance on the rest of the data centre. Secondly, the consolidation of disparate platforms onto a unified hardware layer means that physical utilisation can be better managed, leading to increased energy efficiency. Thirdly, virtualisation allows guest operating systems

Fig. 1.2 Virtualisation
overview

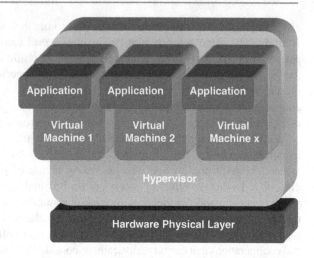

to be stored as snapshots to retain any bespoke configuration settings, which allows images to be restored rapidly in the event of a disaster. This feature also facilitates the user capture of provenance data so that particular situations can be realistically recreated for forensic investigation purposes or to recreate a specific experimental environment. Virtualisation is discussed in more detail in Chap. 4.

1.6 Autonomic Computing

As computing technology becomes more complex, there is a corresponding desire to delegate as much management as possible to automated systems. *Autonomic computing* attempts to specify behaviours that enable the self-management of systems. Self-configuration, self-healing, self-optimising and self-protection (otherwise known as self-CHOP) are the four principles defined by IBM's autonomic computing initiative (IBM Research 2012). If we consider the cloud computing concept of elasticity, we can see that to obtain the 'resource-on-demand' feature will require a variety of computational resources to be configured and, once running, optimised for performance.

If we now consider a grid architecture as a computational resource, then the operations described above will need to take into account some more aspects particular to the technologies involved, including disparate and heterogeneous hardware and software standards. Finally, if we add to the mix hardware virtualisation, there will be a requirement to instantiate and migrate virtual machines (VM) across disparate hardware, dynamically as demand dictates. Such is the complexity of myriad physical and virtualised hardware architectures and software components, that it is essential that this management is automated if true, seamless elasticity is to be realised.

We have now explored the key concepts and technologies that have shaped the emergence of cloud computing, so we shall now explore a more formal definition and observe how this informs the present description of cloud computing architectures.

1.7   Cloud Computing: A Definition

It won't take you long to find a number of 'definitions' of cloud computing. The World Wide Web is awash with attempts to capture the essence of distributed, elastic computing that is available as a utility. There appears to be some stabilisation occurring with regard to an accepted definition, and for the purposes of this book, we'll be persevering with that offered by the National Institute of Standards and Technology (NIST):

> Cloud computing is a model for enabling ubiquitous, convenient, on-demand network access to a shared pool of configurable computing resources (e.g., networks, servers, storage, applications, and services) that can be rapidly provisioned and released with minimal management effort or service provider interaction. This cloud model is composed of five essential characteristics, three service models, and four deployment models.
>
> NIST, US Department of Commerce, http://csrc.nist.gov/publications/nistpubs/800-145/SP800-145.pdf

The essential characteristics that NIST's definition refers to are as follows:

- *On-demand self-service*. Traditionally, hosted computing has enabled consumers to outsource the provision of IT infrastructure, such as data storage, so that hardware purchases could be minimised. However, whilst these solutions allowed customers to increase the storage available without purchasing any extra hardware, the request for data storage was typically an order that was fulfilled some time later. The time lag between request and actual availability meant that such increases had to be planned for and could not be depended upon as a reactive resource. Cloud computing should incorporate sufficient agility and autonomy, that requests for more resource are automatically and dynamically provisioned in real time, without human intervention.
- *Broad network access*. As a utility, cloud computing resources must be available over networks such as the Internet, using established mechanisms and standard protocols. Access devices can include (though are not limited to) personal computers, portable computers, mobile phones and tablet devices.
- *Resource pooling*. This characteristic brings together aspects of grid computing (where multiple compute resources are connected together in a coordinated way) and hardware virtualisation. The virtualised layer enables the resources of a cloud computing provider to be pooled together into one large virtual resource, enabling large-scale efficiencies to be achieved by the dynamic management of hardware and virtualised resources. This results in the appearance of homogenous resources to the consumer, without indicating the physical location or granularity of that resource.
- *Rapid elasticity*. Requests for extra resource are self-managed and automatic in relation to demand. From the consumer's perspective, the supply of compute resources is limitless.
- *Measured service*. In the same way that energy usage can be monitored, controlled and reported, cloud computing resource providers dynamically optimise the underlying infrastructure and provide a transparent metering service at a level of abstraction that is relevant to the consumer.

Fig. 1.3 Cloud service
models

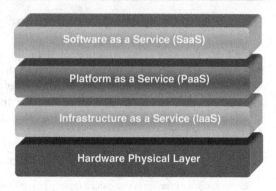

One theme that is emerging here is that of abstraction; the characteristics above are reliant upon a fundamental architecture of hardware resources that are discrete and varied, upon which there is an abstraction layer of software that realises the characteristics of cloud computing. The physical hardware resource layer includes processor, storage and networking components, and the abstraction layer consists of at least a self-managed virtualisation infrastructure.

1.8 Cloud Computing Service Models

Of course, in cloud-speak we refer to services, and there are three categories of service model described by NIST as illustrated in Fig. 1.3. Working from the physical layer upwards, the first service model layer is known as Infrastructure as a Service (IaaS).

IaaS is usually the lowest level service available to a cloud computing consumer and provides controlled access to a virtual infrastructure upon which operating systems and application software can be deployed. This can be seen as a natural extension of an existing hardware provision, without the hassle and expense of buying and managing the hardware. As such, there is no control over the physical hardware, but the consumer retains control over operating system parameters and some aspects of security. There is a trend emerging for 'bare metal' services, where access to the hardware at its most basic is provided, but this is more akin to traditional data centre or 'hosting' services. For the majority of potential cloud consumers, there is a desire to move away from as much of the detail as possible and therefore progress upwards through the cloud service model stack.

Platform as a Service (PaaS) sits atop IaaS. This layer is ready for applications to be deployed, as the necessary operating system and platform-related tools such as language compilers are already installed and managed by the cloud computing provider. Consumers may be able to extend the existing tool set by installing their own tools, but absolute control of the infrastructure is still retained by the provider. Thus, the consumer has control over application development, deployment and configuration, within the confines of the hosted environment. This situation has most in common with traditional web hosting, where consumers rented remote servers that had existing development platforms installed upon them. The key difference with cloud computing in this case, however, is the rapid provisioning or elasticity; classic web hosting relied upon manual management of provisioning and therefore required human intervention if demand increased or decreased.

Finally (for the NIST definition), there is Software as a Service (SaaS). This service model abstracts the consumer away from any infrastructure or platform level detail by concentrating upon the application level. Applications are available via thin client interfaces such as internet browsers or program interfaces such as mobile phone apps. Google's Gmail is one popular example of a cloud computing application. An organisation can adopt Gmail and never concern itself with hardware maintenance, uptime, security patching or even infrastructure management. The consumer can control parameters within the software to configure specific aspects, but such interventions are managed through the interface of the application. The end user gets an email service and does not worry as to how it is provided.

So far, we have described the essential characteristics of cloud computing and then three different service models. As the abstraction concept develops, consumers are finding new ways of using cloud computing to leverage business advantage through the creation of a Business Process as a Service model (BPaaS). Strictly speaking, this sits within SaaS and is not a fourth layer which would fall outside of the NIST definition. We shall revisit this service model later in Chap. 4, so for the time being, we shall consider the models by which cloud computing can be deployed.

1.9   Cloud Computing Deployment Models

A *public cloud*, as its name implies, is available to the general public and is managed by an organisation. The organisation may be a business (such as Google), academic or a governmental department. The cloud computing provider owns and manages the cloud infrastructure. The existence of many different consumers within one cloud architecture is referred to as a multi-tenancy model.

Conversely, a *private cloud* has an exclusive purpose for a particular organisation. The cloud resources may be located on or off premise and could be owned and managed by the consuming organisation or a third party. This may be an example of an organisation who has decided to adopt the infrastructure cost-saving potential of a virtualised architecture on top of existing hardware. The organisation feels unable to remotely host their data, so they are looking to the cloud to improve their resource utilisation and automate the management of such resources. Alternatively an organisation may wish to extend its current IT capability by using an exclusive, private cloud that is remotely accessible and provisioned by a third party. Such an organisation may feel uncomfortable with their data being held alongside a potential competitor's data in the multi-tenancy model.

Community clouds are a model of cloud computing where the resources exist for a number of parties who have a shared interest or cause. This model is very similar to the single-purpose grids that collaborating research and academic organisations have created to conduct large-scale scientific experiments (e-science). The cloud is owned and managed by one or more of the collaborators in the community, and it may exist either on or off premise.

Hybrid clouds are formed when more than one type of cloud infrastructure is utilised for a particular situation. For instance, an organisation may utilise a public cloud for some aspect of its business, yet also have a private cloud on premise for data that is sensitive. As organisations start to exploit cloud service models, it is increasingly likely that a hybrid model is adopted as the specific characteristics of each of the different service models are harnessed. The key enabler here is the open standards by which data and applications are implemented, since if portability does not exist, then vendor lock-in to a particular cloud computing provider becomes likely. Lack of data and application portability has been a major hindrance for the widespread uptake of grid computing, and this is one aspect of cloud computing that can facilitate much more flexible, abstract architectures.

At this point, you should now have a general understanding of the key concepts of cloud computing and be able to apply this knowledge to a number of common use cases in order to hypothesise as to whether a particular cloud service model might be appropriate. The next part of this chapter will dig a bit deeper into the deployment models and explore some finer-grained challenges and opportunities that cloud computing presents.

1.10   A Quick Recap

Before we proceed, let us just quickly summarise what we understand by cloud computing:

- It's a model of computing that abstracts us away from the detail. We can have broad network access to computing resources without the hassle of owning and maintaining them.
- Cloud computing providers pool resources together and offer them as a utility. Through the use of hardware virtualisation and autonomic computing technologies, the consumer sees one homogenous, 'unlimited' supply of compute resource.
- Computing resources can be offered at different levels of abstraction, according to requirements. Consumers can work at infrastructure level (IaaS) and manage operating systems on virtualised hardware, at platform level (PaaS) using the operating systems and development environments provided, or at application level (SaaS), where specific applications are offered by the provider to be configured by the consumer.
- Cloud computing provides metered usage of the resource so that consumers pay only for what they use. When the demand for more computing resource goes up, the bill increases. When the demand falls, the bill reduces accordingly.
- Cloud computing can be deployed publicly in a multi-tenancy model (public cloud), privately for an individual organisation (private cloud), across a community

of consumers with a shared interest (community cloud), or a mixture of two or more models (hybrid cloud).

1.11 Beyond the Three Service Models

The explanations and discussions so far have allowed us to gain a broad understanding of cloud computing. However, like most things in life, it isn't that simple. When chief executive officers declare that an organisation will embrace 'the cloud', the chief information officer (CIO) may be less enthusiastic. We shall now consider more deeply some of the business drivers and service models for cloud adoption and explore the issues that these drivers can present.

1.11.1 The Business Perspective

Large IT vendors have realised for some time that new technology is sold most successfully on its ability to improve profitability. Grid computing and service-oriented architecture (SOA) are two relatively recent examples. Grid computing has demonstrated massive benefits when disparate compute resources are harnessed together to do supercomputing on the cheap. The problem was that the software and protocols that made these large distributed systems perform were inaccessible to those outside of the grid community. Vendors such as IBM and Oracle have both attempted to sell the advantages to business of grid computing, but the lack of realisation of the concept of utility (which informed the selection of the name 'grid') has meant that insufficient consumers were interested and the ultimate benefits could not be enjoyed.

SOA has had a similar 'reduce your business costs' drive over the years, with many organisations reporting an overall increase in expenditure after the costs of migrating to SOA have been accounted for. So what is different about cloud computing?

One of the attractions of cloud computing is the rapid provisioning of new compute resources without capital expenditure. If the marketing director makes claims about a new market niche, then it is much more cost-effective to experiment with new products and services, since cloud computing removes traditional barriers such as raising capital funds, lengthy procurement procedures and human resource investment. Also, if cloud computing is already part of the organisation's IT infrastructure, then new requests merely become additional demands upon the systems, rather than designing and specifying new systems from scratch. Business agility is therefore one key driver for the adoption of cloud computing.

The other key business driver is the potential reduction in ongoing capital expenditure costs afforded by cloud computing. As the use of IT becomes more sophisticated, greater demands are placed upon IT fundamentals such as data storage, and if the requirements fluctuate significantly, the pay-per-use model of cloud computing can realise operational savings beyond the costs of the potential extra hardware requirement.

1.12   When Can the Service Models Help?

1.12.1 Infrastructure as a Service

As described earlier, IaaS is about servers, networking and storage delivered as a service. These resources will actually be virtualised, though the consumer wouldn't know any different. The resources may come with or without an operating system. IaaS is a form of computing rental where the billing is related to actual usage, rather than ownership of a discrete number of servers. When the consumer wants more 'grunt', the IaaS management software dynamically provisions more resources as required. Typically, there will be an agreed limit between the consumer and the provider, beyond which further authorisation is required to continue scaling upwards (and thus incur extra cost). IaaS is particularly suited to organisations who want to retain control over the whole platform and software stack and who need extra infrastructure quickly and cheaply. For instance, the research and development department of an organisation may have specific applications that run on optimised platforms. Sporadically, applications are required to process massive data sets. Using a cloud, it would cost the same to have 500 processors run for 1 hour, as it does to run 1 processor for 500 hours, so the research unit opts for speed without having to invest in hardware that would be nominally underutilised.

1.12.2 Platform as a Service

PaaS has parallels with web hosting, in that it is a complete set of software that enables the complete application development life cycle within a cloud. This includes the tools for development and testing as well as the actual execution environment. As with IaaS, the resources are dynamically scaled, and for the most part, this is handled transparently by the cloud provider without making any extra demands upon the developer. For specialist applications that require low-level optimisation, either IaaS or a private cloud is more suitable. One of the potential drawbacks of PaaS is lack of portability and therefore vendor lock-in, as you are developing applications with the tool sets that are supplied by the cloud provider. If, at a later date, you would like to move provider or you want to use another cloud service concurrently, there may be a substantial effort required to port your application across to another vendor's cloud platform. PaaS is a good option if your existing application's development environment is matched by that of a cloud provider or if you would like to experiment with new products and services that can be rapidly composed from pre-existing services that are provided by the platform.

1.12.3 Software as a Service

In some ways, SaaS is the easiest way into cloud computing. You see some software and you try it out for a limited time. If you like it, you continue and start paying to use it, otherwise you look for something else. The software automatically scales to the number of users you have (but you don't notice this), and your data is backed up. You will probably have to invest a bit of time in getting your existing data into the application, and any tweaks to existing systems that you have may also require some work to get them to connect to your new cloud application. SaaS is useful if you are in the situation whereby a legacy application you own has been replicated by a SaaS provider or if a particular SaaS application offers a capability that you don't currently have but can see the business benefit of having it. Customer Relationship Management (CRM) is one example; many organisations operate without CRM systems as they can be expensive and it is impossible to justify the initial investment. Salesforce.com saw the opportunity to bring enterprise-level CRM to the masses via SaaS and has subsequently opened up their own platform, Force.com, as part of a PaaS service model.

Applications like CRM SaaS have enabled organisations to abstract themselves away from the infrastructure headaches, and as a result, they can think more about the actual business workflows that take place. Whilst it would seem that SaaS is all about pre-packaged software, the vendors have realised that consumers should be able to configure these offerings so that the application can be suitably customised to integrate with existing systems. This has led to a new interest in the abstraction of business process management (BPM), whereby organisational units create high-level process descriptions of their operations, within software that interfaces the process descriptions to an underlying, transactional code base. This offers substantial benefits including:

- No knowledge of the underlying program code is required.
- Process descriptions are closer to the real operations and are easier to derive and communicate between business users.
- Process optimisation and waste identification is simplified and easier to implement.
- Process commonality is more visible, and therefore, process reuse is more prominent, both internally within an organisation and outside of the normal process boundaries with suppliers.
- Libraries of process descriptions enables the rapid composition of new processes.

From a conceptual stance, Business Process as a Service (BPaaS) might be viewed as a fourth layer, above SaaS, but from an architectural perspective, it is clearly a subset of SaaS as Fig. 1.4 illustrates.

BPaaS creates new opportunities for organisations to exploit the cloud, as the abstraction away from technical and integration issues gives organisations a new way to conduct their business. This topic will be explored more fully in Chap. 10, which is all about *enterprise* cloud computing.

Fig. 1.4 Business process as
a service (BPaaS) in the
context of the cloud
computing stack

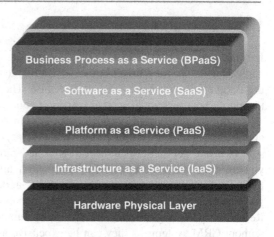

1.13   Issues for Cloud Computing

As with any new approach or technology, there are limits by which benefits can be
realised, and a new way of working may introduce additional risks. Cloud computing is no different in this respect, particularly as the model is still maturing.

From a consumer's perspective there is a great deal of focus upon security and
trust. Many users are ambivalent about where 'their' data is stored, whereas other
users (specifically organisations) are more sceptical about delegating the location of
the data along with the management processes that go with it. For many smaller
organisations, the cloud computing providers will be bringing enterprise-level security
to the masses as part of the offering. Most private individuals and small businesses
are unaware of the risks of lost data and the adverse impact that it can have upon
daily operations. As a consequence, it is likely that they have not put the appropriate
security measures in place. In this case, a move towards the cloud can bring real
benefits.

However, there may be specific legislation that exists to govern the physical
location of data; a multi-tenanted public cloud may place your data in a country that
is outside the scope of the jurisdiction that you need to comply with. Additionally,
the notion of service as a core component of the cloud leads to new service composition from readily available services. The use of third-party services potentially
introduces security and privacy risks, which may therefore require an additional
auditing overhead if the services are to be successfully and reliably trusted.

Another concern is that of vendor lock-in. If an organisation utilises IaaS, it may
find that the platforms and applications that it builds upon this service cannot be
transferred to another cloud computing provider. Similarly, services at PaaS and
SaaS can also introduce nonstandard ways of storing and accessing data, making
data or application portability problematic.

Quality of service (QoS) is an issue that many organisations already face either
as consumers or providers of services. Whilst cloud computing providers offer

measurement and monitoring functions for billing, it might be considered incumbent upon consumers to develop their own monitoring mechanisms to inform any future actions.

Much has been claimed about the potential energy-saving opportunities of organisations moving to the cloud. The ability to pool resources and dynamically manage how these resources are provisioned will of course permit computing resource usage to be more optimised. However, there is an assumption that this occurs at a certain scale, and perhaps less obviously, it is dependent upon the service model required. For instance, an IT department may decide to evaluate the potential of hardware virtualisation as part of a private cloud. The hardware already exists, and the maintenance costs are known. In theory, the more flexible provisioning that cloud architectures offer should release some extra compute resources. In terms of any investment in cooling, for example, then better utilisation of the existing hardware will come cheaper than the purchase of additional air-conditioning units.

Unfortunately, it is only through the provision of compute resources on a massive scale that significant amounts of resource can be redeployed for the benefit of others. The private cloud may be able to scavenge extra processor cycles for heavier computational tasks, but storage management may not be that different from that achieved by a storage area network (SAN) architecture. Thus, significant energy savings can only be realised by using the services of a cloud provider to reduce the presence of physical hardware on premise.

It follows therefore, that it is the massive data centres who offer SaaS that can maximise scalability whilst significantly reducing energy usage. For everyone else, energy reduction might not be a primary motivator for adopting a private cloud architecture.

Of course, as organisations move to the cloud, there is a heightened awareness of measures of availability and the financial impact that a temporary withdrawal of a service might incur. Good practice would suggest that there should be 'no single point of failure', and at first glance a cloud-based system would offer all the resource redundancy that an organisation might want. However, whilst the IaaS, PaaS or SaaS may be built upon a distributed system, the management and governance is based upon one system. If Google or Microsoft went bust, then any reliance upon their comprehensive facilities could be catastrophic. This risk gets greater the higher up the cloud stack that the engagement occurs—if Salesforce.com collapsed, then a great deal of an organisation's business logic would disappear along with the data, all wrapped up in a SaaS application.

Software bugs are a major concern for all software development activity, and many instances of 'undocumented features' occur only when an application is under significant load. In the case of a distributed system, it is not always practical to recreate the open environment conditions, so there remains the potential risk that something catastrophic might occur. Hardware virtualisation can be a way of containing the scope of software bugs, but as many SaaS vendors created their offerings before the widespread use of virtualisation, this form of architectural protection cannot be relied upon. This is clearly a case for open architectural standards for cloud architectures to be established.

As cloud use increases, organisations will place ever-increasing demands that present significant data transfer bottlenecks. Additionally, the distributed architecture of a cloud application may result in a data transfer that would not have occurred had the application been hosted in one physical space. Even though network speeds are getting faster, in some cases the volume of data to be transferred is so large that it is cheaper and quicker to physically transport media between data centres. Of course this only works for data that is not 'on demand' and therefore is relevant when data needs to be exported from one system and imported into another.

With regard to the benefits of scalability, the case for optimising processor cycles across a vast number of units is clear; processors can be utilised to perform a computation and then returned back to a pool to wait for the next job. However, this does not translate as easily to persistent storage, where in general the requirement just continues to increase. Methods for dealing with storage in a dynamic way, that preserve the performance characteristics expected from an application that queries repositories, have yet to be developed and remain a potential issue for cloud computing going forward.

1.14   Summing Up

Cloud computing is a new delivery model for IT that uses established IT resources. The Internet, hardware virtualisation, remote hosting, autonomic computing and resource pooling are all examples of technologies that have existed for some time. But it is how these technologies have been brought together, packaged and delivered as a pay-per-use utility that has established cloud computing as one of the largest disruptive innovations yet in the history of IT. As organisations shift from concentrating on back-office processes, where transactional records are kept and maintained, towards front-end processes where organisations conduct business with customers and suppliers, new business models of value creation are being developed. There is no doubt that the cloud is fuelling this shift.

You've now had a whistle-stop tour of the exciting world of cloud computing. We have covered a lot, and you will probably have some questions that haven't been answered yet. The rest of this book explores a number of important areas in more depth, so that by the end you will not only have a broad understanding of cloud computing, but if you have completed the exercises, you'll be able to implement the technology as well!

1.15   Review Questions

The answers to these questions can be found in the text of this chapter.
1. Explain how energy utility provision has informed the emergence of cloud computing.
2. Briefly discuss the differences between cloud computing service models.

3. Which combination of cloud computing characteristics is the best case for reducing energy consumption?
4. Explain the similarities between grid and cloud computing.
5. Describe the different levels of abstraction that cloud providers can offer.

1.16 Extended Study Activities

These activities require you to research beyond the contents of this book and can be approached individually for the purposes of self-study or used as the basis of group work.

1. You are a member of a team of IT consultants, who specialise in selling IT systems to organisations that have between 100 and 500 staff. Prepare a case for the adoption of cloud computing. Consider the types of IT architecture and systems that might already be in place and whether there are specific business functions made available by cloud computing that an organisation might benefit from.
2. An IT department has decided to investigate the use of cloud computing for application development. What are the issues that they should consider, and how would you advise that they mitigate any risks?

References

Foster, I., Kesselman, C.: The Grid: Blueprint for a New Computing Infrastructure. Morgan Kaufmann Publishers, San Francisco (1999). ISBN 1-55860-475-8

IBM Research: Autonomic Computing. http://www.research.ibm.com/autonomic/ (2012). Last Accessed July 2012

McCarthy, J.: Reminiscences on the History of Time Sharing. Stanford University. http://www-formal.stanford.edu/jmc/history/timesharing/timesharing.html (1983)

Parkhill, D.: The Challenge of the Computer Utility. Addison-Wesley, Reading (1966). ISBN 0-201-05720-4

Business Adoption Models and Legal Aspects of the Cloud

2

What the reader will learn:

- That cloud computing has a number of adoption models
- What is meant by public cloud, and why businesses may choose to adopt this
- What is meant by private cloud, and why businesses may choose to adopt this
- What is meant by hybrid cloud and community cloud, and why businesses may choose to adopt this
- That these new ways of doing business bring with them legal issues that need to be considered as part of any plan to adopt cloud computing

2.1   What Services Are Available?

There are alternative ways a business might adopt cloud computing, and we will be reviewing those approaches in this chapter. As we saw earlier, there are many something-as-a-service options available, and many providers provide all of them, whilst some concentrate on specialist areas like data storage or application platforms.

In a 2011 paper, Li et al. (2010) indicated four general types of service that are currently available from leading cloud providers:

1. Elastic compute clusters which include a set of virtual instances that run a customer's application code.
2. Persistent storage services in which application or other data can be stored in a cluster.
3. Intracloud networks, which connect an application's components.
4. Wide-area networks (WANs) connect the cloud data centres, where the application is hosted, with end hosts on the Internet.

This is a useful categorisation of service types. The other things we will need to consider are metrics. We will need to have some understanding of measures such as performance, cost and availability if we are to have any hope of assessing which

R. Hill et al., *Guide to Cloud Computing: Principles and Practice*, Computer Communications and Networks, DOI 10.1007/978-1-4471-4603-2_2, © Springer-Verlag London 2013

Table 2.1 A summary of the key differences between public and private cloud models

	Public	Private
Network	Internet	Private network
Server and data centre location	Global	In company
Costing	By usage or free	Internal mechanism, often by capacity and processor
Tenancy	Multiple	Single
Scale orientation	Vertical (i.e. user focused)	Horizontal (i.e. application focused)
Key selection rationale	Cost	Security

provider offers the best solution for any of these services. We will examine these in the 'Which Cloud Model?' section (Sect. 2.6) at the end of this chapter.

As we saw in the last chapter, there are many definitions of cloud. Vaquero et al. (2009) attempted to collate these and come up with a single, all-encompassing definition:

> Clouds are a large pool of easily usable and accessible virtualized resources (such as hardware, development platforms and/or services). These resources can be dynamically reconfigured to adjust to a variable load (scale), allowing also for an optimum resource utilisation. This pool of resources is typically exploited by a pay-per-use model in which guarantees are offered by the infrastructure provider by means of customised SLAs.

We must also not forget that to businesses, it matters not how we define cloud computing but rather it matters whether this form of IT supports their business by reducing costs or adding revenue and profit. You will see more of this discussion in Chap. 8. These elements too are reviewed by cloud type.

The three types of cloud adoption we shall review are public, private and hybrid. As the latter is a combination of the other two, it may be worth starting by examining the key differences between typical public and private clouds (Table 2.1).

2.2   What Is Meant by Public Cloud?

The US National Institute of Standards and Technology (NIST) suggests in a recent draft that the definition of a public cloud is as follows:

> The cloud infrastructure is made available to the general public or a large industry group and is owned by an organisation selling cloud services (Mell and Grance 2011).

The authors of this book believe the general public or a large industry group should be replaced with the general public or organisations as there is no evidence that industry groups need to be of any particular size to adopt cloud computing. The key element here is that services are offered by the resource owner (usually referred to as the service provider) to anyone who wants to make use of that service. The service can be any of IaaS, PaaS, SaaS and DaaS (see the previous chapter for definitions). The service provider may charge, usually on a utility basis, but sometimes on a termly basis, or may give the service for free and earn revenue from other income streams, such as advertising.

Table 2.2 Services and estimated number of users of public clouds

Provider	Estimated users (millions, as of 2010)
Hotmail	330
Yahoo	302
Gmail	193
Others	200

2.2.1   Who Is Using Public Cloud?

The short answer is millions of people!

Mail providers can be evasive about the size of their user-base. Specialist email marketing site http://www.email-marketing-reports.com/ gathered some statistics that give us a feel for the scale of the browser-based email usage. These figures are for the 'big 3', and we can safely assume the other providers (such as Excite, AOL, Rediffmail) will amount to >200 million. The dates for these figures are different but all in or after 2010 as illustrated in Table 2.2.

Remember that our definition of cloud services is that a provider owns the resources required to provide a service (such as email) and rents this service to users on a pay-for-use basis. This means there are already at least a billion users of cloud email services worldwide.

We talk about the phenomenon of social networks in the Social, Economic and Political Aspects chapter. Again, the numbers using these services are over a billion. Many will also use email, but nonetheless, when added to other free, privately focused services like image storage and editing, drop boxes for file sharing and presentation tools like Prezi, there is little doubt that public cloud-based services are here to stay. From the business perspective, however, the view is different. As reported in Computerworld (Mearian 2011), some research by TheInfoPro, a market research firm, which approached 247 Fortune 1000 corporations showed that

> 87% of the respondents indicated that they had no plans to use the public cloud for storage-as-a-service. Only 10% said that they would use it.

We should also bear in mind that this sort of large corporation will have been in business for many years and will have invested heavily in IT infrastructure before the cloud existed. They will already have in place their own processes based on internal systems. Heavy investment in enterprise systems like ERP systems such as SAP or PeopleSoft, and RDBMS like Oracle or DB2, not to mention the investment they will have had to make in the specialist people needed to run these business processes, means there is really very little need for them to look elsewhere for solutions. There are, however, two exceptions to this general rule:

- The eternal search for efficiency and cost reduction
- When an innovative solution is only, or primarily, available from a service provider

We have also seen that security and ownership of the data storage are big issues for all potential cloud users. Even if the search for value leads a corporation to begin to use virtualisation to maximise resource usage, they will often prefer to keep that transformation in-house to keep a tight control of security. Set in this context, the indications that large corporates are not racing to take up public cloud offerings are not surprising. For such organisations, private or hybrid clouds may be more appealing (see sections below).

For small-to-medium businesses (SMEs), the argument for adopting public cloud appears a little easier to win. Especially at the micro end, with less than ten employees, businesses are very unlikely to be able to attain the sorts of economies of scale that the megacorporations can achieve with their large-scale IT systems. However, if they, in effect, 'club together and share', they can achieve significant economies of scale. The fact that this collaboration is enabled by a for-profit-making service provider is not consequential.

When you add to this the ease of access to on-demand services which are paid for on a utility basis, the argument is even stronger. If some service providers are to be believed SMEs need never employ an IT specialist again since all their business needs can be made available after signing up and simply completing a series of online questions which act as setup wizards for this application or the other.

Of course life is not always that simple. Apart from the ever-present concern about security (see below) being just as relevant to SMEs as to large corporations, there is the age-old debate between whether you should adapt your business processes to allow the use of off-the-shelf software or keep your processes but have to build, or at least tailor, the software. In terms of IT spent, the former is usually seen as the cheaper, but if your processes are part of what gives you competitive advantage, you may be willing to pay for the privilege of using unique software.

Most of these IT strategy-type questions are not new. The control and specialisation which comes from in-house IT solutions has always been balanced against the savings that can come from off-the-shelf solutions. What is new to cloud, however, is that the cash-flow improvement, at least in the short term, can be very significant as costs become revenue rather than capital, spreading the load over years rather than needing high-cost up-front payments.

The other advantage of the move to pay-for-use is the flexibility that it gives a small firm. Should your business suddenly begin to take off and you need more in the way of IT infrastructure and services, you just pay more to your service provider. Conversely, if part of your business fails, you can stop the IT costs immediately, as opposed to being left with expensive servers doing nothing. Both ways seem to significantly reduce the risks involved in an SME opting to use an IT service.

As usual with business decisions, the preferred solution will be a balance of risks and expected benefits. For SMEs, the balance may seem slightly more biased towards the benefits outweighing the risks. However, every company will be different, and contextual issues like company culture, national norms, sector best practice and government and legal guidelines will all play important parts in the decision-making process.

2.2.2   Another Easy Win for SMEs

One area traditionally less well attended to by smaller organisations is disaster recovery (DR). Even backup and recovery strategies may be relatively unsophisticated. An occasional take backup stored in a fireproof safe may well keep a company's vital data safe, but recovering the data after, for example, a catastrophic server failure, can take days as a new server is purchased, commissioned and brought back to the state of its predecessor.

Major corporations have business continuity plans that look to keep their core operations active with as little as a few minutes between disaster and response. But they have to pay—considerably—for this sort of service. For a multinational bank, for example, this expense is almost a no-brain decision. They can't afford to lose the business that would occur whilst their systems were down.

For an SME, however, a DR plan revolving around a multisite fully mirrored server solution can be seen as a nice-to-have extra as the expense is high and what it buys may never be needed. Cloud provides a small business with an easier, less costly way to run at least two live data centres with automatic failover. This dramatically reduces mean time to recovery (MTTR)—the time between system failures and recovery.

With the cloud, backup need never be to slow tapes. It can be easily automated to happen without human intervention by uploading backup data to a cloud data centre. A centre which will itself have built-in redundancy, meaning you automatically get multiple copies of your valuable data.

2.2.3   Who Is Providing Public Cloud Services?

Those who have seen Larry Ellison's 2009 tirade lampooning cloud computing as nothing other than a hyperbole (see YouTube) may be surprised to see that Oracle now provide pay-for-use services in the cloud (http://cloud.oracle.com).

Other corporates with long track records in the IT arena also now have public cloud offerings and are joined by some newer names. Just as examples, these well-known brands all offer some sort of cloud service now: IBM, AT&T, Fujitsu, Microsoft, HP and Rackspace. And there are many smaller, new market entrants too. Competition is already hot, which is a good indicator that the cloud is well on its way to being accepted by the market.

When we see that these different providers are moving in the same immature market, we should perhaps be a little cautious about predicting the future. Many examples exist of one brand of technology winning out over others and not necessarily because of its excellence. Perhaps the most famous marketing war like this was that between Sony's Betamax and JVC's VHS video formats. The public chose VHS and Betamax died. But there were many people who lost money by investing in Betamax before it declined.

The same thing could happen with cloud. These providers of services do not currently abide by any universally accepted standards. Getting tied into one provider is indeed a risk that needs to be considered. There is a fuller review of interoperability issues in the hybrid section.

2.2.4   Security: The Dreaded 'S' Word

As we will see in the Cloud Security and Governance chapter, privacy and security are big concerns for all potential users of cloud. All the anxieties that may be expressed are most acute with public cloud, where the profitability of the service provider is the key driver to all technology decisions. As Kaufman (2010) puts it,

> To achieve the gains afforded through virtualisation, such providers are colocating virtual machines (VMs) from disparate organisations on the same physical server. From a profit/loss perspective, this matching seems to provide a win-win scenario for both the user and service provider. However, this operational profile introduces a new era of security concerns.

As we have said elsewhere, there isn't much new, in terms of technology, with cloud. There is no real reason why cloud platforms should not be as secure as a traditional platform. Indeed, in some cases, it may be more secure. For example, a server in a locked room may not be as well protected as the Google data centres, as described in this YouTube clip:

http://www.youtube.com/watch?v=1SCZzgfdTBo

In these places, biometrics, multi-checkin and log-in make access to hardware from outsiders virtually impossible—probably far more secure than an average SME's premises.

Of course, one of the aspects about public cloud is that services are accessed through the Internet: an Internet that is available worldwide to both friend and foe. This shared remote access model can potentially allow cyberattacks. All this means that security can be an issue with cloud, but there are issues with current IT infrastructures too.

The perception of insecurity is, however, probably the biggest barrier to cloud adoption. For the non-technically minded amongst business decision-makers, it is not difficult to understand why they may be wary about parcelling up their valuable data and giving it to another company to look after, instead of having it sit on a server behind a locked door on their site. These doubts are compounded when you explain that their data will be multi-tenanting, sharing the same physical resources, perhaps, as their biggest competitor. How could that be seen as a sensible move?

Nor is it just data that can be worrisome. Even IT-literate decision-makers are likely to have grown up in an era when modems went down, when Internet connections broke and when speed of transmission plummeted. How can it be sensible to replace your reliably performing single-purpose system connected to a few clients in a small LAN, all under the control of your network team, with a barely understood worldwide web of entangled connections? Why move ERP from in-house to in-Indonesia or some other foreign domain?

It is not this book's place to counter these concerns. The major service providers will fight that battle, but we do need to be aware that security can be a human problem, rather than a technical one.

2.3   What Is Meant by Private Cloud?

The technology stack need be no different to that used by service providers in public cloud solutions. The US National Institute of Standards and Technology (NIST) suggests in a recent draft that the definition of private cloud is as follows:

> The cloud infrastructure is operated solely for an organisation. It may be managed by the organisation or a third party and may exist on premise or off premise.

The key element here is that the resource owner (known as the service provider in public cloud) is the organisation that is using the services. The service can be any of IaaS, PaaS, SaaS and DaaS (see earlier chapters for definitions), and there may be internal charging mechanisms for these services, but they are not normally made available to anyone outside of the organisation and hidden behind a firewall.

2.3.1   Who Is Using Private Cloud?

Because of the expense involved in creating multi-server operations, early adopters tend to be large organisations with existing infrastructures that lend themselves to the adoption of a cloud platform to increase server efficiency (and thus reduce costs) and allow broader availability to systems within the organisation. We must also remember that organisations have been using some of the building blocks, such as virtualisation and SaaS, for years without calling it cloud.

There is an argument that private cloud is not really that different to the ways large organisations typically manage their infrastructures. Stand far enough away and the technology of a large server farm making good use of virtualisation looks very similar to a cloud. To make matters worse, the organisation doesn't even get the advantages of flexibility, which come from sharing resources, nor do they benefit from the move to revenue costing that is also one of cloud's oft-trumpeted advantages.

Whether or not a move to a private cloud will be beneficial to an organisation depends upon many things, but their existing infrastructure is one of the key ones. A recent big spend in modernising the company data centre can be an indicator that investing in cloud is not an immediate need. If it is time to upgrade anyway, then perhaps internal cloud is a solution worth reviewing.

Especially in the current economic conditions, companies are looking at all their costs to see if they can run more efficiently. IT is no different to any other part of the business in this. Most big organisations depend upon a set of core IT processes. The question being asked is 'are we paying too much for this service?' and that question plays into the hands of those arguing the benefits of cloud computing.

Gartner (2010) suggests that

> … cloud computing has become more material, because the challenges inherent in managing technology based on the principles of previous eras — complex, custom, expensive solutions managed by large in-house IT teams — have become greater, and the benefits of cloud computing in addressing these challenges have matured to become more appropriate and attractive to all types of enterprises.

The question on the lips of many larger organisations' CIOs will not be private versus public but rather legacy versus private. The ability of a cloud infrastructure to flexibly move computing resources to deal with spikes in workload means that cloud-based data centres can run much more efficiently than existing ones, and that may be the biggest single factor in the decision.

For organisations who have taken the decision that cloud will be their preferred technology solution, the question of public versus private is likely to force them to think about the value of security to their business. Private allows, or at least seems to allow, organisations to have greater control over their data. There are, however, many more barriers to private since in-house expertise in virtualisation and operations automation may not currently exist and will be expensive to acquire. Moreover, a move to public cloud can happen much more quickly and allows for maximum flexibility in resource management. The ultimate question, therefore, is likely to be how much are we willing to spend to maintain control over our data?

A whole later chapter is reserved for further investigation into enterprise cloud, and many of the issues which surround the process of adopting a private cloud in a large organisation are covered there.

2.3.2 Who Is Supplying Private Cloud?

Most of the big players are now fully committed to selling products or services badged as cloud. Even Oracle, once more famous for laughing at cloud, sells cloud-related services and products, mostly private cloud solutions. They say

> Cloud computing promises to speed application deployment, increase innovation, and lower costs, all while increasing business agility. It also can transform the way we design, build, and deliver applications....
> (http://www.oracle.com/webapps/dialogue/ns/dlgwelcome.jsp?p_ext=Y&p_dlg_id=92 70949&src=7054580&Act=13&sckw=WWMK10058758MPP002.GCM.9322)

IBM has been in cloud from very early days. Lotus Notes has now become iNotes, and one prong of the IBM cloud marketing campaigns is clearly aimed at public, with the catchy strapline of

> Install nothing. Access everything.

But IBM clearly recognises the need for private cloud too. They have a suite of underpinning technologies they call SmartCloud Foundations which they describe as

> an integrated set of technologies for enabling private and hybrid clouds, and the virtualisation, automation and management of service delivery. SmartCloud Foundation capabilities allow organisations to easily build and rapidly scale private cloud environments.
> (http://www.ibm.com/cloud-computing/us/en/)

HP is a big player too, playing heavily on the reputation for cloud to be rapid and flexible; they can deliver private cloud computing services within 30 days (http://www.hp.com/hpinfo/newsroom/press/2010/100830a.html).

On their website, their senior vice president and general manager, Technology Services, HP, uses the concept of an 'internal provider':

> To better serve the needs of their enterprises, clients are asking us to help them become internal service providers with the ability to deliver applications through a highly flexible private cloud environment.

Citrix too has been in the market since it really started. Their solutions also play on the speed of change possible from cloud:

> With CloudStack, customers can quickly and easily build cloud services within their existing infrastructure and start realizing the benefits of this transformative service delivery model within minutes—without the overhead of integration, professional services and complex deployment schedules.
> (http://www.citrix.com/English/ps2/products/product.asp?contentID=2314749)

An interesting development with Citrix is their CloudBridge technology which tackles the perceived security issues in public cloud head-on and seeks to help create secure hybrid solutions:

> Citrix CloudBridge lowers the risk and reduces the effort and cost for enterprises to move production workloads to the cloud by …. making the cloud provider network look like a natural extension of the enterprise datacenter network.
> (http://www.citrix.com/site/resources/dynamic/salesdocs/Citrix_NetScaler_Cloud_Bridge.pdf)

As well as suppliers of hardware and software, consultancies too are very much in the market for helping customers migrate to a cloud solution. And it isn't just Western companies who are pushing cloud. TCS and Infosys in India, for example, are major global players.

Simply type private cloud supplier in a Google search, and (at the time of writing) 95 million hits are reported. There can be no doubt that the cloud market is well and truly active!

2.4 What Is Meant by Hybrid Cloud?

NIST definition:

> Hybrid cloud. The cloud infrastructure is a composition of two or more clouds (private, community, or public) that remain unique entities but are bound together by standardized or proprietary technology that enables data and application portability (e.g., cloud bursting for load balancing between clouds).

The key aspect is that hybrid includes some mix of public and private cloud in a non-specified ratio.

2.4.1 Who Is Using Hybrid Cloud?

If an organisation has a steady and quantifiable use of IT resources, they are able to adopt private cloud, gaining the benefits of efficiency and availability, without missing the other strength of cloud—flexible scalability.

If, on the other hand, like many organisations, they have spikes of activity, planned or not, then public cloud's ability to offer unlimited and immediate scalability on an occasional basis may well appeal. Building your systems to cope with standard workloads in-house and extend outwards when required should allow for the best of both worlds. Sensitive systems can be kept entirely in-house if required.

Some e-commerce organisations can adopt a hybrid approach to help with the activity associated with the front-end during peak shopping periods whilst maintaining secure back-end services in their own private cloud. This prevents them having to invest in many servers which may be idle for long periods just to cope with occasional high loads.

The other likely driver towards a hybrid approach is the organisation's existing infrastructure and their IT strategy. Hybrid may well be an interim approach which means that wholesale in-house architectural changes do not need to happen immediately as some changes are contracted out to service providers and some existing systems continue to function. Interoperability between these different systems here is a key issue (see below).

Another way that hybrid is likely to happen is by accident. An organisation with its own private cloud platform for its main systems may, for example, decide that Google's Gmail email solution is the right one for their organisation. The security risks with noncritical systems like email will seem relatively minor, and the cost-effectiveness of such a solution may attract many organisations. Part of their IT stack then becomes private, part public—de facto a hybrid cloud solution.

2.4.2   What Are the Issues with Hybrid Cloud?

Whilst suppliers, such as Citrix and their CloudBridge, will be keen to suggest that hybrid offers the best of both private and public worlds, it is also arguable that it is the worst of both. After all, as we saw in the private section above, one of the biggest drivers for private solutions is the ability to control your own, independent data centre for security reasons. Claybrook (2011) suggests

> The challenges of building a bridge between private and public clouds are real.
>   (http://www.computerworld.com/s/article/9217158/Cloud_interoperability_Problems_ and_best_practices)

The report goes on to quote Joe Skorupa, a Gartner vice president, as saying that

> ... users and cloud vendors are in very different places on this issue [interoperability], and true cloud interoperability will likely not occur for some time -- if ever. Standards are nascent and will take years to fully develop.

The lack of standards is indeed likely to be a major stumbling block when it comes to trying to pass data, which will usually be encrypted, between different systems in a hybrid cloud solution. It is not unusual in IT for technology to get so far ahead of standards. And in the absence of standards, there is little reason for the various providers to ensure ease of communications between themselves and other providers. Indeed, the cynical amongst us may even think that these different approaches can help tie in the customer to a provider.

The two key proprietary virtualisation technologies (VMWare and Hyper-V) will be trying to keep their own customers whilst also fighting off open-source alternatives in the PaaS area. As trust is one of the likely decision factors for cloud platform providers' customers, some form of industry-wide standard is being actively sought. Unfortunately, however, there are several agencies keen to seek to take the lead in this area. At the time of writing, these included:

- IEEE, self styled as 'the world's largest professional association advancing technology for humanity'
- Open Grid Forum
- Cloud Security Alliance
- NIST

All these agencies are themselves liable to lobbying from the industry. This lobbying is generally for financial reasons, but it is also true that individual providers naturally believe their particular solutions are the best! It is unlikely that a truly global and agreed standard will happen for a few years yet, so interoperability is likely to remain one of the biggest barriers to hybrid adoption.

2.5   What Is Meant by Community Cloud?

NIST definition:

> The cloud infrastructure is shared by several organisations and supports a specific community that has shared concerns (e.g., mission, security requirements, policy, and compliance considerations). It may be managed by the organisations or a third party and may exist on premise or off premise.

The key aspect here is that of inter-organisational collaboration. Community cloud is just like a private cloud except that several organisations share the responsibility for resourcing the cloud, instead of just one.

2.5.1   Who Is Using Community Cloud?

Trust between companies operating in a competitive marketplace is not a usual phenomenon, and so community is not a realistic option for them. However, organisations which are about care and support have naturally tended to help each other in the past. Charitable organisations, for example, have been coming together to share all sorts of resources, including IT.

One example is the International HIV/AIDS Alliance which is a partnership for '… everyone who works with and for NGOs and CBOs and is involved in community and health system strengthening worldwide'.

Whilst the political advantages which come from small charities coming together as a single pressure group are their reason d'être, the support provided by IT across the partnership can also be important. Working with Cisco, the alliance has implemented online collaboration and SaaS platform:

Fig. 2.1 AIDS Alliance website home page (last accessed 22 May 2012)

http://www.aidsalliance.org/includes/Document/Uploaded/IHAA_CISCO_D1.pdf

The vision expressed by Sam McPherson, associate director, International HIV/ AIDS Alliance, is

> We want to exploit the technology available to us and truly become a collaborative organi-
> sation. By using the full complement of WebEx solutions, we hope to move closer toward
> our vision of a world in which people do not die of AIDS.

One major problem is that not all third sector organisations are as forward thinking as the International HIV/AIDS Alliance (Fig. 2.1). Many charitable organisations are small and not cash rich and are therefore afraid of the costs associated with IT systems (Maison 2011). In a recent survey of nearly 160 charities, *the Guardian* found

> Eight of 10 people said that technology could help build the 'big society'. Yet only one in
> three have the time or confidence to try out new tools like cloud computing.
>
> http://www.guardian.co.uk/voluntary-sector-network/2011/jun/01/charities-
> save-money-cloud

Other first movers in the area of community cloud are governmental organisations. Sometimes the key driver here is the need, traditionally difficult to address with different organisations with disparate IT systems, to share information. In the UK, for example, the police service is separated into constabularies, and they have their own budgets and have met their information system needs with different solutions. This can make sharing information about a suspect difficult when they cross boundaries between constabularies. The matter gets yet more complicated should the suspect be apprehended and taken to court, as the court systems will also be different, not to mention prison systems should they be found guilty.

In the USA, firms like IBM have been quick to spot how they can offer a service to governmental organisations. In a recent press release, they say

> IBM has launched a new Federal Community Cloud specifically designed to help federal government organisations respond to technology requirements more quickly. The secure, private cloud environment is part of IBM's established and dedicated Federal Data Centers (FDC) that provide secure and comprehensive certified computing capabilities to federal government clients.

In the UK there is G-Cloud. This is a government-funded initiative to gain the benefits that cloud can give whilst attempting to save the public purse £200m/annum by 2014/2015: http://gcloud.civilservice.gov.uk/ The G-Cloud program is a cross-government initiative; collaboration across departments, and throughout the public sector, being encouraged and enabled by cloud.

Reported in *the Guardian* in January 2012 (Best 2012), Liam Maxwell, the UK Cabinet Office's director of ICT futures, foresees

> "In two or three years' time what we now call IT, the delivery of those disaggregated services like hosting, networking, end user devices, support, all of those, will become core commodity services and will be bought 'like stationery'".

2.6   Which Cloud Model?

Of course, the answer to the question 'which type of cloud' may well be none. Richard Stallman, founder of GNU, argued that cloud was a trap in an article in *the Guardian* (Johnson 2008). He argued

> 'One reason you should not use web applications to do your computing is that you lose control', he said. 'It's just as bad as using a proprietary program. Do your own computing on your own computer with your copy of a freedom-respecting program. If you use a proprietary program or somebody else's web server, you're defenceless. You're putty in the hands of whoever developed that software.'

Before 2010, there were many such warning sirens. Larry Ellison, Oracle's CEO and co-founder, is also famously quoted as saying that cloud is 'nonsense'. And yet, now, Oracle is a leading player in cloud services to corporates.

If we examine the sales statistics from the cloud service providers, there can be little doubt that many CIOs, IT Managers and IT Consultants are now seriously

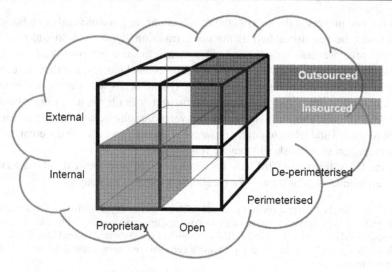

Fig. 2.2 Jericho Cloud Cube Model (2010)

considering cloud platforms as one of their options when looking at how to deliver their IT strategies. So, how do they decide which cloud adoption model to use?

We have identified already that cloud security is seen as a major concern by many organisations. At least whilst the platform is still quite new, many will adopt a 'wait and see' approach—especially if their existing infrastructure is adequate. Some, seeking to gain some advantage from early adoption, may see the advantages of cloud but still want to be cautious about how they look after their data and internal systems. For them, probably starting with pilot projects to test the water, private cloud may well seem more attractive.

The Jericho Forum proposed a framework Fig. 2.2 (Opengroup 2010) which is intended to help organisations find the most appropriate cloud 'formations' for their own particular business need. 'Formations' is a nice way of describing the many alternative solutions available in a mix-and-match environment. Every organisation is likely to be different.

The Forum describes itself as '…an international IT security thought-leadership association dedicated to advancing secure business in a global open-network environment', so it is not surprising to see that security figures highly in their proposed decision-making process.

The cube usefully expresses the considerations that need to be made when deciding which approach to take. The dimensions are described below.

- Internal/external here is the same as private/public clouds.
- Proprietary/open is, as with other software, whether or not the software or platform is open source or not. Also important in the cloud is how open the data standards adopted by a supplier are. Really we are talking about how much tie-in the supplier has over the customer, and whether that is an issue of concern or not.

- Perimeterised/de-perimeterised is about where the IT services exist. If a company keeps all its data behind a firewall within its own private network, for example, we would call that perimeterised. The Jericho paper interestingly refers to this as a mindset. This is very import as an organisation's culture will impact heavily upon their willingness to expose, or not, their systems to external access.
- Insourced/outsourced is about who does the work in the cloud. Entirely insourced means that the organisation employs the people directly. The use of contractor or specialist consultants allows for a control to be maintained within the organisation whilst certain specialist skills are outsourced, often temporarily whilst in-house staff gain the skills themselves.

This cube is an excellent start, but other important factors in the decision about which cloud adoption model to select are not covered but need reviewing.

2.6.1   Internal Factors

1. *Existing infrastructure and IT portfolio.* 'If it ain't broke, don't fix it.' Cloud has some potential benefits, but as with all new technologies, it has risks too. If the organisation's IT is delivering what it should, as well as it should, then there is probably nothing for a CIO to do other than keep their eye on the cloud space.
2. *Capability.* Rightly or wrongly, CIOs in organisations with a long history of managing their own IT systems with their own employees may feel that some of the marketing hype about the cloud's approachability and ease of use does not apply to them. Their CEOs and CFOs may actually disagree if there is board level dissatisfaction with existing internally supplied services.
   Start-ups, on the other hand, will have none of these prejudices. The ability to implement sophisticated enterprise-style systems with no in-house expertise may well be seen as the single biggest reason for opting into public cloud services.
3. *Emphasis on costs.* It may seem obvious that companies will always look to run as efficiently as possible, but in a time of economic hardship such as most of the world is enduring as we write, it is the case that efficiencies are more aggressively sought. Being new, we have no real evidence as to whether cloud is truly a cheaper alternative long term, but we do know that moving away from big capital expenditure IT projects towards pay-for-use will move costs away from a company's fixed assets and into revenue costs, spreading the cash flow over many years as it does so. This drive to efficiency can point towards public cloud where the nature of the shared capacity leads to significantly more savings than would private cloud.
4. *Performance and scalability.* Again, there are not enough studies carried out to suggest how cloud performs in comparison to in-house client/server technology. The most obvious point is that a reputable cloud provider will always be running on high-performance equipment in order to enable them to support many users. However, how big a 'slice' of that platform a customer gets is variable.

The other aspect of this comparison is that a recently upgraded internal infrastructure will perform better than an ageing one and will therefore be less likely to be outshone by cloud. If performance is paramount to a business, the likelihood is that they would adopt private cloud, where they can manage the performance themselves and ensure that nothing can cause degradation.

It is probably true that a need for scalability is a significant driver towards adopting cloud. If an organisation understands its business well and it is relatively stable, it can plan what capacity is required and purchase as and when required. Many organisations, however, go through unexpected sharp up- and downturns in their OLTP traffic in step with the business performance. Not having to purchase extra capacity 'just in case' in such circumstances can make public cloud more appealing.

2.6.2 External Factors

1. *Publicly available bandwidth.* Cloud computing requires reliable, high-performance access to the Internet to work effectively. In some luckier Western countries, this is not a problem with almost country-wide broadband coverage. In other nations, however, the Internet is only available through mobile telephones or private networks. Organisations which have their own private networks in these countries will be able to decide on a cloud adoption model as described elsewhere, but those with limited or poorly performing access may be constrained to only using public cloud SaaS options, such as email and document sharing.
2. *The competition.* It is the nature of a competitive market that organisations will monitor what each other is doing. They need to ensure that no-one steals a march in adopting some new technology that may give competitive advantage. Sustainable competitive advantage in the IT arena is an impossible dream as every advance can be replicated by the competition given time. However, to not seek at least temporary advantage is, in actual fact, to allow oneself to go backwards, as everyone else in the market will be looking for the next new advance. Of course, caution is needed. Just blindly adopting an approach because a competitor has it is a recipe for disaster. However, if your major competitor suddenly starts using public cloud for some of their IT needs, it may well be the case that you should at least review the potential advantages to your organisation.
3. *Suppliers' and purchasers' expectations.* The balance of power between your organisation and its customers on the one hand and its suppliers on the other will impact your decision-making. When electronic data interchange (EDI) came to the fore in the 1980s, it was seen by adopters as a cost-reducing technology which would speed the order-to-delivery process. Typically the early adopters were large companies in particular markets. The motor trade was one such market, and early adopters were the big automobile manufacturers. In order to ensure that their suppliers would adopt this new technology, some manufacturers began to dictate that all their orders for parts would be delivered electronically. In a market where the customer was king, this meant that part manufacturers had to adopt EDI practices or else face bankruptcy.

Similar pressures will begin to bear on companies dealing with organisations which are using the public cloud to manage all or part of their own supply chain. In those circumstances, the decision to use public cloud might be made for you by default.

There are many other business reasons for and against which model to adopt, and we investigate some more detailed investment appraisal approaches in Chap. 8.

2.7   Legal Aspects of Cloud Computing

The law about cloud computing, because of the relative newness of the concept, is largely uncertain, and, as is often the case in a rapidly moving field like IT, the lawyers and legislators are having difficulty keeping up with the changes. However, there are some elements that are clear.

2.7.1   A Worldwide Issue

In March 2010, in the USA, the ITIF president Robert D. Atkinson said, 'There is no way a law enacted at the dawn of the digital age can guide law enforcement officials and protect privacy rights in an age of cloud computing and the wireless Internet, and as billions of electronic exchanges occur every hour' (ITIF Press Release 2010).

One reason that cloud is going to be problematic to law makers is borne of its very essence—global, shared, distributed and replicated data which may reside anywhere in the world. Several of the leading players in the spread of cloud have formed a pressure group in the USA to try and push legislators to recognise that current legal frameworks are not cloud friendly. They are called the Digital Due Process (DDP) group and their aim is to

> ...simplify, clarify, and unify the ECPA [Electronic Communications Privacy Act] standards, providing stronger privacy protections for communications and associated data in response to changes in technology and new services and usage patterns, while preserving the legal tools necessary for government agencies to enforce the laws, respond to emergency circumstances and protect the public. (DDP Website 2011)

Naturally, when organisations like Amazon, Facebook, Google and IBM (all fierce competitors in the cloud market) can agree to come together to lobby government, we can see that there is a lot of commercial interest in getting the legislation changed. We are, however, still at the stage where we will have to wait and see what the law makers do in response. This all sounds very American, but we should acknowledge that in terms of cloud, where the USA goes, so, often, follows Europe and the rest of the world. China is a noticeable exception, having a massive internal market for cloud technology, but with its own particular legal frameworks which do include filtering out certain cloud content before it crosses into China.

Because of the inherently international nature of cloud computing, commentators are suggesting that the world needs international treaties to allow for the free movement of information across borders, in the same way agreements protecting commercial bank transfers between organisations in different nations allows the globalisation of trade in goods.

Policing, too, is difficult when the cybercrime is so international in nature. There are international agreements already in place. The Budapest Convention, for example, allows police to access servers in other countries. However, cybercriminals can move data and applications from one server to another, across national boundaries, very easily and quickly, which makes the work of the police extremely difficult.

This uncertainty is doubtless adding to the perceived level of risk for organisations thinking of using the cloud. Compared to current service-focused IT provision, they see cloud as less transparent and may legitimately feel less protected by the law. Particularly when organisations are talking about handing over vital or sensitive information to service providers, their concerns are understandable. Moreover, even if the service providers themselves do act as their customers wish, there have been cases where governments and their legal systems have forced service providers to hand over data stored in the cloud.

When this happens, there may well be no impetus for the service provider to fight any subpoena as the information is not theirs and they can blame the state for them having to pass the data over. The legal position is made even trickier by the fact that the law that exists, created in a different era, states that data handed over to a third party in the normal course of business can be subpoenaed without notice. What customers are doing with cloud service providers is passing data on to third parties but for storage, not for sharing, as was the norm when the laws were first couched (Gruenspecht 2010).

2.7.2 The Current Legal Framework for Cloud

The uncertainties outlined in the above section may be one reason for an organisation being wary of investing in the cloud. However, elsewhere in this book, we have seen its many advantages, and as with all business decisions, organisations will just weigh benefits against risk. Other players, such as governmental institutions, will also provide input to the decision-making. In the EU, for example, the Commission President indicated that he foresaw that digital commerce would be a significant area of growth for Europe:

> Half of European productivity growth over the last 15 years was driven by information and communication technologies. This trend is set to intensify. Our European Digital Agenda will deliver a single digital market worth 4% of EU GDP by 2020 (Barroso 2010).

Many companies have already committed to cloud. They will therefore need to work within the existing legal framework. Uncertainty is not an excuse to ignore the laws that do exist.

Remember that one of the building blocks of cloud, particularly the public aspects thereof, is the idea of pooling resources and charging them out on a pay-for-use basis. The service provider will typically offer certain guaranteed services, and the service contract will usually include service-level agreements (SLAs). The guarantees are usually expressed in measurable terms, some examples of which include:

- Availability of the service
- Minimum performance benchmarks
- Minimum help-desk response time

These SLAs are part of normal contract law. The jurisdiction in which any legal disputes will be settled is often stipulated within the SLA itself but if it isn't determining the appropriate jurisdiction can be a lengthy (and expensive) precursor to any actual legal action. The question, in short, is the following: Which national, or subnational, laws apply? Those of the providing company's head office? Those of the customer? Those of the location of the data centre? The safest advice to give, therefore, is to ensure that jurisdiction is explicitly agreed in the SLA.

2.7.3   Privacy and Security

As we cover in the Security and Governance chapter of this book (Chap. 10), there is much for potential cloud adopters to worry about in terms of privacy and security. This section only covers the legal aspect of these concerns.

Until legislation specific to cloud computing is forthcoming, both service providers and their customers need to rely heavily on their SLAs to effectively deal with security risks, a process that requires an element of trust from the customer perspective. Further to the comments above about the EU putting cloud high on their economic policy agenda, the EU has created a body called the European Network and Information Security Agency (ENISA) to review and respond to cybersecurity issues within the European Union. Its website says it is

> ... the 'pace-setter' for Information Security in Europe, and a centre of expertise. The objective is to make ENISA's web site the European 'hub' for exchange of information, best practices and knowledge in the field of Information Security.

ENISA's cloud computing risk assessment report (http://www.enisa.europa.eu/ activities/risk-management/files/deliverables/cloud-computing-risk-assessment) states 'loss of governance' as one of the biggest single risks for cloud adopters. The customer passes responsibility for security to the service provider, who may not provide adequate guarantees in their SLAs. Any adopter therefore needs to carry out a risk assessment, perhaps as discussed in the ENISA report, and must ensure that their privacy protection is built into the SLA.

Suppliers of cloud infrastructure and services are not going to allow a perceived lack of security to prevent them from maximising profits. If you Google 'cloud security IBM' and then repeat for the major cloud players, you will see many pages on each site dedicated to explaining the supplier's security. And current security specialists, too, have noticed how cloud is becoming important. McAfee recently released its Cloud Security Platform, for example, and Symantec's have their Symantec.Cloud.

But these are still all sales pitches, and some caution needs to be taken. With the best will in the world businesses do not, and should not, blindly believe suppliers' claims. Again, until legislation catches up, it is the customers' task to ensure that they have contracts which ensure their data is secure and that services are delivered as promised.

2.8   Summary

In this chapter, we explored the different methods by which cloud computing can be adopted by organisations and by individuals. The adoption types we examined were public, private, hybrid and community. These terms will be used throughout this book and are in wide usage in the computing arena and have become the de facto way of describing the differing approaches. The ways that these are implemented technically are explored in the next part of the book, whilst the business aspects are explored in Part III.

We also analysed the way that these adoption types may be used by different types of business, from small to enterprise sized. We have a chapter in Part III which discusses large-scale enterprise cloud in more detail.

One of the major difficulties for organisations trying to decide whether to adopt cloud computing is which model to adopt. We began to explore tools to assist in analysis of the major factors and looked at the Jericho Cloud Cube Model. A more detailed review of the financial and investment appraisals issues is to be found in Chap. 8.

2.9   Review Questions

The answers to these questions can be found in the text of this chapter.
1. List the types of service that are available from cloud providers today, being clear that you understand the differences between them.
2. How might cloud be an easy solution for smaller businesses looking for business continuity and disaster recovery?
3. What is meant by hybrid cloud?
4. Is a community cloud a public or private cloud solution? Or both? Or is it something else?
5. Why is the policing of cloud seen as problematic for many law makers?

2.10   Extended Study Activities

These activities require you to research beyond the contents of the book and can be tackled individually or as a discussion group.

2.10.1 Discussion Topic 1

What factors are suitable for inclusion in an SLA between cloud provider and customer? You should not only review the factors themselves but also decide on their relative importance and how they might be measured and monitored. You should also consider what the likely impact of requiring extremely demanding levels would be on cost.

We saw that SLAs are key for organisations in terms of ensuring satisfactory levels of service from providers. Some of the more obvious factors are around performance and availability. Five 9 s are industry-speak for as available as possible and mean that a system is up and running 99.999% of the time. However, availability levels set so high are extremely expensive to enable, as the provider will need many layers of redundancy built into their offering.

Measurement too can be a problem. The organisation may have in mind that performance can be measured in terms of user-click-to-returned dataset times. But for cloud applications, the timings can be out of the provider's hands since much will depend upon local Internet speeds and connections.

2.10.2 Discussion Topic 2

Many commentators see hybrid as the likely model for cloud adoption in the long term, allowing companies to use the best of both public and private platforms. In an era when many applications are built with data sharing built in, you should explore the significant challenges that will be faced by organisations with mixed public–private application portfolios.

When attempting this question, you should look to see what standards are in place for cloud computing. If you advise your organisation to use Salesforce CRM, for example, what pressure does that put on other organisational systems in terms of preventing needless data duplication? Is there a threat that cloud could actually result in more siloed data and less sharing?

References

Barroso, J.M.D.: State of the Union 2010 Strasbourg, 7 Sept 2010. http://europa.eu/rapid/pressReleasesAction.do?reference=SPEECH/10/411 (2010). Last accessed 22 May 2012

Best, J.: G-Cloud will lead to shorter contracts and IT 'bought like stationery'. Guardian Professional, Thursday 26 Jan 2012. http://www.guardian.co.uk/government-computing-network/2012/jan/26/gcloud-contracts-liam-maxwell-procurement (2012)

Claybrook, W.: Cloud interoperability: problems and best practices. ComputerWorld, June 2011. http://www.computerworld.com/s/article/9217158/Cloud_interoperability_Problems_and_best_practices (2011)

DDP Website.: http://digitaldueprocess.orgspecific page; http://digitaldueprocess.org/index.cfm?objectid=99629E40-2551-11DF-8E02000C296BA163 (2011)

Gartner, Inc.: Gartner Says Worldwide Cloud Services Market to Surpass $68 Billion in 2010. Gartner press release, Stamford, 22 June, 2010. http://www.gartner.com/it/page.jsp?id=1389313 (2010)

Gruenspecht, J.: "Reasonable" grand jury subpoenas: asking for information in the age of big data. Harv. J. Law Technol. 24(2), 543–562 (2010). http://jolt.law.harvard.edu/articles/pdf/v24/24HarvJLTech543.pdf

ITIF Press Release: ITIF Calls for Updates to Privacy Laws, 30 Mar, 2010. http://www.itif.org/pressrelease/itif-calls-updates-privacy-laws (2010). Last accessed 22 May 2012

Johnson, R.: Cloud computing Is a trap, warns GNU founder Richard Stallman, guardian.co.uk, Monday 29 Sept 2008. http://www.guardian.co.uk/technology/2008/sep/29/cloud.computing.richard.stallman (2008)

Kaufman, L.M.: Can public-cloud security meet its unique challenges? IEEE J. Security Priv. **8**(4), 55–57 (2010). ISSN: 1540–7993

Li, A., Yang, X., Kandula, S., Zhang, M.: Comparing public cloud providers. IEEE Internet Comput. **15**(2), 50–53 (2010)

Maison, A.: How charities could save money by getting on 'the cloud'. Guardian Professional, Wednesday 1 June 2011. http://www.guardian.co.uk/voluntary-sector-network/2011/jun/01/charities-save-money-cloud (2011). Last accessed 22 May 2012

Mearian, L.: Fortune 1000 firms shun public cloud storage. ComputerWorld, May 2011. http://www.computerworld.com/s/article/356680/Survey_Big_Firms_Shunning_Public_Cloud_Storage (2011). Last accessed 22 May 2012

Mell, P., Grance, T.: The NIST Definition of Cloud Computing, NIST Special Publication 800–145 (Draft). Recommendations of the National Institute of Standards and Technology. http://csrc.nist.gov/publications/nistpubs/800-145/SP800-145.pdf (2011). Last accessed 22 May 2012

Opengroup: Cloud Cube Model - Selecting Cloud Formations for Secure Collaboration April 2009, The Jericho Forum, a Forum of The Open Group Available online from: https://collaboration.opengroup.org/jericho/index.htm (2010). Last accessed 22 May 2012

Vaquero, L.M., Rodero-Merino, L., Caceres, J.: A break in the clouds: towards a cloud definition. ACM Comput. Commun. Rev. **39**(1), 50–55 (2009). doi:10.1145/1496091.1496100. ISSN:0146–4833

Social, Economic and Political Aspects of the Cloud

3

What the reader will learn:

- Cloud computing will impact not only on business but also on our society, economy and politics.
- 'Green IT', or sustainable IT, will benefit from cloud computing.
- New business models created by changes in technology can have a significant effect on our society.
- Governments all over the world are looking to cloud to help make their interaction with society more efficient and, sometimes, more democratic.
- People are using cloud to help empower themselves.

3.1 How IT Has Historically Made an Impact on Society

That technology can make enormous changes to human society is not in doubt. Where would we be without the invention of the wheel? But deep-seated changes have also happened as a result of advances in computing.

There are good texts about the history of computing, for example, A Brief History of Computing, Gerald O'Regan, Springer (2008). Conversely, as there is a strong argument that cloud only really started around 2008, there is not much of a history of cloud to examine. We can, however, learn from what happened in the past when new IT became commonplace.

Many of the early developments in computing were driven by military or commercial needs. The large mainframe computers that were the primary form of computing were so expensive that only wealthy corporations or governments could afford to purchase and run them. Ordinary people would react to computing with a sense of awe and, not understanding it, might well be wary or even frightened by it.

R. Hill et al., *Guide to Cloud Computing: Principles and Practice*, Computer Communications and Networks, DOI 10.1007/978-1-4471-4603-2_3, © Springer-Verlag London 2013

In this era, middle managers who needed information to help them make business decisions would think nothing of having to wait for days for the data they needed. The request would need to be coded, probably into COBOL, then perhaps handed to a punch-card operator who would punch the programme, and then on to await an allotted, and very valuable, processing slot. Output from this request would probably be on a continuous run of sprocket-holed paper, along with many other outputs. A further wait might ensue whilst awaiting the specialist paper decollator or burster.

With the advent of personal computing in the 1980s, managers were able to collect and manipulate data without waiting for the still very powerful mainframe. The relational database, with its English-like SQL language, also helped empower decision-makers. Critical information could be delivered in a few seconds, and organisations could gain competitive advantage by accessing information swiftly. Moreover, new information might be uncovered by using data mining techniques.

At this stage, computing was still a very expensive discipline. Personal computers could cost around 10% of the US median salary. Despite Moore's Law bringing us evermore powerful processors, the price was now nearer 1% of median income. In many nations, the PC has become just another household electric item, as well as an office-based workstation.

The acceptance of PCs into the household was doubtless aided by the transition from text-based interaction to the graphical user interface, such as that provided by Microsoft Windows or Apple Mac. The trend towards ease of use allowed noncomputer literate people to become familiar with the benefits that a home computer provided.

And then came access to the Internet to make PCs even more useful in a social context, as well as at work. Now, whole generations of geographically dispersed families and friends keep in touch with tools like email and Skype. Online search tools, such as Google, mean that no-one ever needs not to know any fact.

It isn't all benefits though. Concerns about the often secretive elements of early computing were common. In his paper, Models for the social accountability of computing, 1980, Bob Kling said:

> Unlike many technologies, however, computing generates problems which are generally subtle, private, and potential rather than dramatic, public, and probably harmful.

As we have seen elsewhere, security is still at the top of the worry-list for many people. In broadening the potential participation of citizens, cloud is also collecting more and more information about individuals. And organisations worry about where, physically, their critical data is being stored.

Society's attitude to computing has changed significantly in the past few decades. In some countries, it is the computer illiterate who is unusual. People are no longer frightened by the technology itself. Children are exposed to ICT at a very early age and so computer usage becomes the norm.

There have been measures of attitude to computing (ATC) in the past. Perhaps the first was Lee's Social Attitudes and the Computer Revolution (1970) in which he examined attitudes to computers. Interviews he carried out gathered sentiments like 'they are going too far with these machines' and 'they create unemployment'.

People did say positive things too, but it would be hard to envisage getting too many answers like 'there is something strange and frightening about these machines'. In a more recent paper, Wang (2007) points out that both technology and society have changed dramatically since Lee and he proposed a three-dimensional model for measuring ATC: senses of benefit, harm and dependence. They found respondents saying things like: 'I can't live without my computer for a single day'; 'When using computers, I feel the computer and I become one, and I forget myself'; 'I'd rather browse or chat on the Internet than go on an excursion.' These findings illustrate the way that we have changed our views on computing over the years.

But we started by saying we would try to learn from previous ICT trends to help us guess about the future of cloud. So, when we see that people were expressing concerns about security in the 1980s, and yet we see how the computing has become commonplace, perhaps we should be cautious about dismissing cloud merely on the grounds of security. If the benefits can be cheaply made to outweigh the potential risks, and those risks are managed as well as possible, it seems likely that our society will continue to want to acquire the latest technology in this area.

3.2 The Ethical Dimension

As we saw in the previous section, society's first reaction to computing advances, as it has been with many previous advances, has often been one of scepticism or concern. IT professionals are now far more aware of this public image, and organisations like the BCS and IET address this by expecting members of the professional body to follow a code of ethics.

As we shall see in the later discussion about politics in the cloud, there are potential benefits to be accrued from using the cloud to increase citizen participation in decision-making. There are, however, threats from the same process. Prime amongst them is perhaps that of privacy infringements that can happen when gathering data for political reasons.

Society will also need to take care with cloud availability if an increasing number of services are made available through cloud technologies. There are two key potential issues about ensuring the fairness of access that need to be noted:

1. Even in technologically advanced countries where the infrastructure might be in place to allow all people access to the cloud, there are many people who are either computer illiterate or prefer to use nonelectronic communications.
2. A few countries do have an infrastructure that would allow universal access, but many, including some of the biggest countries, are a long way from that situation.

Cloud-based health advice is now becoming commonplace, for example, in the UK, there is NHS Direct (http://www.nhsdirect.nhs.uk/) which provides 'health advice and reassurance, 24 hours a day, 365 days a year'. This is a prime example of the use of cloud to share vital information widely and efficiently.

UK health officials (http://www.guardian.co.uk/healthcare-network/2011/may/12/european-ehealth-week-neelie-kroes) believe ICT-enabled self-care could potentially reduce GP visits by 40% and hospital admissions by 50% (Kroes 2011).

However, we are a long way from replacing doctors' surgeries, drop-in centres or telephone help. In many Western countries, interaction with a healthcare professional is still seen by many as the only way to seek medical help with the expectation that the state will supply that service.

But in countries without this tradition or where qualified help is limited, cloud, especially in mobile form, can indeed work for the good of remote information-poor areas.

Universities have a long track record of investigating the ways that ICT can be put to sound, ethical use, and this is continuing in the cloud era. Professor Andy Dearden from Sheffield Hallam University, for example, examines designs for applying interactive systems to promote social change and development, which he calls e-SocialAction. He is working on Bridging the Global Digital Divide and leads a research project looking at Practical Design for Social Action, which is investigating technology design in voluntary groups, trade-unions, community groups, campaigning organisations and NGOs.

He describes one project (Rural e-services: Participatory co-design of Sustainable Software and Business Systems in Rural Co-operatives) which is examining ways of improving the dissemination of agricultural advice in a rural area of India:

> This project has been working with marginal farmers in Sironj, Madhya Pradesh, India, to explore how participatory approaches to ICT design and participatory approaches to social development can be combined. Together [with other partners], we have designed and implemented a new communications system using mobile camera phones and web systems to improve the flow of agricultural knowledge and advice between the advisors in the crop-producer's co-operative, and the farmers in the villages around Sironj.

3.3   Social Aspects

It can be argued that society began to view computing as an everyday tool after the GUI tools like Windows and Apple GUI began to become widely available. These interfaces suddenly made the computer far more approachable to nonspecialists.

Other changes in the last couple of decades have also helped with this integration of computing into society. Perhaps the most significant is the introduction of mobile computing. From the earliest 'luggable' laptops to today's iPads and smartphones, the trend has been to allow people to access music, information and many other digital artefacts from more and more places. If we are lucky enough to live where there is good broadband coverage and own any of these devices, we need never not know a fact. We can always Google and find out.

People born in the West during the last 20 years are not likely to be so worried by IT. Indeed there is much evidence that IT changes are actively sought as people try to acquire the latest and best new iPhone or netbook. Those people demand changes. They no longer wait for the vendors; they let the vendors know what they expect to be in the latest release of the devices or software.

This change in approach to computing in general is an essential precursor to the other changes we have seen in the more recent past, and which we now examine in more detail.

3.3.1 Web 2.0

Much has been written about Web 2.0. There is a little about it in Chap. 7 in which we look at intelligent web systems. The key point is that the change from Web 1.0 to 2.0 saw a change in approach from the web as solely a provider of static information to a place for interaction with dynamic data. Web 2.0 is all about allowing and encouraging users to interact with websites.

Of course Web 2.0 was with us before the term cloud was first used. Tim O'Reilly was explaining, in his paper 'Design Patterns and Business Models for the Next Generation of Software', what Web 2.0 is in 2005. Many people see cloud as post 2008. But there can be no doubt that cloud has broadened the user-base of Web 2.0 applications and will continue to do so as it too grows.

O'Reilly goes on to suggest a Web 2.0-specific marketing strategy:

> ...leverage customer-self service and algorithmic data management to reach out to the entire web, to the edges and not just the center, to the long tail and not just the head.

Amazon bookstore customers will recognise that this is indeed their strategy and that they carry it out extremely successfully.

Again, Amazon bookstore was with us well before cloud. And yet, it is in the cloud: You can access it with only a browser or even just with an e-book, and they provide you with services which you pay for as and when you use them.

Now, of course, with EC2, cloud drive and S3, Amazon is heavily involved with aspects of the cloud that makes them one of the leading service providers, not just a seller of books and CDs.

It is probably in the field of social media and networking that the most change has happened as a result of first Web 2.0 and the cloud.

Facebook, Myspace and its equivalents such as Orkut are now part of everyday life for many. Twitter has also enjoyed a rapid growth in popularity. These can all be seen as social phenomena that have rooted themselves in the cloud, together with other 'free' services like Flickr or Shutterfly for storing and sharing your photographs and DropBox or Google Drive for storing and sharing your files.

In the chapter about data in the cloud, we talk about the problems of perception of a lack of security that service providers need to get over with their customers. Why would a sceptical businessmen trust them with his data rather than having it where he can see it—on his own system?

Interestingly, the success of the services mentioned above just demonstrates that many people do not have a problem trusting the likes of Google, Amazon, Shutterfly Inc. and DropBox Inc. with their personal information, photographs and other digital belongings. This willingness to trust cloud services as an individual may just be that the scale of the risk is seen as less to a person with their photographs than to a business with their commercial secrets. But it may also be a precursor to an overall change in mindset. The longer the young people using these services continue to do so without problems, the more likely they are to become decision-makers in organisations, meaning they may be more willing to take 'risks' with their corporate data and opt for cloud storage.

3.3.2 Society in the Clouds

Social network services (SNSs) help people find others with common interests, background or affiliations. They provide forums for discussion and debate, exchange of photographs and other digital media and personal news.

Some of the established service providers in this domain can boast some staggering figures in terms of users and usage. In June 2011, for example, there were, worldwide, 1 trillion pageviews, as per Google's report in support of their DoubleClick ad campaign (http://www.google.com/adplanner/static/top1000/).

Even more remarkable is that this figure was achieved from 880 million unique visitors. That is almost three times the entire population of the US! It isn't far short of the population of India. There is only China that has a population that is noticeably larger, and at the time of writing, Facebook was banned in China. Further, this is bigger than the number of registered users, so somewhere over 100 million non-registered visitors are hitting Facebook via advertisements and as a result of queries in search engines.

Professionals have their own SNS; LinkedIn, with more than 100 million users worldwide, is seen by many as the place to find professional employment. Some employers will only interview potential employees if they have a LinkedIn profile.

Cyworld, the largest SNS in South Korea, by 2005 had 10 million users, which was a staggering quarter of the population of South Korea (Ahn et al. 2007).

One US survey of over 900 teens came up with these statistics (Lenhart and Madden 2007):

1. More than half (55%) of all of online American youths ages 12–17 use online social networking sites.
2. Further 91% of all social networking teens say they use the sites to stay in touch with friends they see frequently.
3. 82% use the sites to stay in touch with friends they rarely see in person.
4. 72% of all social networking teens use the sites to make plans with friends.
5. 49% use the sites to make new friends.

The sheer scale of the user-base, together with the modes of use, point to SNSs making a significant difference to the way society works. In the way that cloud simplifies access to this sort of service, this trend can only increase. Who knows how our society will change as a result?

This is not to say that businesses aren't engaging with SNSs. The commonly quoted example is targeted marketing. Because the target audience are identifying their own preferences, affiliations and interests, marketeers are able to get the message to only people who may be interested. This makes such campaigns far more efficient in terms of cost per response.

Other parts of business too are beginning to use SNS tools: Human relations and customer service, for example, are departments that can easily benefit from using SNS to keep in touch with employees and customers alike.

Social media is far more than just SNS. More than 1 billion photos and 40 million user-created videos had been uploaded and contextually tagged in photo- and video-sharing sites like YouTube and Flickr.

3.4   Political Aspects

Many commentators are pointing to social media available from mobile communication devices as a force for empowerment for entire populations. Futuristic novels in the past, like Orwell's Nineteen Eighty-Four, have depicted those in power using ICT technologies to monitor and control their populations. In actual fact, we are seeing trends which indicate the reverse may be true, thanks to ubiquitous cloud-based technologies.

Using a variety of cloud tools, people can rapidly come together to highlight, discuss and actively promote solutions to specific issues. Pressure groups form which can drive the political decision-making process or, at the very least, give it a push in a particular direction. Political scientists would point out that the sort of pluralist model that is encouraged can damage a society's political apparatus, but here we are just observing the phenomenon.

In the UK, there are many online pressure groups, some not so obvious as others. One example of an effective advocacy group is that of the mother's lobby. As the Guardian reported in December 2008 (Pidd 2008):

> The global online poll of more than 27,000 people in 16 countries revealed that UK housewives spend 47% of their free time surfing the Internet, compared with 39% for students around the world and 32% for the unemployed.

As Gordon Brown, whilst he was Prime Minister, observed, the group has more members than all UK political parties added together. This has meant that politicians like to join in to try and get their message across to a wider audience. Both Brown and Cameron have recently agreed to do 'live chat' shows hosted by Mumsnet. The 2010 general election was even called the Mumsnet election by some journalists, so prominent was the attention politicians were paying to the site. But this very platform also provides the potential to pressure politicians on particular issues.

It isn't always politicians that are targeted. This is an excerpt from the Mumsnet's 'About us' page (http://www.mumsnet.com/info/aboutus):

> In January 2010, the Outdoor Advertising Association pulled posters for a £1.25 million campaign that unwisely declared 'Career women make bad mothers' after an outcry and mass letter-writing campaign on Mumsnet. The OAA issued a formal apology, stating: 'We did not intend to cause any offence'. The advertising agency responsible for the campaign replaced the posters with new ones stating: 'Sexist adverts damage us all'.

Mothers are just one example. Many other groups are springing up, in no small part because of the liberating environment offered by the cloud. There are campaigning groups which support anything from hospital patients to animal rights activists and many, many others. In a list entitled 'British Government and Politics on the Internet', Keele University School of Politics, International Relations and Philosophy identifies hundreds of politically orientated sites (http://www.keele.ac.uk/depts/por/ukbase.htm).

The UK suffered from riots in a few centres in August 2011. Many people quickly blamed Twitter as a major contributor, claiming that messages incited the violence to continue. These riots had no particular political focus, although the death of a Tottenham man at the hands of the police was no doubt a catalyst.

Twitter was used extensively to spread the news of the riots, as one would now expect of any newsworthy events. But after the event, Professor Rob Procter of the University of Manchester, who led a team of academics conducting an analysis of 2.6 million riot-related tweets, found that:

> Politicians and commentators were quick to claim that social media played an important role in inciting and organising riots, calling for sites such as Twitter to be closed should events of this nature happen again. But our study has found no evidence of significance in the available data that would justify such a course of action in respect to Twitter. In contrast, we do find strong evidence that Twitter was a valuable tool for mobilising support for the post-riot clean-up and for organising specific clean-up activities.
> (Reported on the Guardian website: http://www.guardian.co.uk/uk/series/reading-the-riots)
> (Bell and Lewis 2011)

Human nature being what it is, there will certainly be some evil by-products, but we are already seeing how useful Facebook can be in terms of exerting political pressure. As reported in the medical journal The Lancet (June 2011):

> The Taiwan Society of Emergency Medicine has been in slow-moving negotiation with the Department of Health for the past several years over an appropriate solution to emergency-room overcrowding. A turning point was reached on Feb 8, 2011, when an emergency physician who was an active social network user and popular blogger among the emergency-room staff created a Facebook group called 'Rescue the emergency room'.
> Within a week about 1,500 people—most of the emergency department staff around Taiwan—became members of this group and started discussing actively and sharing their experiences. One of the members then posted the group's concerns and problems on the Facebook profile of the Taiwanese Minister of Health.

In short, Facebook cut through bureaucratic obfuscation and made a positive change happen.

In their 2009 EU-sponsored report, Public Service 2.0: The Impact of Social Computing on Public Services, Huijboom et al. suggest that the following may be future benefits to accrue from the use of social media in the political arena:

Transparency
- Social computing applications may enhance transparency of citizen demand and government services and processes, as public-sector information is easier to collect, structure and disseminate.
- This process is likely to empower citizens to hold their public officials to account.

Citizen-centred and user-generated services
- Forms of social computing can stimulate the accessibility and personalisation of some public services because groups of users are enabled to create those public services themselves or tailor them to their preferences

Improvement of efficiency (cost/benefit)
- Social computing trends may enhance the efficiency of public value production as the knowledge needed to create public value can be built up efficiently (e.g. efficient allocation)

In terms of international relations, online cooperation can remove both organisational and geographical barriers, although there are still other barriers such as language which may be more difficult to overcome. Even language barriers may eventually be removed. As a start, the Dudu social network is attempting to become a truly multilingual SNS. The BBC's Simon Atkinson filed this in October 2011:

> Billing itself as the world's first multilingual social network, Godudu hopes to take on the likes of Facebook by offering real-time translation that it says will allow people to communicate beyond language barriers.

There is some evidence that the recent Arab Spring events have been at the very least supported by the use of social media. Some commentators see SNSs as a key enabler. We do need to be cautious about attributing too much to what is just a communications medium, however. There does need to be an underlying sense of purpose or belief that can be called upon in cloud-based campaigns.

Twitter as a large-scale political tool was first used during the 2009 Iranian election. The highlight was when the US State Department asked social networking site Twitter to delay scheduled maintenance to avoid disrupting communications amongst tech-savvy Iranian citizens as they took to the streets to protest at the re-election of President Mahmoud Ahmadinejad.

This point is ably exemplified by Anderson et al. (2011) when she said:

> In Tunisia, protesters escalated calls for the restoration of the country's suspended constitution. Meanwhile, Egyptians rose in revolt as strikes across the country brought daily life to a halt and toppled the government.

And then she points out that the year being described is 1919 and the media spreading the encouraging messages are telegraph and newspapers. In other words, we should always remember that SNS is only a communication channel and its advantage over previous channels is merely its speed and popularity.

That being said, Twitter and Facebook were very powerful tools to allow citizens to express their views and, almost as importantly, to let the outside world know what was happening. In some countries, these tools helped pile unstoppable pressure upon failing governments. In others, with stronger, more authoritarian regimes, these sites are dangerous places to be seen as Facebook spying is part of the information-gathering process used by the regimes' protectors.

Philosophical debates abound at this time as to the significance of cloud or what is more generally described as cyberspace. Does society need to control the cloud's content, or is society shaped by it? Sterner (2011) puts it thus:

One perspective generally holds that cyberspace must be managed in such a way that conforms it to society's existing institutions, particularly in matters related to national security. Another philosophy holds that cyberspace is fundamentally reordering society and that, in doing so, it will unleash new possibilities in the story of human liberty.

The recent rise to prominence of Wikileaks (http://wikileaks.org/About.html) has certainly helped to focus minds in regimes used to the near certainty of their information remaining secret. This organisation tends to polarise views. Their declaration is that:

> The broader principles on which our work is based are the defence of freedom of speech and media publishing, the improvement of our common historical record and the support of the rights of all people to create new history. We derive these principles from the Universal Declaration of Human Rights. In particular, Article 19 inspires the work of our journalists and other volunteers. It states that everyone has the right to freedom of opinion and expression; this right includes freedom to hold opinions without interference and to seek, receive and impart information and ideas through any media and regardless of frontiers.

If it was a simple as this, however, they would not have caused such a furore as they have in even liberal democracies. For example, as a result of sites like Wikileaks, US Secretary of State Hilary Clinton, in a speech in February 2011, called for:

> ...'a serious conversation' about rules to ensure an open Internet, noting it had helped power the pro-democracy uprising in Egypt but also served as a tool for terrorists and repressive governments. [...]

She went on to say that:

> To maintain an Internet that delivers the greatest possible benefits to the world, we need to have a serious conversation about the principles that will guide us. What rules exist – and should not exist – and why; what behaviors should be encouraged and discouraged, and how.

These comments are as reported by Mary Beth Sheridan in the Washington Post, Feb. 2011, in the article Clinton calls for 'serious conversation' about Internet freedom.

Reporting in The Telegraph, in the UK, Robert Winnett described the potential for Wikileaks to even affect the outcome of wars. In July 2010 he wrote that:

> Wikileaks published 90,000 documents – mostly reports detailing operations by American and other allied forces in Afghanistan between 2004 and 2009.

And that:

> The Taliban has issued a warning to Afghans whose names might appear on the leaked Afghanistan war logs as informers for the Nato-led coalition.

He goes on to report a high-ranking US military man, Admiral Mike Mullen, as saying:

> Mr Assange [Wikileak founder] can say whatever he likes about the greater good he thinks he and his source are doing, but the truth is they might already have on their hands the blood of some young soldier or that of an Afghan family.

And this was because the leaked documents might reveal information about:
- Names and addresses of Afghans cooperating with Nato forces
- Precise GPS locations of Afghans
- Sources and methods of gathering intelligence

The debate, at its heart, seems to revolve around two key questions:
- Does anyone in public life have the right to maintain secrets?
- Does anyone have the right to put people's lives at risk for the mere principle of publishing everything it can?

The authors feel that this textbook is not the place for our views. However, these issues are great as the subject matter for debates and essays, as you will gather from the exercise session at the end of this chapter.

As an interesting footnote on Wikileaks, they are clearly a cloud-based service provider which offers '…a high security anonymous drop box fortified by cutting-edge cryptographic information technologies'. Moreover, they 'operate a number of servers across multiple international jurisdictions and we do not keep logs'. In this way they are using the cloud to protect the anonymity of their contributors, even, to some extent, from themselves. And yet, they too feel under threat from a variety of agencies and are struggling to find the most secure cloud-based mechanisms to ensure theirs is a secure system.

3.5   Economic Aspects of Cloud Computing

Since economics can mean many different things, we will confine ourselves to the definition in Merriam-Webster:

> A social science concerned chiefly with description and analysis of the production, distribution, and consumption of goods and services.

Probably the most obvious possible contribution to economic models comes from the globe-spanning, border-less nature of cloud. The term globalisation has been with us for many years now and describes the fact that the world's economy is becoming increasingly integrated. This is driven by relaxations in the flow of capital and moves towards freer trade and the ability to utilise the cheapest labour possible, wherever that is in the world, as opposed to being restricted to being tied to the geographic location of a producer.

Cloud can accelerate the globalisation trend in two distinct ways:
- By enabling inter-organisational collaborations across borders.
- In its own right, platform as a service allows the spread of services and software without physical boundaries.

Since the former is covered in our Business chapters (Part III), we will concentrate here upon the latter.

Globalisation of services, in just the same way as many products now are, is fast becoming the norm. Whilst there may always be a place for your local solicitor, financial advisor or accountant, it is also true that these services are now available through the cloud in many parts of the world.

One example can be found in accountancy, where, in the UK, Liquid Accounts (http://www.liquidaccounts.net/) offers:

> …easy to use, UK-based online accounting software for SME's, accountants and book-keepers from £20 per month

This is clearly an example of a cloud service with a monthly fee rather than an annual accounting fee and obviates the need to buy accounting software.

There are many other such examples. Accountancy is a well-established service industry. But then, so is the creation of and implementation of software applications. The latter can gain significant sales benefits and customer tie-in through the adoption of a software or application as a service approach. Even the infrastructures that allow cloud to work are a marketable service, as described in the Economist magazine, February 2011:

> LIKE oil or pork bellies, computing capacity is now a tradable commodity. February 14th saw the launch of SpotCloud, the world's first spot market for cloud computing. It works much like other spot markets. Firms with excess computing capacity, such as data centres, put it up for sale. Others, which have a short-term need for some number-crunching, can bid for it.

Opportunities exist, then, for the service sector to become truly global. When the service is not located in one geographic location, barriers to trade can disappear. After all, the cloud effectively hides data and application location behind their distributed nature. If I buy some spare capacity at one service provider, who is to know? Which nation's laws will we need to follow, if any? Will I pay any trade-related tax, such as value added tax (in the United Kingdom)?

And then, if the cloud is to become a big free-trade market, it is likely to behave differently to the markets we are more used to. For a start, there will be few economies of scale and few barriers to entry. Anything your application can do, I can replicate in mine. Whilst the large players will doubtless play on their premium quality brand status, the others will need to be one of many smaller fish in a very big ocean. The cloud will allow smaller companies of niche products to sell low-volume goods and services in a cost-effective way. This effect is known as the long tail.

Furthermore, the very way that business is carried out can change. Look, for example, at the changes to the business model for selling music. The de facto norm of customers walking into a shop to buy a CD is being replaced today with iPod and iPod-like environments where the consumer has an unlimited selection and can buy just a single track, rather than a full album.

Prior to this revolution, our selection of music to purchase was typically based more upon what CDs were physically available in the store you visit. In as much as Top 10 charts are actually good indicators of popular taste, they were often actually driven by supply push, rather than demand.

Without actual shelves, a retailer no longer needs to worry about what is actually going to be profitable. Server space is the only real barrier to the size of their stock. This means they can afford to risk supplying unheard of artists at little cost to themselves. In turn this has seen the business of recording change significantly. Some artists will not even bother with contracts with traditional labels.

As well as this change brought about by one innovative approach to selling music, we can expect to see many other changes in all the entertainment industries. Film on Demand is already available in some places. Technologies are already in place that mean that anyone can wake up at 3 a.m. in the morning in more or less any country in the world and 'rent' the latest James Bond film to try and lull them back to sleep.

Although we have said it before, it is worth reminding ourselves that these changes were not as a result of cloud computing since many happened before 2008. However, the entertainment industry is just as valid an application as a service as any other, and as cloud becomes more widely adopted, it will doubtless add impetus to the existing changes in the way we do business.

Other changes can begin to occur when the cloud approach is adopted. Sellers of services and applications are less liable to cash flow problems since payments are regularly coming from customers (or they don't get the service!) The 30-day (which can mean 90 real days) payment problem which hampers many businesses disappears.

Costs to market are also likely to be less, especially for the niche software provider. They will be renting space from providers, rather than having to find up-front investment into hardware. Many service providers allow free, or very cheap, access to services in the development phase, thus supporting product creation.

All this means that the way we do business generally would be affected by the changes in methods of working as a consequence of broad adoption of cloud computing. There are, however, significant barriers to complete globalisation. Not least of these is that a large proportion of the world's population do not have access to the Internet.

India was recently quoted as having 100 million Internet users (http://www.internetworldstats.com/stats3.htm) which is a massive market by anyone's standards. But it still leaves more than 9/10th of the nation's population unable to gain any benefits from cloud. A good many of those Indians do, however, have access to mobile phones. Mobile aware cloud is clearly going to be a very import part of the growth of cloud-based economics.

Governments, many of whom are early adopters of cloud technology, will play a large part in the way that cloud is adopted worldwide. As Kushida et al. (2011) say:

> As with the previous computing platforms – mainframes, PCs, and networks of PCs – cloud computing is becoming a baseline for national and corporate IT infrastructure against which other forms of infrastructure and service delivery must be measured. In this respect it is likely that cloud computing will become an important component of national critical infrastructure. Control of cloud infrastructure will matter to national governments.

Breznitz et al. (2011) point out that:

> According to the prevailing economic thinking, public policies should set market-friendly 'rules of the game' and then stay out of the way. This fantasy is far from an apt description of the world, whether in the financial sector or in the ICT domain...

This leads us to one of the biggest uncertainties for cloud computing adopters: the legal and accounting frameworks they will be expected to work in. Legal aspects of the cloud are investigated in more detail in the Business and Law chapter, but the operating framework for a company whose product is in essence everywhere around the globe is a tricky one. The current international trading regulations were not built for border-free trade. This has to be a case of watch this space.

3.6   Cloud and Green IT

Green IT can mean many different things to many people. Just to clarify, in this section we will be looking at how cloud might assist organisations in their quest to save power costs of a variety of sorts. Sometimes this is referred to as sustainable IT.

Worrying about efficiency of our computing devices is not new and certainly pre-dates cloud computing. The 1992 Energy Star programme was an international attempt to help organisations select more efficient computers and monitors. It became, and still is, an important way to inform purchasing decisions for a broad range of electrical goods.

Concerns about climate change have helped move Green IT up the agenda for many governments and organisations. Recently we began to see Board-level appointments, demonstrating the importance that companies are now placing on sustainability. In 2009, for example, Siemens appointed a Chief Sustainability Officer (CSO) to their management board. The press release states:

> Efficient sustainability management requires clear structures and a consistent integration of the sustainability strategy in our company's organisation. Here we have taken another important step at Siemens with the appointment of Managing Board member Barbara Kux as Chief Sustainability Officer. The Sustainability Office ensures that our sustainability activities are closely interconnected with the operating units.

Obviously, the remit here is far greater than just computing, but since a sizeable portion of a typical organisation's electricity bill is as a direct result of computing, this is an area that will doubtless be an important area for investigation for any CSO.

Another sign of the importance of sustainability is the prominence of the subject on consultancy websites. The big players all have Green IT expertise and are able to offer help on reducing carbon footprints. An example of how sustainability is now part of the marketing message can be seen by reviewing the interesting Green Cube, which is on the CapGemini site: http://www.capgeminigreen.com/greencube. You could review some of the case studies on this site.

Some may wonder what all the fuss is about. After all, our laptops hardly use any energy do they? But the large servers that support an organisation's systems actually do cost a large proportion of an organisation's carbon footprint. Studies suggest that an average server can run at only 15% efficiency. If that is the case, it means many organisations could probably run one server instead of five separate ones, making huge energy savings. Typically, server power can account for 25% of total corporate IT budgets, and their costs are expected to continue to increase as the number of servers rise and the cost of electricity increases faster than revenues.

This is a strong argument for virtualisation. This technology allows you to run several virtual servers on one actual server. One of the main arguments used in the sale of virtualisation products such as VMWare and Hypervisor is this potential saving.

If you are an organisation in this position, it may be relatively easy, therefore, to combine servers using virtualisation and thence save energy. Although we have said in our chapter on underpinning technologies that virtualisation is key to cloud computing, we might still ask how cloud might help in the search for sustainability.

Smaller businesses do not necessarily have the computing needs to enable a server to be running at full efficiency. And this is where cloud helps: Many companies share the resources of the service provider's infrastructure. The service providers will be seeking to run as efficiently as possible as this will directly affect their bottom-line profitability.

As well as the hardware benefits, there are carbon savings to be found in cloud applications. The major advantage of many cloud tools, starting from Google Drive innovative approach to shared documents, is the built-in collaborative working. A plethora of business tasks are now available in the cloud allowing travel-free collaboration. Examples include brainstorming, mind mapping, systems design and process design.

There exist many cloud-based tools that can reduce an organisations costs and carbon footprint. Think, for example, of the air miles saved when geographically remote businesses work together using Skype or any of the other collaboration tools. Salespeople sending data back to their base through cloud systems no longer have to plan journeys around the need to have time in the office, but rather can plan the most efficient routes.

Is cloud, then, inherently better for the planet? We do need to be careful when jumping to this sort of conclusion. There may be other factors to consider when balancing overall good. Moreover, there are many business drivers in IT infrastructure decisions, and greenness is often not paramount amongst them.

One argument might be that IT itself is inherently a non-sustainable addition to any process. Picture an office using green pens and recycled paper for their processes, with paper moving by foot or bicycle. Now compare that to the typical office today: Paperless turns out to be a largely unachievable dream, so the paper still exists, but we also have expensive to create machinery which contains toxic substances, contributes to a high proportion of an organisation's energy bills, and which will need to be disposed of as waste in 3–5 years time.

We need to be conscious of what are the real arguments for and against sustainability in IT. Sustainability is used as a marketing buzzword in IT.

Moreover, there is the problem of general awareness. When driving a car many people now realise that it is more fuel efficient not to accelerate and brake harshly and to reduce the average speed you travel at. How many of us, however, think about the extra disk reads and CPU usage caused by just playing around with data? The costs are hidden.

So where are the costs? One paper (Brill 2007) suggests that:

> The largely invisible costs of providing power, cooling and environmental site support infrastructure are increasing far faster than the performance gained from buying new servers.

The paper continues by projecting that:

...the 3-year cost of powering and cooling servers (OpEx + amortized CapEx) is currently 1.5 times the cost of purchasing server hardware. Future projections extending out to 2012 show this multiplier increasing to 22 times the cost of the hardware under worst case assumptions and to almost three times under even the best-case assumptions. (Brill 2007)

The financial aspects of investment appraisal are discussed in Chap. 8. Here we will just explore what this means in terms of sustainability. Other papers, as outlined by Ruth (2009), suggest that IT infrastructure accounts for about 3% of global electricity usage and of greenhouse gasses. Gartner et al. (2007) suggested the level of CO_2 emissions from IT was running at about 2% and that equals the contribution of the aviation industry, which has historically had much bad press from the green lobbies. To help with scale, Schmidt et al. (2009) point out that worldwide power consumption by servers approximately equates to the consumption of the whole of the polish economy.

Whether or not there is a proven case for IT's claims to enhance productivity, it is clearly here to stay, at least in the short-to-medium term. The green pen and paper is not often considered as a serious alternative when organisations look to improve their systems. So the thrust has to be making IT as green as possible.

Governments across the globe are creating measures to cut carbon emissions by industry, but some of the measures may seem to be unfair to rapidly expanding data centre businesses. As the Financial Times reported (2011):

Information technology companies are becoming reluctant to build big data centres in the UK because of uncertainties and additional costs created by the government's carbon reduction commitments.

Whilst there may be a net increase in efficiency through the shutting of many inefficient small data centres, those smaller centres belonging to SMEs are often less harshly hit by the measures than the large centres. Moreover, in continuing to offer this amalgamation service, the large centres increase in size and therefore in energy usage year on year. Since government measures often rank businesses according to their success in reducing carbon, this expansion could be costly in terms of levies.

As we have seen elsewhere in this book, cloud computing can have significantly different meanings. A small company which uses a private cloud is likely to have a significantly different power usage per user than a large organisation which uses entirely a public cloud. Moreover, some organisations will be using software as a service, whilst others will be more closely tied to the service provider and adopt an infrastructure as a service approach.

With this in mind, it is perhaps too simplistic to make claims about cloud computing's green credentials. Intuitively it may seem that combining processing is bound to improve efficiency. But we are in danger of forgetting that there is a cost of a globalised approach to data storage in terms of transporting the data. Far more energy sapping switching and routing is required to put and get data than might be the case if your data is stored on your own PC or local server.

One detailed study by Baliga et al. (2010) suggests:

under some circumstances cloud computing can consume more energy than conventional computing where each user performs all computing on their own personal computer (PC).

As that paper goes on to suggest, optimum greenness will probably be a result of a mixture of approaches rather than simply going for one single approach:

Significant energy savings are achieved by using low-end laptops for routine tasks and cloud processing services for computationally intensive tasks, instead of a midrange or high-end PC, provided the number of computationally intensive tasks is small.

So it is clear that the jury is out at the minute about how Green Cloud actually is. Governments continue to attempt to reduce our carbon outputs, and it may well be that legislation is the single biggest driver in the use, or not, of cloud towards green ends.

3.7   Review Questions

The answers to these questions can be found in the text of this chapter.
1. How has the public reaction to ICT in general changed over the past few decades? How will those changes help, or hinder, the adoption of cloud?
2. What impact has Web 2.0 had on the way society interacts with technology?
3. Give an example of how a social networking tool has been used to apply political pressure on decision-makers.
4. Describe ways that cloud-based technologies are likely to accelerate the trend to globalisation.
5. Explain how the virtualisation that may be involved in cloud platforms might help reduce energy consumption.

3.8   Extended Study Activities

These activities require you to research beyond the contents of this book and can be approached individually for the purposes of self-study or used as the basis of group work.

3.8.1   Discussion Topic 1

How much impact did cloud computing have upon what has been described as The Arab Spring? When answering this question, you might like to start by attempting to define what is meant by cloud in this case. You can debate whether you consider social networking technologies as part of the cloud.

3.8.2 Discussion Topic 2

Is cloud computing inherently better for the planet? A starting point here is the section in this chapter, but as you will see, there are arguments for and against this proposition, and there is much information in the public domain that could help you form a reasoned judgement on this question.

References

Ahn, Y., Han, S., Kwak, H., Moon, S., Jeong, H.: Analysis of topological characteristics of huge online social networking services. In: Proceedings of the 16th International Conference on World Wide Web (WWW '07), pp. 835–844. ACM, New York (2007). doi:10.1145/1242572.1242685, http://doi.acm.org/10.1145/1242572.1242685. Last accessed 12 May 2012

Anderson, L.: Demystifying the Arab spring: parsing the differences between Tunisia, Egypt, and Libya. Foreign Affairs (New York, N.Y.) Vol 90, Issue 3 (2011)

Atkinson, S.: Middle East firms eye social media profit potential. BBC Online News, 25 October 2011. http://www.bbc.co.uk/news/business-15435768 (2011). Last accessed 12 May 2012

Baliga, J., Ayre, R., Hinton, K., Tucker, R.S.: Green cloud computing: balancing energy in processing, storage, and transport. Proc. IEEE **99**(1), 149–167 (2011). Issue Date: Jan 2011

Ball, J., Lewis, P.: Reading the riots study to examine causes and effects of August unrest. guardian.co.uk, Monday 5 Sept 2011: http://www.guardian.co.uk/uk/2011/sep/05/reading-riots-study-guardian-lse (2011). Last accessed 12 May 2012

Brill, K.: Data Center Energy Efficiency and Productivity. The Uptime Institute, Santa Fe (2007). http://www.warmtraining.org/gov/pdf/WhitePaper_DataCenters.pdf. Last accessed 12 May 2012

Breznitz, D., Kenney, M., Rouvinen, P., Zysman, J., Ylä-Anttila, P.: Value capture and policy design in a digital economy. J. Ind. Compet. Trade **11**(3), 203–207 (2011)

Gartner, Inc.: Gartner Estimates ICT Industry Accounts for 2 Percent of Global CO$_2$ Emissions, Press Release, Stamford, 26 April 2007. http://www.gartner.com/it/page.jsp?id=503867 (2007). Last accessed 12 May 2012

Huijboom, N., van den Broek, T., Frissen, V., Kool, L., Kotterink, B., Nielsen, M., Millard, J.: Public Service 2.0: The Impact of Social Computing on Public Services. EUR Number: 24080 EN (2011)

Keele University. British Government and Politics on the Internet. http://www.keele.ac.uk/depts/por/ukbase.htm#groups (2011). Last accessed 12 May 2012

Kling, R.: Models for the social accountability of computing. Telecommun. Policy **4**(3), 166–182 (1980)

Kroes, N.: How eHealth can lead to a healthier Europe. Guardian Professional, Thursday 12 May 2011

Kushida, K., Murray, J., Zysman, J.: Diffusing the cloud: cloud computing and implications for public policy. J. Ind. Compet. Trade, doi:10.1007/s10842-011-0106-5. Springer, Dordrecht (2011)

Lee, R.S.: Social attitudes and the computer revolution. Public Opin. Q. **34**(1), 53–59 (1970)

Lenhart, A., Madden, M.: Teens, Privacy and Online Social Networks: How Teens Manage Their Online Identities and Personal Information in the Age of MySpace. Pew Internet and American Life Project 2007, Washington, DC (2007)

O'Regan, G.: A Brief History of Computing. Springer, London (2008)

O'Reilly, T.: What Is Web 2.0: Design Patterns and Business Models for the Next Generation of Software. http://oreilly.com/web2/archive/what-is-web-20.html (2005). Last accessed 12 May 2012

Palmer, M.: IT sector fears impact of carbon targets. Financial Times, 28 Aug 2011. http://www.ft.com/cms/s/0/cc219a30-cf3b-11e0-b6d4-00144feabdc0.html#axzz1rGsuyOa7 (2011). Last accessed 12 May 2012

Pidd, H.: UK housewives are world's top internet surfers. guardian.co.uk, Wednesday 31 December 2008. http://www.guardian.co.uk/technology/2008/dec/31/internet-housewives (2008). Last accessed 12 May 2012

Ruth, S.: Green IT more than a three percent solution? Internet Comput. IEEE **13**(4), 74–78 (2009). doi:10.1109/MIC.2009.82. http://ieeexplore.ieee.org/stamp/stamp.jsp?tp=&arnumber=5167271&isnumber=5167256

Schmidt, K., Kolbe, Z.: Sustainable information systems management. J. Bus. Inf. Syst. Eng., Gabler Verlag **1**(5), 400–402 (2009)

Sheridan, M.: Hilary Clinton's speech, comments are as reported by Mary Beth Sheridan in the Washington Post, Feb 2011 in the article: Clinton calls for 'serious conversation' about Internet freedom. http://www.washingtonpost.com/wp-dyn/content/article/2011/02/15/AR2011021504505.html (2001). Last accessed 12 May 2012

Sterner, E.: Wikileaks and Cyberspace Cultures in Conflict. George C. Marshall Institute, Feb 2011. http://www.marshall.org/pdf/materials/931.pdf (2011). Last accessed 12 May 2012

Syed-Abdul, S., Lin, C., Scholl, J., Fernandez-Luque, L., Jian, W., Hsu, M., Liou, D., Li, Y.: Facebook use leads to health-care reform in Taiwan. The Lancet **377**(9783), 2083–2084 (2011)

Wang, L.: Attitudes toward computers: a new attitudinal dimension. Cyberpsychol. Behav. **10**(5), 700–704 (2007)

Winnett, R.: Wikileaks Afghanistan: Taliban 'hunting down informants'. The Telegraph, 30 Jul 2010

Part II
Technological Context

Cloud Technology

4

What the reader will learn:

- Essential web technology for the cloud
- How virtualisation supports the cloud
- About distributed programming and the MapReduce algorithm
- How to create a desktop virtual machine
- How to create a simple MapReduce job

4.1 Introduction

If we are asked to sum up cloud computing in four key words we might arguably choose 'web', 'elasticity', 'utility' and 'scalability'. In this chapter, we are going to look at the technology underlying the cloud. Cloud applications are accessed via the web, and web technology is integral to the cloud, so we will begin with a brief review of the current state of web technology. We will then move on to virtualisation, a key cloud technology which has many benefits including improved use of resources. Virtualisation can be used to provide the elasticity required to offer cloud computing as a utility. We then turn our attention to the MapReduce programming model, originally developed by the founders of Google and now used to provide scalability to many of the distributed applications which are typical of the cloud and simply too big to be handled in a user-friendly time frame by traditional systems.

At the end of this chapter, you will be guided through the process of creating your own virtual machine (VM) using VMWare and the open source Ubuntu (Linux) operating system. You will then run a simple MapReduce job using your virtual machine. We will use this VM again in later chapters.

R. Hill et al., *Guide to Cloud Computing: Principles and Practice*, Computer Communications and Networks, DOI 10.1007/978-1-4471-4603-2_4, © Springer-Verlag London 2013

4.2   Web Technology

A feature of web and cloud applications is that a number of separate technologies are required to work together. A minimum web application is likely to use HTTP, XHTML, CSS, JavaScript, XML, server programming (e.g. PHP) and some mechanism to persist data (to be examined in detail in a later chapter). We will introduce these technologies in a brief way here; if you are already familiar with web technology you can safely skip this section. On the other hand, if you are completely new to web technology, you may prefer to begin by working through the basic tutorials for HTML, CSS, JavaScript and XML at the excellent W3 site: http://www. w3schools.com/.

4.2.1   HTTP

Cloud systems are built on the World Wide Web, and the web is built on the underlying network communication system known as HTTP or Hypertext Transfer Protocol. HTTP is the key to building cloud systems, and at a low level, each interaction in a cloud application uses HTTP (Nixon 2009).

Berners-Lee (who originally proposed the World Wide Web) and his team are credited with inventing the original HTTP. The first version had just one method, namely, GET, which was used when a user made a request for a web page from a server. A number of other methods have since been added including:

- HEAD which asks the server for information about a resource
- PUT which stores data in a resource
- POST which sends data to a program to be processed on the server
- DELETE which deletes the specified resource

HTTP uses a simple request/response cycle which allows two parties, often referred to as the client and the server, to communicate. The client drives the communication by sending requests to the server. The server processes the request and sends responses, which may contain content such as HTML. A response may contain status information and the content requested in the message body.

HTTP requests are centred on a particular resource. We can think of a resource as anything on the network that has a name. Every HTTP request is either asking to retrieve data from a resource or sending data to a resource.

Each HTML request that you generate using a browser or application has three parts:

1. A request line consisting of the HTTP method, the URL of the resource and the protocol version (usually HTTP 1.1)
2. A series of header lines containing metadata about the resource
3. The body consisting of a stream of data

A typical HTTP request might look like:

```
GET/cloud/book/chapter4 HTTP/1.1
User-Agent: Mozilla/5.001 (windows; U; NT4.0; en-US;
rv:1.0)
Host: cloud-principles-practices.appspot.com
```

Table 4.1 Common HTTP
status codes

Status code	Description
200	OK
301	Moved permanently
401	Unauthorised
403	Forbidden
404	Not found
500	Internal server error

When a server responds, the first line includes a 3-digit status code (frequently encountered codes are summarised below) and message indicating whether or not the request succeeded, for example,

`HTTP/1.1 200 OK`

Other codes, which you have probably encountered, are shown in Table 4.1

An important aspect of the HTTP is that you are unable to store mutable state; that is, we cannot assign values to variables or store anything to be shared between different calls to the same function. Everything that is needed by a server process must be sent explicitly as a parameter.

4.2.2 HTML (HyperText Markup Language) and CSS (Cascading Style Sheets)

Web pages are written using HTML also originally proposed by Berners-Lee. HTML is used to describe the structure of the page and includes structural elements such as paragraphs (e.g. <p></p>), headings (e.g. <h1></h1>) and lists (e.g. <li></li>).

CSS is a technology which allows us to create styles which define how HTML elements should look. The combination of HTML and CSS allows web page developers to separate structure from appearance. The 'separation of concerns' is an important principle in many areas of software engineering and is central to the development of cloud systems.

All pages on a site are usually styled in the same way, and styles are generally not specific to a single web page. CSS allows us to define our style information and then apply it to many pages across a site. So, for example, should we wish to present our pages in a different way to distinct user groups, the required changes may be limited to a small number of CSS pages rather than updating all the pages on our site. The separation of structure from appearance can be translated into the separation of the logic of our cloud application to the rendering of the pages to be presented to our users.

Separating style information lets you write it once and use it on all pages instead of coding it again and again. This also relates to another important principle of software engineering, namely, 'Don't Repeat Yourself' or DRY. When the DRY principle is applied successfully, modifications are localised and should not occur in unrelated elements. DRY aims to reduce repetition of all kinds of information but is particularly important to multi-tier web or cloud architectures where the improvements in maintainability become critical to success.

4.2.3   XML (eXtensible Markup Language)

XML is a technology introduced by the W3C to allow data to be encoded in a textual format which is readable to both humans and machines. XML simplifies and standardises the exchange and storage of data and has become a standard way of representing data. In XML, the tags relate to the meaning of the enclosed text, making XML self-explanatory. XML allows for a hierarchical approach, is portable and interoperable and has been used to create a wide variety of markup languages including XHTML which is simply HTML in XML format.

The Document Object Model (DOM) allows for machine navigation of an XML document as if it were a tree of node objects representing the document contents, and there are many tools and libraries freely available in many programming languages which will parse XML. Unsurprisingly, XML is widely used in cloud systems. XLM does, however, have some disadvantages and in particular is criticised for being 'tag heavy'; indeed, a significant fraction of an XML file can be taken up by the tags.

4.2.4   JSON (JavaScript Object Notation)

JSON is an increasingly popular lightweight alternative to XML and is directly based on data structures found in the JavaScript language (although JSON is language independent). JSON is built on two human readable structures, namely, a collection of name/value pairs or an ordered list of values.

4.2.5   JavaScript and AJAX (Asynchronous JavaScript and XML)

JavaScript is a programming language which normally runs in the client's browser and allows the web page to be updated by traversing and updating the DOM tree. This means that the programmer is able to dynamically update an XHTML document by navigating the tree and then applying insert, delete or update operations to elements, attributes (including style information) or contents. JavaScript can also add important functionality such as the ability to validate user input before an HTTP request is sent to the server.

XMLHttpRequest is a JavaScript object which manages HTTP requests and has the useful capability of working outside the normal browser request/response cycle. The technology surrounding the XMLHttpRequest is known as AJAX and allows for partial page updates which in turn improve the user experience and allow for web applications to work in a comparable manner to desktop applications. Such web applications are sometimes referred to as Rich Internet Applications (RIA). However, the asynchronous nature of the HTTP calls adds complexity to web application programming, and as pages may be updated without changing the URL in the user's browser, special consideration needs to be given to handling the user's back button and bookmarking capability. Furthermore, older browsers do not support the technology so developers must check the browser type and version when using AJAX.

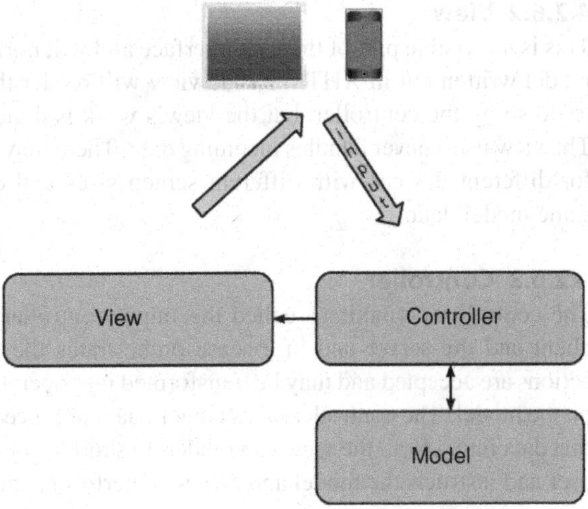

Fig. 4.1 MVC

4.2.6   Model-View-Controller (MVC)

MVC is a standard architecture for separating components in an interactive application. The architecture was first described well before the World Wide Web in 1979 by Trygve Reenskaug but in recent years has proved increasingly popular in the development of web applications. MVC is interpreted and applied in slightly different ways, but here we use it to refer to the separation of application data (contained in the model) from graphical representation (the view) and input-processing logic (the controller). A simple summary of MVC is given in Figure 4.1.

The controller implements logic for processing the input, the model contains the application data and the view presents the data from the model. An MVC application consists of a set of model/view/controller triples responsible for different elements of the user interface. MVC is a natural way to write cloud applications, and so it is worth briefly describing the three components in more detail.

4.2.6.1 Model
We mentioned earlier that HTTP does not allow us to assign values or store information between requests. In a cloud application based on MVC, the model is responsible for maintaining the state of the application, whether this is just for a small number of request/response cycles or if we need to persist data in a permanent way, for example, using a server database. The model is, however, more than just data as the model is responsible for the enforcement of the business rules that apply to the data. The model acts as a 'gatekeeper' and a data store. Note that the model is totally decoupled from the interface and works instead with the underlying data, often stored in a database. As our application is based on HTTP, the server must wait for requests from the client before it can send its response.

4.2.6.2 View

This is the visible part of the user interface and will normally be based on data in the model written out in XHTML. The view will render the XHTML when instructed to do so by the controller, but the view's work is done once the data is displayed. The view itself never handles incoming data. There may be many views, for example, for different devices with different screen sizes and capability, which access the same model data.

4.2.6.3 Controller

The controller (sometimes called the 'input controller') is the bridge between the client and the server and in a sense orchestrates the whole application. Interface actions are accepted and may be transformed into operations which can be performed on the model. The controller takes content data produced by the model and translates that data into a form the view can render. In short, a controller accepts input from the user and instructs the model and a view to perform actions based on that input.

4.3   Autonomic Computing

Autonomic computing seeks to improve computer systems by decreasing human involvement in their operation with the ultimate goal of producing systems which manage themselves and adapt to unpredictable changes. The advantages become significant in a large data centre of hundreds or thousands of nodes. In this environment, machine failures are not rare events but are regular occurrences which must be managed carefully.

Autonomous or semi-autonomous machines rely on three elements: monitoring probes and gauges, an adaption engine and on effectors to apply any required changes to the system. Decisions made by an autonomic system are usually based on a set of predefined policies. IBM's Autonomic Computing Intuitive defines four properties of autonomic systems, namely, self-configuration, self-optimisation, self-healing and self-protection.

4.4   Virtualisation

Virtualisation refers to the process where abstract or virtual resources are used to simulate physical resources. Virtualisation can be of great benefit to cloud systems as it can improve resource pooling and enable rapid and elastic resource provisioning. These benefits make for agile, flexible networks leading to significant cost reductions. In typical cloud computing applications, servers, storage and network devices may all be virtualized (Goldne 2008).

Virtualisation has a long history in the software industry and the term has been used in a variety of ways. The earliest type of virtual machine dates back to IBM in the 1960s which aimed to maximise use of expensive mainframe systems through multitasking. We will briefly introduce the main types of virtualisation in the following sections.

4.4.1 Application Virtualisation

Application virtualisation, sometimes called a 'process virtual machine', provides a platform-independent programming environment which hides the details of the underlying hardware and operating system. The Java Virtual Machine (JVM) is a commonly cited and popular example of an application virtual machine. The JVM provides an environment in which Java bytecode can be executed. The JVM can run on many hardware platforms, and the use of the same bytecode allows for the 'write once run anywhere' description which is highly appealing to application developers. Java bytecode is an intermediate language which is typically compiled from Java, but a number of other languages such as Python (Jython) or Ruby (JRuby) can also be used.

4.4.2 Virtual Machine

In the cloud context, 'virtual machine' is usually taken to mean a software implementation of a machine with a complete independent operating system, which executes programs like a physical machine. This type of virtualisation began with work in the Linux community but has lead to a variety of commercial and open source libraries.

The virtual machine may have a number of virtual components including:

- 'Virtual processors' which share time with other virtual machines on the physical processor
- 'Virtual memory' which are normally implemented as a slice of physical RAM on the host machine (not to be confused with common use of 'virtual memory' referring to the combination of various types of storage media)
- 'Virtual hard disk' which is typically one or more large files on the physical disk
- 'Virtual network' based on a network interface controller (NIC)

In the next chapter, we will see how vendors such as Amazon use the power of virtualisation to offer users access to cloud-based resources such as compute power (e.g. Amazon EC2) or storage (e.g. Amazon S3) which they can rent from Amazon at an hourly rate.

4.4.3 Desktop Virtualisation

In desktop virtualisation, the user is provided with access to a virtual machine over which they may have complete control. This can be very useful, for example, in an organisation where users have very limited rights in terms of program installation and configuration on local machines, they can be given complete freedom to install their own programs on a virtual machine. Furthermore, the virtual machine can run an entirely different operating system to that of the host, so users can choose and configure their preferred environment. Virtual machines can be copied, moved or destroyed as required, and a 'snapshot' can be taken of a machine at any time so that the user can save and return to a particular environment. This capability also provides for a useful and safe way of testing new upgrades and environments. Examples of the technology include VMWare Workstation, Microsoft VirtualPC and Oracle Virtual Box. At the end of this chapter, you will create your own desktop virtual machine using VMWare.

4.4.4   Server Virtualisation

Server virtualisation applies the same principle as desktop virtualisation but to the server environment. Server virtualisation allows entire operating systems, applications and accessories to be packaged into a set of files that can be moved or copied and then run on common hardware in any compatible virtualized environment. Virtual machines allow us to decouple the computing infrastructure from the physical infrastructure, potentially leading to a number of important benefits in the running of a data centre.

4.4.4.1 Efficiency

It has been estimated that most servers are highly underutilised and run at about 15% of their total capacity. Virtualisation allows for a more efficient use of machine resources which can lead to a reduction in power consumption, cooling and space requirements (see also Chap. 3). This improved use of resources can make a big difference to the overall energy consumption of a large data centre, and it has been suggested that virtualisation can be an important component in achieving reduced carbon emissions from the IT industry.

4.4.4.2 Isolation

Virtualisation means that secure, encapsulated clones of your entire work environment can be created for testing and backup purposes leading to improved maintenance, flexibility and high availability. The failure of one virtual machine should not affect any of the other machines running on the same host. This has important and beneficial implications for vendor's offering cloud based resources which are available to multiple tenants. Thus, for example, if a user of an Amazon EC2 machine accidentally corrupts their operating system or runs a program with an infinite loop, it should not have a detrimental effect on other users running virtual machines in the same data centre.

4.4.4.3 Mobility

Virtual machine mobility enables applications to migrate from one server to another even whilst they are still running. For example, with systems such as vSphere, virtual machines can be configured to automatically restart on a different physical server in a cluster if a host fails. This capability can be a critical component in the provision of autonomic computing as well as leading to the following advantageous outcomes:

- A reduction in the number of servers required
- Data centre maintenance without downtime
- Improved availability, disaster avoidance and recovery

- Simplification of data centre migration or consolidation
- Data centre expansion
- Workload balancing across multiple sites
  There are, of course, some disadvantages:
- Virtual servers require a hypervisor to keep track of virtual machine identification (see below), local policies and security, which can be a complex task.
- The integration of the hypervisor with existing network management software can be problematic and may require changes to the network hardware.

4.4.5 Storage Virtualisation

Storage virtualisation provides different servers access to the same storage space. Data centre storage is comprised of storage area networks (SAN) and network-attached storage (NAS). In a cloud computing environment, a network can be enabled to address large virtual pools of storage resources. Storage virtualisation allows for the use of all the multiple disk arrays, often made by different vendors and scattered over the network, as if they were a single storage device, which can be centrally managed.

4.4.6 Implementing Virtualisation

As mentioned above, multiple virtual machines can run simultaneously on the same physical machine, and each virtual machine can have a different operating system. A virtual machine monitor (VMM) is used to control and manage the virtual machines on a single node. A VMM is often referred to as a hypervisor (see below). At a higher level, virtual machine infrastructure managers (VIMs) are used to manage, deploy and monitor virtual machines on a distributed pool of resources such as a data center. Cloud infrastructure managers (CIM) are web-based management solutions specifically for cloud systems.

Virtualisation management is the technology that abstracts the coupling between the hardware and the operating system, allowing computing environments to be dynamically created, expanded, shrunk, archived or removed. It is therefore extremely well suited to the dynamic cloud infrastructure. Load balancing is of course an important part of this management and soon becomes critical in the prevention of system bottlenecks due to unbalanced loads.

4.4.7 Hypervisor

Generally, virtualisation is achieved by the use of a hypervisor. The hypervisor is a software that allows multiple virtual images to share a single physical machine and to logically assign and separate physical resources. The hypervisor allows the computer hardware to run multiple guest operating systems concurrently. As mentioned above, each of the guest operating systems is isolated and protected from any others and is unaffected by problems or instability occurring on other virtual machines

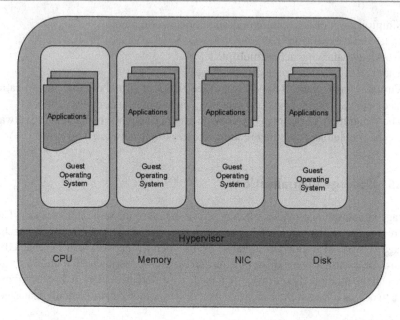

Fig. 4.2 Hypervisor (bare metal)

running on the same physical machine. The hypervisor presents the guest operating systems with an abstraction of the underlying computer system and controls the execution of the guest operating system.

Many powerful hypervisors including KVM (Kernel-based Virtual Machine), Xen and QEMU are open source. VMWare is currently the market leader in the field of virtualisation and many of its products are based on open source. Amazon uses a modified version of Xen.

Figure 4.2 shows a high-level view of a hypervisor where the machine resources of the host are shared between a number of guests, each of which may be running applications and each has direct access to the underlying physical resources.

4.4.8 Types of Virtualisation

Virtualisation can be classified into two categories depending on whether or not the guest operating system kernel needs to be modified. In full virtualisation, a guest operating system runs unmodified on a hypervisor. In the case of para-virtualisation, there is no need to emulate the entire hardware environment. Para-virtualisation requires modifications to the guest operating system kernel so that it 'becomes aware' of the hypervisor and can communicate with it. Guest operating systems using full virtualisation are generally faster.

Figure 4.3 shows the situation where the hypervisor is running on a hosted operating system. This is the type of hypervisor we will be using in the exercise at the end of this chapter.

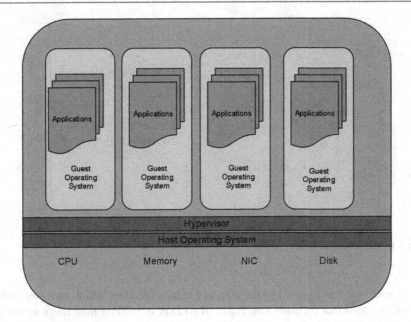

Fig. 4.3 Hosted hypervisor

4.5 MapReduce

MapReduce was originally introduced by Google as a distributed programming model using large server clusters to process massive (multi-terabyte) data sets. The model can be applied to many large-scale computing problems and offers a number of attractive features such as automatic parallelisation, load balancing, network and disk transfer optimisation and robust handling of machine failure. MapReduce works by breaking a large problem into smaller parts, solving each part in parallel and then combining results to produce the final answer (White 2009).

MapReduce runs on top of a specialised file system such as the Google File System (GFS) or the Hadoop File System (HDFS). Data is loaded, partitioned into chunks (commonly 64 MB) such that each chunk can replicate. A key feature of MapReduce is that data processing is collocated with data storage, and as a distributed programming paradigm, a number of advantages are evident when compared to the traditional approach of moving the data to the computation including:

1. Scalability
2. Reliability
3. Fault tolerance
4. Simplicity
5. Efficiency

All these advantages are obviously very relevant to the cloud, where processing large amounts of data using distributed resources is a central task. Unsurprisingly, MapReduce is a programming model used widely in cloud computing environments for processing large data sets in a highly parallel way.

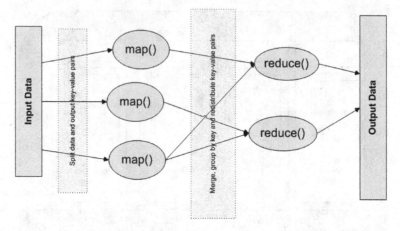

Fig. 4.4 MapReduce overview

MapReduce was inspired by the map and reduce functions which are commonly found in functional program languages like LISP. In LISP, a map takes an input function and a sequence of values and then applies the function to each value in the sequence. Reduce combines all the elements in the sequence using an operator such as * or +. In MapReduce, the functions are not so rigidly defined, but programmers still specify the computation in terms of the two functions map and reduce, which can be carried out on subsets of total data under analysis in parallel. The map function is used to generate a list of intermediate key/value pairs, and the reduce function merges all the intermediate values associated with same intermediate key.

When all the tasks have been completed, the result is returned to the user. In MapReduce, input data is portioned across multiple worker machines executing in parallel; intermediate values are output from the map worker machines and fed to a set of 'reduce' machines (there may be some intermediate steps such as sorting). It is, perhaps, useful to think of MapReduce as representing a data flow as shown in Figure 4.4 rather than a procedure. Jobs are submitted by a user to a master node that selects idle workers and assigns each one a MapReduce task to be performed in parallel. The process of moving map outputs to the reducers is known as 'shuffling'.

4.5.1   MapReduce Example

The canonical MapReduce example takes a document or a set of documents and outputs a listing of unique words and the number of occurrences throughout the text data. The map function takes as its key/value pair the document name and document contents. It then reads through the text of the document and outputs an intermediate key/value listing for each word encountered together with a value of 1. The reduce phase then counts up each of these individual 1's and outputs the total value for each word. The pseudocode for the functions is shown below. The map function takes the name of the document as the key and the contents as the value.

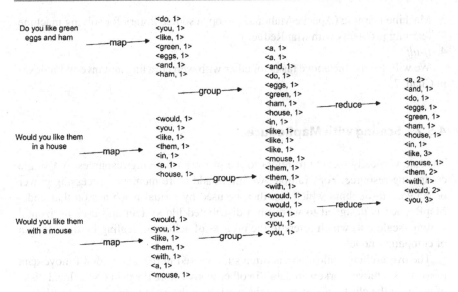

Fig. 4.5 MapReduce word count example

```
map(document_name, document_contents) {
    for each word w in document_contents
        emit_intermediate(w, 1)
}
reduce(a_word, intermediate_vals) {
    result = 0
    for each value v in intermediate_vals
        result += v
    emit result
}
```

Figure 4.5 shows a simple example with the three input files shown on the left and the output word counts shown on the right.

The same kind of process can be applied to many other problems and is particularly useful where we need to process a huge amount of raw data, for example, from documents which have been returned by a web crawl. To create an inverted index (see Chap. 7) after a web crawl, we can create a map function to read each document and output a sequence of <word, documentID> pairs. The reduce function accepts all pairs for a given word and output pairs of <word, documentIDList> such that for any word, we can quickly identify all the documents in which the word occurs. The amount of data may be simply too big for traditional systems and needs to be distributed across hundreds or thousands of machines in order to be processed in a reasonable time frame. Other problems which are well suited to the MapReduce approach include but are not limited to:

1. Searching
2. Classification and clustering

3. Machine learning (Apache Mahout is an open source library for solving machine learning problems with MapReduce)
4. *tf-idf*

We will discuss the above tasks together with web crawling and inverted indexes in Chap. 7.

4.5.2 Scaling with MapReduce

To scale vertically (scale up) refers to the process of adding resources to a single computing resource. For example, we might add more memory, processing power or network throughput which can then be used by virtual machines on that node. MapReduce is designed to work on a distributed file system and uses horizontal scaling (scale out) which refers to the process of achieving scaling by the addition of computing nodes.

The overarching philosophy is often summarised in the adage 'don't move data to workers – move workers to data'; in other words, store the data on the local disks of nodes in the cluster and then use the worker on the node to process its local data. For the kind of problem typical of MapReduce, it is simply not possible to hold all the data in memory. However, throughput can remain reasonable through use of multiple nodes, and reliability is achieved through redundancy. Rather than use expensive 'high end' machines, the approach generally benefits from standard commodity hardware—a philosophy sometimes summarised as 'scale out not up'. In any MapReduce task, coordination is needed, and a 'master' is required to create chunks, balance and replicate and communicate with the nodes.

4.5.3 Server Failure

Where processing occurs on one powerful and expensive machine, we might reasonably expect to run the machine for several years without experiencing hardware failure. However, in a distributed environment using hundreds or thousands of low-cost machines, failures are an expected and frequent occurrence. The creators of MapReduce realised they could combat machine failure simply by replicating jobs across machines. Server failure of a worker is managed by re-executing the task on another worker. Alternatively, several workers can be assigned the same task, and the result is taken from the first one to complete, thus also improving execution time.

4.5.4 Programming Model

The MapReduce model targets a distributed parallel platform with a large number of machines communicating on a network without any explicit shared memory. The programming model is simple and has the advantage that programmers without expertise in distributed systems are able to create MapReduce tasks. The programmer only needs to supply the two functions, map and reduce, both of which work with key value pairs (often written as <k, v>). Common problems can be solved by writing two or more MapReduce steps which feed into each other.

4.5.5 Apache Hadoop

Hadoop is a popular open-source Java implementation of MapReduce and is used to build cloud environments in a highly fault tolerant manner. Hadoop will process web-scale data of the order of terabytes or petabytes by connecting many commodity computers together to work in parallel. Hadoop includes a complete distributed batch processing infrastructure capable of scaling to hundreds or thousands of computing nodes, with advanced scheduling and monitoring capability. Hadoop is designed to have a 'very flat scalability curve' meaning that once a program is created and tested on a small number of nodes, the same program can then be run on a huge cluster of machines with minimal or no further programming required. Reliable performance growth should then be in proportion to the number of machines available.

The Hadoop File System (HDFS) splits large data files into chunks which are managed by different nodes on the cluster so that each node is operating on a subset of the data. This means that most data is read from the local disk directly into the CPU, thus reducing the need to transfer data across the network and therefore improving performance. Each chunk is also replicated across the cluster so that a single machine failure will not result in data becoming inaccessible.

Fault tolerance is achieved mainly through active monitoring and restarting tasks when necessary. Individual nodes communicate with a master node known as a 'JobTracker'. If a node fails to communicate with the job tracker for a period of time (typically 1 min), the task may be restarted. A system of speculative execution is often employed such that once most tasks have been completed, the remaining tasks are copied across a number of nodes. Once a task has completed, the job tracker is informed, and any other nodes working on the same tasks can be terminated.

4.5.6 A Brief History of Hadoop

Hadoop was created by Doug Cutting (also responsible for Lucene) who named it after his son's toy elephant. Hadoop was originally developed to support distribution of tasks associated with the Nutch web crawler project. In Chap. 7, we will discuss Lucene and Nutch in more detail and will use Nutch to perform a web crawl and create a searchable Lucene index in the end of chapter exercise.

Yahoo was one of the primary developers of Hadoop, but the system is now used by many companies including Facebook, Twitter, Amazon and most recently Microsoft. Hadoop is now a top-level Apache project and benefits from a global community of contributors.

4.5.7 Amazon Elastic MapReduce

Elastic MapReduce runs a hosted Hadoop instance on an EC2 (see Chap. 5) instance master which is able to provision other pre-configured EC2 instances to distribute the MapReduce tasks. Amazon currently allows you to specify up to 20 EC2 instances for data intensive processing.

4.5.8 Mapreduce.NET

Mapreduce.NET is an implementation of MapReduce for the .Net platform which aims to provide support for a wide variety of compute-intensive applications. Mapreduce.Net is designed for the Windows platform and is able to reuse many existing Windows components. An example of Mapreduce.Net in action is found in MRPGA (MapReduce for Parallel GAs) which is an extension of MapReduce specifically for parallelizing genetic algorithms which are widely used in the machine learning community.

4.5.9 Pig and Hive

Pig, originally developed at Yahoo research, is a high-level platform for creating MapReduce programs using a language called 'Pig Latin' which compiles into physical plans which are executed on Hadoop. Pig aims to dramatically reduce the time required for the development of data analysis jobs when compared to creating Hadoops. The creators of Pig describe the language as hitting 'a sweet spot between the declarative style of SQL and the low-level, procedural style of MapReduce'. You will create a small Pig Latin program in the tutorial section.

Apache Hive which runs on Hadoop offers data warehouse services.

4.6   Chapter Summary

In this chapter, we have investigated some of the key technology underlying computing clouds. In particular, we have focused on web application technology, virtualisation and the MapReduce model.

4.7   End of Chapter Exercises

Exercise 1: Create your own VMWare virtual machine

In this exercise, you will create your own virtual machine and install the Ubuntu version of the Linux operating system. In later chapters, we will use this same virtual machine to install more software and complete further exercises. Note that the virtual machine is quite large and ideally you will have at least 20 GB of free disk space and at least 2 GB of memory. The machine may run with less memory or disk space, but you may find that performance is rather slow.

4.8 A Note on the Technical Exercises (Chaps. 4, 5, 6, 7)

As you will already be aware, the state of the cloud is highly dynamic and rapidly evolving. In these exercises, you are going to download a number of tools and libraries, and we are going to recommend that you choose the latest stable version so that you will always be working at the 'cutting edge'. The downside of this is that we cannot guarantee that following the exercise notes will always work exactly as described as you may well be working with a later version than the one we used for testing. You may need to adapt the notes, refer to information on the source web pages or use web searches to find solutions to any problems or inconsistencies you encounter. The advantage of this is that you will be developing critical skills as you go through the process which would be an essential part of your everyday work should you be involved in building or working with cloud systems. Anyone who has developed software systems will know that it can be very frustrating and at times may feel completely stuck. However, you are often closer to a solution than you might think, and persisting through difficulties to solve a problem can be very rewarding and a huge learning opportunity.

4.9 Create Your Ubuntu VM

(1) Install VMWare Player on your machine: http://www.vmware.com/products/ player/ You may need to register with VMWare but VMWare Player is free.
  (a) Click on download and follow the instructions until VM Player is installed.
(2) Go to www.ubuntu.com
  (a) Go to the Ubuntu download page.
  (b) Download the latest version of Ubuntu (e.g. ubuntu-11.10-desktop-i386.iso).
  (c) Save the .iso file to a folder on your machine.
(3) Open VMplayer. Be aware that this process can be quite lengthy.
  (a) Select 'Create New Virtual Machine' (Fig. 4.6).
  (b) Select 'Installer disc image file(iso)' and browse to the folder where you saved your Ubuntu .iso file. Select next.
  (c) Enter a name for your VM and a username and password for the main user on your Linux VM.
  (d) Select a location where your VM will be stored: You will need plenty of disk space (~5 GB).
  (e) You now need to select additional disk space for the VM to use. If you have plenty of space you can go with the recommendation (e.g. 20 GB). It is probably best to select at least 8 GB. Select 'Split virtual disk into 2 GB files'. Select next.

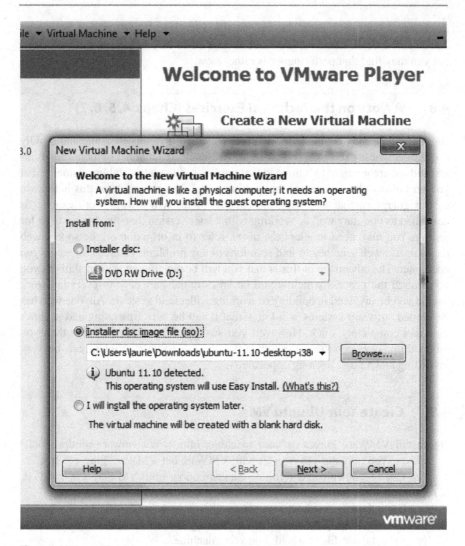

Fig. 4.6 VMware Player

(f) Check the options you have selected and select Finish. If you want to run
the VM as soon as it is ready leave the 'Power on this virtual machine after
creation' selected.
(4) Your machine will now be created. This will take some time depending on the
configuration of your underlying hardware.
(5) You may be asked to select your country so that the keyboard layout can be set
appropriately. You can test your keyboard to check it works as expected.

4.10 Getting Started

Your machine is now ready to use.

1. Once your Ubuntu VM has loaded up inside VMWare, log on using the ID and username you gave when creating the VM. VMWare tools should be automatically installed and you may need to restart your machine a number of times. Once complete, you should now be able to maximise the size of your VM screen.

2. Also in the Virtual Machine menu you should see 'power options' where you can 'power off', 'reset' or 'suspend' your virtual machine. 'Suspend' is often a useful option as it will maintain the particular state that your virtual machine is in and restore it to that state next time you 'resume' the virtual machine.

3. If you wish to copy your virtual machine, perhaps to a USB memory stick, you should first suspend or power off the virtual machine. You then need to locate the folder where you created the virtual machine and copy the entire folder to the required destination. You can then start the virtual machine on another computer, providing that VMware Player is installed by locating the file ending with .vmx and double clicking on that file. Note that if something goes wrong later on, you can switch to using this copy. You can of course take a copy of the virtual machine at any point during your development.

4.11 Learn How to Use Ubuntu

In this tutorial and others that follow, we will be using the Ubuntu virtual machine. If you are not familiar with Ubuntu, it will be well worth getting familiar with the basics. There are many guides available, and a good starting point is the Ubuntu home page (http://www.ubuntu.com/ubuntu) where you can take a 'tour' of the important features. In your virtual machine, there is also help available, just click on the 'dash home' icon on the top left and type help and select the help icon (Fig. 4.7).

So take some time to explore the environment and get used to Ubuntu. Actually most of the features are quite intuitive, and you can learn by just 'trying'. In terms of the tutorials in this book, we will only be using a small subset of the available commands and applications. In particular you will need to:

- Be able to browse, copy, move, delete and edit files.
- Use the archive manager to extract zipped files.
- Use the terminal to send basic Unix commands including:
- ls to list the contents of a folder (traditionally referred to as 'Directory' in Unix)
- cd to change directory
- pwd to identify your location in the directory structure

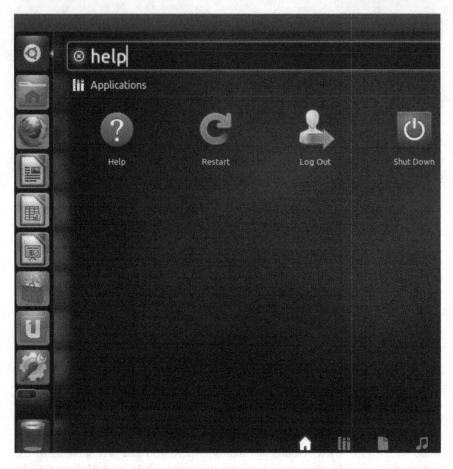

Fig. 4.7 Finding assistance from the Ubuntu home screen

4.12 Install Java

We will be using Java for a number of the tutorial exercises. Java is a freely available programming language. We are going to install the java SDK from Oracle which is suitable for all the tutorial material in this book. These notes are partly based on information from the Ubuntu community at https://help.ubuntu.com/community/Java. If you encounter problems you may want to check the site for any updates.

1. Download the latest Oracle JDK 7 for Linux from http://www.oracle.com/technetwork/java/javase/downloads/java-se-jdk-7-download-432154.html (e.g. jdk-7-linux-i586.tar.gz) in your Ubuntu VM.
2. You will have to agree to Oracle Binary Code License to download this.
3. Locate the file by clicking on the home folder icon and then selecting the 'Downloads' folder (Fig. 4.8).

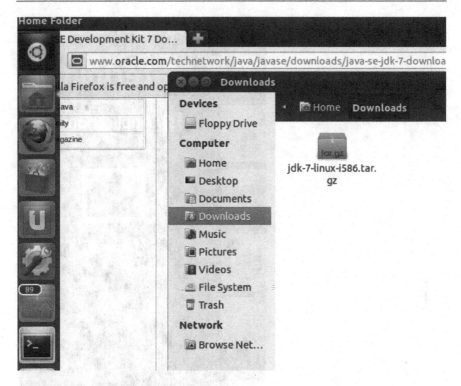

Fig. 4.8 Downloads folder illustrating the Oracle Java Development Kit archive

4. Right click on the file and select 'open with archive manager'.
5. In the archive manager select 'extract' and save. Select 'show the files' once the extraction is complete.
6. A new folder called 'jdk1.7.0' or similar should have been created. Rename this folder to 'java-7-oracle' by right clicking and selecting 'rename'.
7. In your Ubuntu virtual machine open a terminal session. To get a terminal session just click the Ubuntu logo in the side bar and type 'terminal' and then click on the terminal icon (Fig. 4.9). Move to the directory where you extracted the files.
8. Now type the following commands one at a time. Enter your password if prompted and follow on-screen instructions where required. Make sure you type these exactly, including the case.

```
user@ubuntu:~$ sudo mkdir -p/usr/lib/jvm/
user@ubuntu:~$ sudo mv java-7-oracle//usr/lib/jvm/
user@ubuntu:~$ sudo add-apt-repository ppa:nilarimogard/
webupd8
user@ubuntu:~$ sudo apt-get update
user@ubuntu:~$ sudo apt-get install update-java
user@ubuntu:~$ sudo update-java
```

Fig. 4.9 Invoking a terminal
session in Ubuntu

9. If prompted, select the Java version you just updated (/usr/lib/jvm/jdk1.7.0).
10. Answer Y if prompted to continue with the Java install.
11. Type the following commands to set the JAVA_HOME

```
user@ubuntu:~$ JAVA_HOME=/usr/lib/jvm/java-7-oracle
user@ubuntu:~$ export JAVA_HOME
user@ubuntu:~$ PATH=$PATH:$JAVA_HOME/bin
user@ubuntu:~$ export PATH
```

4.13 MapReduce with Pig

In this tutorial we are going to implement the classic word count program using Pig
Latin.
1. Open your home folder and create a new folder called 'Pig'.
2. In your virtual machine, use a browser such as Firefox to go to http://www.
apache.org/dyn/closer.cgi/pig, select a suitable mirror and then download the latest stable release of pig e.g. pig-0.9.2.tar.gz.

Fig. 4.10 Ubuntu download

3. Open the home folder and then the download folder to see the downloaded pig file (Fig. 4.10).
4. Right click on the file (e.g. pig.0.9.2.tar.gz) and select 'open with archive manager'.
5. In the archive manager select 'extract' and allow the current folder as the destination folder. Select 'show the files' once the extraction is complete.
6. The archive manager will extract the file to a folder called pig-0.9.1 or similar. The only file we need for this tutorial is the .jar file. Locate this file (e.g. pig.0.9.1.jar), right click and select 'copy' and paste the file into the pig folder you created earlier.
7. We need a text file which we can use to count the words. You can use any text file you like but in this example we will copy over the NOTICE.txt file from the extracted folder to the pig folder for testing purposes.
8. We are now going to create our first Pig Latin program. To do this, we first need a text editor so select the 'dash home' icon, type 'text' and select the text editor.
9. Paste in the following code (originally from http://en.wikipedia.org/wiki/Pig_(programming_language)) and save the file as wordCount.pig

```
A = load 'NOTICE.txt';
```

```
  B=foreach A generate flatten(TOKENIZE((chararray)$0))
as word;
  C=filter B by word matches '\\w+';
  D=group C by word;
  E=foreach D generate COUNT(C) as count, group as word;
  F=order E by count desc;
  store F into 'wordcount.txt';
```
10. Open a terminal and navigate to the pig folder.
11. Type in the following command to run your word count program using pig
    ```
    java -Xmx512M -cp pig-0.9.1.jar org.apache.pig.Main
    -x local wordCount.pig
    ```
12. Once the program has finished running you should see a new folder called wordcount.txt. Navigate into the folder and open the contents of the file. Compare your output with the text file you used and hopefully you will see that the program has been successful and the frequency of the words has been counted and placed in order.
13. Try and run the program with another text file of your choice.
14. Alter the program so that it orders the output by word rather than frequency.
15. Alter the program so that only words starting with a letter above 't' are output.

4.14 Discussion

You might be thinking that actually the program seemed to take quite some time to complete this simple task on a small text file. However, notice that we are running the Pig Latin program using the 'local' mode. This is useful for testing our programs, but if we were really going to use pig for a serious problem such as the results of a web crawl, we would switch to 'hadoop' mode. We could then run the same Pig Latin program, and the task would be automatically parallelized and distributed on a cluster of possibly thousands of nodes. This is actually much simpler than you might expect, especially when vendors such as Amazon offer a set of nodes pre-configured for MapReduce tasks using pig.

4.15 MapReduce with Cloudera

Should you wish to experiment with MapReduce a nice way to start is to visit the Cloudera site (http://www.cloudera.com/) where you can download a virtual machine with Hadoop and Java pre-installed. Cloudera also offer training and support with a range of MapReduce related tasks.

References

Goldne, B.: Virtualization for Dummies. Wiley, Chichester (2008)

Nixon, R.: Learning PHP, MySQL, and JavaScript. O'Reilly Media, Inc, Sebastopol (2009). This is a useful introduction to developing web applications with the popular PHP language

White, T.: Hadoop: The Definitive Guide, 2nd edn. O'Reilly Media, Sebastopol (2009)

Cloud Services

5

What the reader will learn:

- How service-oriented architectures relate to cloud computing
- About the 'cloud stack'
- Details of the three service models
- About the kind of services that are being offered by the major vendors
- How to create a basic cloud application on Google App Engine

5.1 Introduction

Wikipedia defines cloud computing as:

> the delivery of computing as a service rather than a product, whereby shared resources, software, and information are provided to computers and other devices as a metered service over a network (typically the Internet). (http://en.wikipedia.org/wiki/Cloud_computing)

The Gartner Group similarly lists 'service based' as one of the key defining attributes of cloud computing. Indeed, we could say that one of the defining characteristics that makes cloud computing different from traditional software development and deployment is the focus on service delivery. The National Institute for Standards and Technology (NIST) also sites services as an essential component of cloud computing and defines three service models.

In this chapter we are going to explore the different ways in which you can build and use services in the cloud. We will examine what is known as the SPI model where the letters stand for 'services', 'platforms' and 'infrastructures' and see how the model applies to the systems currently available in the cloud. As an emerging and rapidly advancing area, a number of key terms used in cloud computing do not yet have an agreed designation. However, NIST provides the most widely used definitions, particularly relating to the SPI model, and so we include them in the relevant sections below. We also include a number of example technologies for each

R. Hill et al., *Guide to Cloud Computing: Principles and Practice*, Computer Communications and Networks, DOI 10.1007/978-1-4471-4603-2_5, © Springer-Verlag London 2013

of the service types. However, the list is far from exhaustive, and of course, new services and providers are continually emerging and transforming the rapidly changing 'cloudscape'. At the end of this chapter, you will develop the virtual machine you created previously and then use it to create and deploy your own applications in the cloud. We should note that although we do touch on data storage issues in this chapter, the topic is discussed in detail in Chap. 6.

There are a number of technologies which have been identified as precursors to cloud computing such as grids, utility computing, autonomic computing and virtualisation. Perhaps the most relevant to cloud services is the development of web services and service-oriented architectures (SOAs). We begin this chapter by examining these technologies which are still highly relevant to the ongoing evolution of cloud services.

5.2   Web Services

A web service refers to software which provides a standardised way of integrating facilities offered by web applications and supports communication between organisations without requiring detailed knowledge of how the services are implemented or even which language or platform they are implemented on. Services should perform easily describable, focused and isolated tasks such that they are independent of the particular state of other services. Unlike traditional client–server architectures, web services provide a programmatic and machine-friendly interface rather than a graphical user-friendly interface presented in a browser or desktop application.

XML is the typical format of communication for web services which provides the significant advantage of platform independence. The Web Service Description Language (WSDL) can be used to describe the services available, to structure requests and responses and to provide information regarding the kind of protocol needed in order to invoke the service. Implementations for working with WSDL based on C#, Java and other languages are available.

Many web services are completely free, whereas others may charge for their use. If you create a web service, it is obviously useful if you can publish this fact such that potential users are able to locate, evaluate and use the web service you are offering. The most widely used directory of web services is available via UDDI (Universal Description, Discovery and Integration) specification which defines a way to publish and discover information about web services. SOAP (Simple Object Access Protocol) is a standardised XML format commonly used to tag the information and transport the data. The collection of standards (developed by the World Wide Web Consortium (W3C)) used for web services are collectively known as the WS* stack.

Perhaps it is easier to understand web services by looking at some examples. If you go to the home page of WebserviceX.NET (http://www.webservicex.net), hundreds of web services are listed. You can search by keyword or browser by popularity or subject category. You should be able to see commonly used examples such as barcode generators, currency converters and suppliers of weather data. If you are interested, you can use the site to obtain the WSDL service description together with the required SOAP structuring and other useful information regarding the services.

5.3   Service-Oriented Architecture

The goal of service-oriented architecture is to bring together various pieces of functionality to form new applications which are built largely from existing software services. SOA provides a set of methodologies for designing software as a set of loosely coupled interoperable services suitable for use in a distributed computing environment. In a somewhat similar way to other software engineering approaches such as object orientation, service-oriented architectures enable us to create components or building blocks that make sense to human users and designers and can be reused for different purposes. The complex internal working of the components is hidden, and a simple interface with well-defined behaviour is presented. The services are self-contained modules that provide standard business functionality and are independent of the state or context of other services. Services are described in a standard definition language and have a published interface.

The W3C refers to SOA simply as:

> A set of components which can be invoked, and whose interface descriptions can be published and discovered. (http://www.w3.org/TR/ws-gloss/)

SOA enables communication between providers and consumers and gives a mechanism to manage available services. The communication should be in the form of loosely coupled services or software functionalities that can be reused for different purposes. In summary we can say that an enterprise application that follows the SOA paradigm is a collection of services that together perform complex business logic.

5.4   Interoperability

Interoperability is a key SOA requirement. SOA components should be independent of programming language and platform and should be unassociated with each other. SOA aims to allow users to combine or mesh collaborating services from a number of sources to build new, potentially complex applications. SOA allows organisations to expose and access an application's services and to consume information bound to those services using well-defined interfaces.

5.5   Composability

Applications are frequently built from a collection of components: a feature called composability. A composable system uses components to assemble services that can be tailored for a specific purpose using standard parts. One of the compelling advantages of the SOA approach is the way that services can be composed when creating applications. Combining and interleaving of services is the heart of service-oriented computing. SOA implies that services can participate equally well in simple or complex compositions. Composability has been taken to a new level with cloud computing; for example, fundamental computing resources such as storage and processing power are provided as services which can be composed to create a required application environment (see below).

5.6   Representational State Transfer (REST)

Representational state transfer (REST) is a style of software architecture originally introduced by Roy Fielding who was one of the principal authors of HTTP specifications 1.0 and 1.1. As with HTTP, the REST architecture envisions clients and servers in a conversation or request/response cycle. Requests are centred on representations of the resource and use existing HTTP methods. This is in contrast to other systems, such as SOAP where users can define their own methods and resource identifiers. In REST a given URI is used to access the representational state of a resource and also to modify the resource. For example, a URL on the web can be used to provide information to users about the resource or to modify the resource:

- GET is used to transfer the current representational state of a resource from a server to a client.
- PUT is used to transfer the modified representational state of a resource from the client to the server.
- POST is used to transfer the new representational state of a resource from the client to the server.
- DELETE is used to transfer the information needed to change a resource to a deleted representational state.

REST uses HTTP for all CRUD (Create/Read/Update/Delete) operations. REST is an increasingly popular lightweight alternative to mechanisms like RPC (remote procedure calls) and SOAP. Like SOAP and RPC, a 'RESTful' service is platform and language independent but is considered simpler and easier to use. Whilst REST services might use XML in their responses (as one way of organising structured data), REST requests rarely use XML; indeed we can think of the web page itself as the service. A good example is given by a site offering an ISBN service which returns the details of a book on receipt of an ISBN number. Isbndb.com offers such a service which requires you to simply use an HTTP GET with parameters including an access key to allow use of the service (to gain an access key and use isbndb.com, you need to complete the free registration at http://isbndb.com/ and follow the instructions to gain a verified account).

If you enter a URL as shown below:

http://isbndb.com/api/books.xml?access_key=abc123&index1=isbn&value1=9 780045100606

but replace the value for the access key with one you have generated at isnbdb.com, the result returned in XML format as shown below:

```
<?xml version="1.0" encoding="UTF-8"?>
<ISBNdb server_time="2012-02-22T13:19:46Z">
 <BookList total_results="1" shown_results="1">
  <BookData book_id="alan_turing_a04" isbn="0045100608"
isbn13="9780045100606">
```

```
  <Title>Alan Turing</Title>
  <TitleLong>Alan Turing: the enigma of intelli-gence</
TitleLong>
  <AuthorsText>Andrew Hodges</AuthorsText>
  <PublisherText publish-er_id="unwin_paperbacks">
London : Unwin Paperbacks,
   1985.</PublisherText>
 </BookData>
 </BookList>
</ISBNdb>
```

At the end of this chapter, we will build a small web application using Google App Engine (see below) which will use the RESTful service provided by isbndb. com to retrieve and process book information in XML based on ISBN numbers entered by the user.

Unlike SOAP services which require responses packaged in XML, REST does not require the response to be in any particular format. A simple illustration is provided by Twitter which will return the results in various formats (RSS, ATOM and JSON) using the URLs shown below to send a REST request to Twitter's search service.

```
http://search.twitter.com/search.atom?q=turing&count=5
http://search.twitter.com/search.rss?q=turing&count=5
http://search.twitter.com/search.json?q=turing&count=5
```

The 'q' following the question mark is the query term ('turing'), and the count represents the maximum number of items to return.

REST is based on the HTTP protocol and so is a 'stateless' architecture. It is straightforward to make AJAX-based applications RESTful, and returning the response in JSON format makes the applications simple to program whilst minimising the bandwidth required for the response. REST is ubiquitous in cloud services, for example, Amazon.com offers a RESTful API with HTTP verbs for their S3 storage solution (see below).

Resources are the key element of a RESTful approach. Resources are identified by the URLs, and both the state and functionality of the application are represented using resources. SOAs can be built using REST services—an approach sometimes referred to as ROA (REST-oriented architecture). The main advantage of ROA is ease of implementation, agility of the design and the lightweight approach. The latest version of WSDL now contains HTTP verbs and is considered an acceptable method of documenting REST services. There is also an alternative known as WADL (Web Application Description Language).

5.7   The Cloud Stack

It is useful to view cloud offerings as a stack, where each layer has distinct features and capabilities. This is sometimes referred to as the 'cloud ontology', and various models of differing complexity have been proposed. We present a relatively simple model here as shown in Fig. 5.1.

Fig. 5.1 The cloud stack

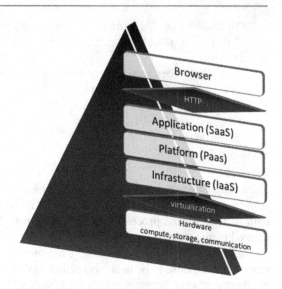

At the top of the stack is the application with the user interface delivered to the user via a web browser. At the base of the stack lies the hardware of the physical machines actually running the application, normally located in a large data centre. Virtualisation technology allows for the abstraction and presentation of the hardware resources in a discrete and scalable manner to the higher layers. Actually, a particular layer can be defined according to the level of abstraction, so we can say that a layer is classified higher in the cloud stack if the services offered by that layer can be composed from the services of the underlying layer. The layer can also be identified according to the type of user targeted by the layer. The service models build on one another and define the areas of responsibility amongst vendors, end users and developers.

In this chapter, we are primarily interested in the three service layers in the middle of the stack, and the following sections describe each of these with examples.

5.8   Software as a Service (SaaS)

The capability provided to the consumer is to use the provider's applications running on a cloud infrastructure. The applications are accessible from various client devices through either a thin client interface, such as a web browser (e.g., web-based email), or a program interface. The consumer does not manage or control the underlying cloud infrastructure including network, servers, operating systems, storage, or even individual application capabilities, with the possible exception of limited user-specific application configuration setting. NIST (http://csrc.nist.gov/publications/nistpubs/800-145/SP800-145.pdf)

Software as a service (SaaS) is a hosted application that is available over the Internet via a web browser. SaaS, sometimes referred to as 'on-demand software', is the most complete of the cloud services. Computing hardware, software and the solution are offered by a vendor. The cloud application layer is the only layer visible to end users who are the target users for this layer. The end user does not manage or control the underlying infrastructure. Their only responsibility is for entering and managing their data based on interactions with the software. The user interacts directly with the hosted software via the browser. We should note that SaaS existed well before the concept of cloud computing emerged; nevertheless, it is now an integral part of the cloud model.

Creating and delivering software via the SaaS layer is an attractive alternative to the more traditional desktop applications which must be installed on the users' machine. With SaaS the application is deployed in the cloud so the work of testing, maintaining and upgrading software is greatly simplified since it can all occur in one place rather than being rolled out to the desktops of potentially thousands of users. Configuration and testing is reduced in complexity due to centralisation and the preset restrictions in the deployment environment. Developers can also use a simplified strategy when applying upgrades and fixes. Furthermore, composition, as discussed above, becomes a straightforward option as soon as the cloud services are developed. Last but not least, the providers also benefit from greater protection to their intellectual property as the application is not deployed locally and pirated versions of the software will be much harder to obtain and distribute.

A number of typical characteristics of SaaS are listed below:
- Software is available globally over the Internet either free or paid for by subscription based on customer usage.
- Collaborative working is easily provided and generally encouraged.
- Automatic upgrades are handled by the vendor with no required customer input.
- All users have the same version of the software.
- The software will automatically scale on demand.
- Distribution and maintenance costs are significantly reduced.

There are a huge variety of SaaS applications already available, and their number appears to be growing at an exponential rate. A small selection of prominent examples of SaaS are discussed below, which hopefully give a good illustration of the SaaS approach. We recommend that you investigate for yourself by viewing the sites mentioned, even if only briefly.

5.8.1 Salesforce.com

Salesforce.com (http://www.salesforce.com) provides the most widely used customer relationship management (CRM) service used for managing financial, logistics and staffing issues related to business system operation. A CRM consists of a set of business processes together with software that helps manage customer-related activities, information and analysis. These activities include:
- Sales
- Marketing and leads
- Content analysis
- Accounts
- Forecasting
- Partnerships and collaboration
- Customer service

Salesforce.com offers a comprehensive list of features which can be integrated with applications from Google. The Salesforce.com SaaS offering is highly customisable and tailored for particular industries.

5.8.2 Dropbox

Dropbox (https://www.dropbox.com) uses cloud storage to enable users to store and share files and folders across the Internet. Dropbox starts with a free tier with up to 2 GB of storage and supports multiple user clients across desktop and mobile operating systems, including versions for Windows, Linux, Mac OS X, Android and iPhone. Any files or folders the user places or updates in the dropbox folder of their local machine are synchronised with the web version. When a user logs onto another machine with dropbox installed, any updates are automatically applied. Dropbox also provides a revision history so that user can revert to older versions of their files. Dropbox currently uses Amazon's S3 storage (see below) although it may switch to a different storage provider in the future.

5.8.3 Google Services

Google (http://www.google.com/services/) offers a wide range of cloud applications including email, web hosting and, of course, searching. A number of Google services target business users, such as Google Analytics which support its targeted advertising business.

Google Docs is somewhat similar to Microsoft Office and contains a word processor, spreadsheet, drawing and presentation program and is free to use up to a certain data size. With Google Docs, collaborators can share documents and work in real time from different locations. REST APIs enable users to directly access the Google Data Protocol (which underlies Google products) and to search Google Docs contents. Once published to the web, the users are provided with the public URL and the HTML code required to embed the document in a web page.

Google Apps Script gives users a high level of control over a number of Google products. Google spreadsheets amongst other products can be accessed and controlled using JavaScript programs which run directly on Google servers. Actually this means that the Google spreadsheet is offering more than 'user-specific application configuration settings' and so strictly speaking is falling outside the NIST definition of SaaS. This is not an uncommon situation for products which otherwise naturally fall into the SaaS category.

5.8.4 Prezi

Prezi (http://prezi.com/) is a collaborative technology, which is free to use when creating and showing publicly available non-linear presentations (a 'prezi') in the cloud up to 100 MB in size. Users may simply replace Microsoft PowerPoint with Prezi for interactive presentations but much more is on offer. The service also allows users to collaborate in real time for editing or brainstorming, and Prezi allows the user to upload video files and image files.

A fee is payable for greater storage and for additional features such as the ability to create Prezis offline and to make the Prezis private.

5.9 Platform as a Service (PaaS)

The capability provided to the consumer is to deploy onto the cloud infrastructure consumer-created or acquired applications created using programming languages, libraries, services, and tools supported by the provider. The consumer does not manage or control the underlying cloud infrastructure including network, servers, operating systems, or storage, but has control over the deployed applications and possibly configuration settings for the application-hosting environment. NIST

For many businesses, specific rather than general requirements may mean that a generic SaaS application will not suffice. PaaS creates a managed environment in the cloud where complex, tailor-made applications can be constructed, tested and deployed. The provider supplies a hardware platform together with software environments specifically designed to support cloud application development. The target users are developers who build, test, deploy and tune applications on the cloud platform (for the end user the result is still a browser-based application). Automatic scalability, monitoring and load balancing are provided so that an increase in demand for a resource such as a web application will not result in degradation in performance (of course, this may mean an increased charge is incurred). PaaS vendors will also ensure the availability of applications, so, for example, should there be any problems on the underlying hardware, the application will be automatically redeployed to a working environment, without a detrimental effect on the end users experience. PaaS should accelerate development and deployment and result in a shorter time to market when compared with traditional software development using an organisations' own data centre.

The developer does not control and has no responsibility for the underlying cloud infrastructure but does have control over the deployed applications. The vendor is responsible for all operational and maintenance aspects of the service and will also provide billing and metering information. The vendor commonly offers a range of tools and utilities to support the design, integration, testing, monitoring and deployment of the application. Typically the tool set will include services to support:
- Collaboration and team working
- Data management—sometimes referred to as data as a service (DaaS)
- Authentication or identification—sometimes referred to as authentication as a service (AaaS)
- Performance monitoring and management
- Testing
- Queue services

- Email and messaging
- User interface components

Often the supporting tools are configured as RESTful services which can readily be composed when building applications. It is important that developers are able to write applications without needing to know the details of the underlying technology of the cloud to which they will be deployed. Standard programming languages are often available, although normally with some restrictions based on security and scalability concerns. Additional support for programming and configuration tasks is often available from a developer community specific to the PaaS offering.

5.9.1   Portability

Portability is a concern to many organisations considering developing PaaS applications due to the differing requirements of the various vendors, so, for example, if you build an application using Google App Engine, there may be significant work involved if you later decide to move to Microsoft Azure. Using an established language like Java goes some way to ameliorate concerns about application portability but does not necessarily eliminate them as the code will often need to be adjusted to fit in with the vendor's particular requirements and it is quite likely that the program will only work within the specific environment. The way in which data is persisted is especially prone to quite distinct strategies between the vendors.

5.9.2   Simple Cloud API

The Simple Cloud aims to provide a set of common interfaces for file storage services, document storage services, simple queue services and infrastructure services, or in their own words, 'the Simple Cloud API brings cloud technologies to PHP and the PHP philosophy to the cloud' (http://simplecloud.org/). Zend has invited the open source community and software vendors of all sizes to participate. IBM, Microsoft, Rackspace, Nirvanix, and GoGrid have already joined the project as contributors.

5.9.3   Java

Many programming languages are available on the various PaaS offerings, but Java would currently seem to be the most popular. Although Java is sometimes referred to somewhat mockingly by developers as 'the COBOL of the twenty-first century', Java is nevertheless a powerful object-oriented language which is freely available and offers a number of attractive features such as automatic memory management. Perhaps most importantly there is a huge pool of developers with Java expertise: currently a reported ten million Java users. The language has particular appeal to those building client–server web applications.

Java applications are typically compiled to form a Java source file to Java bytecode. Once in this format the code can run on any Java Virtual Machine (JVM) regardless of computer architecture. One of the main goals of the language is summarised in the famous 'write once, run anywhere' adage, meaning that code that runs on one platform (e.g. Windows) does not need to be edited to run on a different one (e.g. Linux). Another of the reasons for its appeal is the large number of supporting tools, libraries and frameworks also freely available and generally open source. These include the widely used open source and freely available Eclipse Integrated Development Environment (IDE) which supports rapid development and debugging. The JUnit library (which can be easily integrated into Eclipse) supports test-driven development and an agile approach to software production. The Web application ARchive (WAR) is a standard format used to package and distribute resources used for Java Web applications which aims to facilitate development, testing and deployment.

A number of vendors such as Amazon, Google and VMForce have developed 'plug-ins' for Eclipse so that their Java PaaS offerings can be developed, tested, debugged and deployed in an environment already familiar to many developers. The WAR file format is also frequently used by a number of PaaS vendors, again supporting a familiar style of development and reducing portability concerns.

5.9.4 Google App Engine

A few years ago before cloud really hit the headlines, Google famously gave away stickers saying 'My other computer is a data center'. Google App Engine (GAE) is a good example of PaaS and allows users to write and deploy their applications on the same infrastructure which powers Google's products. We are going to give a little more time here to discuss GAE as this is the product we will use at the end of this chapter when you will develop your own GAE cloud application.

Google, of course, has great flexibility in terms of dynamic reallocation of resources required to meet changing needs and demands. GAE applications are not hosted on a single server but will run in a distributed environment (see Chap. 4) even whilst the developer is completely unaware of the production configuration of the data centres and is totally free from capacity management, server maintenance and load-balancing tasks. As the number of requests for the web application increases, GAE automatically allocates more resources without the developer needing to change their code.

GAE applications can currently be built using three different programming languages:
1. The Python programming language was the first to appear when GAE was initially made available to developers. Python System Development Kit (SDK) is still available and widely used.
2. Java has been added together with integration with Eclipse. Using the Eclipse plug-in developers can run and test their Java applications locally and deploy to the cloud with a single click. Google uses the Java Virtual Machine with the Jetty

servlet engine and a standard WAR file structure. Any programming language which can run on a JVM-based interpreter, such as JRuby, Groovy, JavaScript (Rhino) and Scala, can also be run on GAE although there may be a little more work in terms of initial configuration. GAE also supports many of the Java standards and frameworks such as servlets, the Spring Framework and Apache Struts.

3. Most recently an 'experimental' environment has been added for the new 'Go' (http://golang.org/) concurrent programming language developed by Google.

Java, Python and Go runtime environments are provided with APIs (application program interface) to interact with Google's runtime environment. Google App Engine provides developers with a simulated environment to build and test applications locally with any operating system that supports a suitable version of the Python, Java or Go language environments. However, there are a number of important restrictions. Developers cannot write to the file system, Java applications cannot create new threads, and only a subset of the standard Java classes and packages are available (you can view the list of supported classes at http://code.google.com/appengine/docs/java/jrewhitelist.html).

Restrictions such as these have led to portability concerns, but recently a number of projects such as AppScale have been able to run Python, Java and Go GAE applications on EC2 and other cloud vendors.

The GAE platform also allows developers to write code and integrate custom-designed applications with other Google services. GAE also has a number of composable supporting services including:

• Integrated web services
• Authentication using Google Accounts
• Scalable non-relational, schema-less storage using standard Java persistence models
• Fast in-memory storage using a key-value cache (memcache)
• Task queues and scheduling

GAE allows applications to be served from the developers own domain name although by default this will be the name the developer assigns to their application at appspot.com, for example, http://myApp.appspot.com.

The URL can be shared publicly or selectively. The code required for an application can be stored on Google code which can be managed by various open source version control systems such as SVN (http://subversion.apache.org/).

A great advantage, particularly to new developers, is that you can begin using GAE for free with no credit card required before continuing onto a graduated fee based on usage (this is one of the reasons we choose a tutorial using GAE). At the time of writing, each developer can host up to ten free applications. An application on a free account can use up to 1 GB of storage and up to five million page views a month.

To persist data using GAE, the application must use the provided app engine services. The data store is a key-value storage system similar to Amazon SimpleDB and Windows Azure Table Service (see below). GAE provides high availability by data replication and synchronisation. The memcache service is used to improve performance by using a short term, in memory local cache rather than going to the data store. Although data cannot be read from the file system, it is possible to read files that are packages as part of a WAR.

5.9.5   Google Web Toolkit

Google Web Toolkit (GWT) is a set of open source libraries under Apache 2.0 licence, which allows web developers to write AJAX web applications entirely in Java. GWT will compile the Java to optimised JavaScript code which will run in the user's browser whilst allowing for mature Java testing strategies, for example, using JUnit. GWT aims to improve developer productivity and web application maintenance issues and includes support for asynchronous communication (AJAX), history management, bookmarking, internationalisation and cross-browser portability. A GWT application using HTML5 can have separate views for tablets and mobile phones. There is also a GWT plug-in to the eclipse IDE and a straightforward procedure for deploying GWT applications to GAE.

5.9.6   Microsoft Azure

The Azure Services Platform provides a wide array of Windows-based services for developing and deploying Windows-based applications on the cloud. Whilst Azure is primarily designed as a PaaS offering where users can build host and scale web applications on Microsoft's global data centres, it also includes Infrastructure as a Service (IaaS) features. The platform consists of compute, storage and fabric (network resources). Azure provides scaling, load balancing and a number of support services such as identity and authentication, message encryption, monitoring and management.

Three main brands have been developed:
1. The Windows Azure scalable cloud operating system
2. SQL Azure which is a cloud-based scalable version of Microsoft SQL Server
3. AppFabric which is a collection of services supporting the cloud service

Azure applications are typically written either as a 'web role', a 'worker role' or both. Web role is used for typical web applications that are hosted on servers running Microsoft's IIS web server, whilst the worker role is used for applications that require compute intensive operations. The virtual machine role is currently in beta but enables the developer to deploy a custom-built Windows Server machine image to Windows Azure potentially saving significant time on installation-related tasks.

Azure uses a combination of standard web service technologies REST, HTTP and XML and integrates with Microsoft Visual Studio. By using the Microsoft Azure SDK, developers can create services that leverage the .NET Framework. The aim is to allow developers to be able to choose the language or framework and to integrate public cloud applications with existing applications. These applications have to be uploaded through the Microsoft Azure portal in order to be executed on top of Windows Azure. Additional services are available, such as workflow execution and management, web services orchestration and access to SQL data stores. Microsoft also offers system development kits for other languages such as Java, PHP and Ruby.

5.9.7 Force.com

Force.com from SalesForce.com is an approach to PaaS for developing CRM systems and applications for social enterprise with built-in support for social and mobile functionality. The design of its platform and the runtime environment is based on Java technology. The platform uses a proprietary programming language and environment called Apex Code, which has a reputation for simplicity in learning and rapid development and execution. Users of Force.com can build their own applications which are either stand-alone or integrated with Salesforce.com.

5.9.8 VMForce

Salesfoce.com and VMware have partnered to introduce VMForce, one of the first enterprise cloud platforms for Java developers. VMForce uses Eclipse and allows for development with standard Java Web technology such as JSPs and servlets. Once developed applications can be deployed to the cloud with a single click.

5.9.9 Heroku

Heroku is a cloud platform for instant deployment of Ruby on Rails web applications. Ruby on Rails provides a complete framework for web application development including a template and rendering system and methods to persist and retrieve data. Ruby on Rails is popular amongst developers, has a good track record for rapid web application production and sits particularly well with agile methods of software production. Heroku servers are invisibly managed and applications automatically scaled and balanced.

5.9.10 Cloud Foundry

Cloud Foundry claims to be the first open source scalable PaaS offering, using industry-standard frameworks such as Spring (Java) and Scala and a choice of application infrastructure services. The project was initiated by VMware but has gained broad industry support. The Cloud Foundry aims to minimise restrictions on development and deployment in the cloud so that developers need not be concerned with middleware or vendor infrastructure.

5.10 Infrastructure as a Service (IaaS)

The capability provided to the consumer is to provision processing, storage, networks, and other fundamental computing resources where the consumer is able to deploy and run arbitrary software, which can include operating systems and applications. The consumer does not manage or control the underlying cloud infrastructure but has control over operating systems, storage, and deployed applications; and possibly limited control of select networking components (e.g., host firewalls). NIST (http://csrc.nist.gov/publications/nist-pubs/800-145/SP800-145.pdf)

IaaS provides developers with on-demand infrastructure resources such as compute, storage and communication as virtualised services in the cloud. The provider actually manages the entire infrastructure and operates data centres large enough to provide seemingly unlimited resources. The client is responsible for all other aspects of deployment which can include the operating system itself, together with programming languages, web servers and applications. IaaS normally employs a pay-as-you-go model with vendors typically charging by the hour.

Once connected the developers work with the resources as if they owned them. IaaS has been largely facilitated by the advances in operating system virtualisation which enables a level of indirection or abstraction with regard to direct hardware usage (see Chap. 4). The virtual machine (VM) is the most common form for providing computational resources, and users normally get super-user access to their virtual machines.

Virtualised forms of fundamental resources such as computing power, storage or network bandwidth are provided and can be composed in order to construct new cloud software environments or applications. Virtualisation enables the IaaS provider to control and manage the efficient utilisation of the physical resources and allows users unprecedented flexibility in configuration whilst protecting the physical infrastructure of the data centre. The IaaS model allows for existing applications to be directly migrated from an organisation's servers to the cloud supplier's hardware, potentially with minimal or no changes to the software.

5.10.1 Virtual Appliances

A virtual appliance is a virtual machine image which is designed to run on a particular virtualised platform, typically supplied via IaaS. The virtual appliance may have software such as an operating system, compilers, web server, database system and any required applications already installed, configured and optimised to solve the particular problem for which it was designed. In practice many virtual appliances are often used to run a single application. We can think of an appliance as an application combined with everything else it needs to actually run. Often the operating system is a stripped down version of its all-purpose counterpart, a process sometimes referred to as 'just-enough-operating-system' or 'Juice'. Virtual appliances are normally controlled using a web interface and can be used as a starting point for building a more complex server.

A number of online marketplaces have been set up to allow the exchange of ready-made appliances containing a wide range of operating system and software combinations. VMWare has the largest selection of appliances (available at http://www.vmware.com/appliances/directory/) which can be readily deployed to the VMWare hypervisor. In Chap. 4 tutorial, we used VMWare to create an Ubuntu virtual machine and then installed Java and Eclipse to our machine. An alternative approach would have been to download the appropriate appliance with the software we required already installed.

Amazon Machine Image (AMI) is used to store copies of particular virtual machines which can run on Amazon's Elastic Compute Cloud (EC2) and other IaaS platforms which support the format. Amazon Web Services offer hundreds of ready-made AMIs, which Amazon refers to as 'pre-built solutions' containing common combinations of operating systems and application software.

5.10.2 Amazon Web Services

Amazon Web Services (AWS) is one of the most successful cloud-based businesses based on SOA standards and includes a whole family of related services. The computational needs of an organisation are of course extremely variable, and some applications are likely to be compute intensive, whilst others will emphasise storage. EC2 is renowned for its ability to provide scalable solutions for diverse requirements.

5.10.3 Amazon Elastic Compute Cloud (EC2)

EC2 provides virtualised computing power as a service and is considered the central application of the AWS offering and is often referred to as the 'model example' of IaaS. Users can rent computing power on Amazon's infrastructure and pay with an hourly rate using EC2. EC2 can be customised in a similar way to a physical server and can run a variety of operating systems including Linux, Solaris and Windows server. The users gain administrator privileges and can perform numerous activities on the server such as starting and stopping, configuration and installation of any database system, programming language or software package.

The computing resources available on EC2 instances consist of combinations of computing power and other resources such as memory. EC2 is offered as a metered service, and an EC2 Compute Unit (CU) is used as a standard measure of computing power. EC2 users can select from a number of different instance types to best match particular computing needs. Amazon Auto Scaling is a set of command line tools that allows scaling EC2 capacity up or down automatically and according to conditions specified by the end user.

Standard instances are currently offered with the following resources as illustrated in Table 5.1.

There are many other instance types designed to meet nonstandard requirements. EC2 also offers users the ability to select from a number of regions and within each

Table 5.1 Standard EC2 instance types

Instance type	Memory (GB)	Compute	Instance storage (GB)	Platform
Small	1.7	1 EC2 Compute Unit (1 virtual core with 1 EC2 Compute Unit)	160	32-bit
Large	7.5	4 EC2 Compute Units (2 virtual cores with 2 EC2 Compute Units each)	850	64-bit
Extra large	15	8 EC2 Compute Units (4 virtual cores with 2 EC2 Compute Units each)	1,690	64-bit

region a number of availability zones where the virtual data centres on which the EC2 instances will be running.

5.10.4 Amazon Storage Services

Various forms of data storage are also provided by Amazon 'as-a-service'. Amazon's Simple Storage Service (S3) is a pure object-based storage system which can be accessed via a REST-based web interface. S3 does not provide the ability to run programs and does not even provide any file system or indexing, but has the advantages of reliability, availability and scalability. The user can allocate a block of storage up to 5 TB in size that has a unique user-assigned identifier and can then read or write to the block. S3 is often cited as a good example of a perfectly focused cloud service which does exactly one thing in a very narrow way. The service can then be composed with others to provide the resources required for development.

The S3 user is charged according to the volume of data and network bandwidth used when storing and retrieving data. S3 is a popular choice amongst web application developers and can easily be used to replace existing web hosting infrastructure. The Apache Hadoop file system (see Chap. 4) can also be hosted on S3 for running MapReduce jobs. At the time of writing Amazon S3 is reported to store more than 762 billion objects. Dropbox and Ubuntu One are examples of online backup and synchronisation services which use S3 for storage and transfer. Amazons SimpleDB is a key-value NoSQL data store (see Chap. 6) and Amazon Relational Database Service provides a MySQL database instance in the cloud.

As mentioned above Amazon S3 works over HTTP. Amazon also offers block storage systems where resources appear to be physical discs on the EC2 server. This provides improved performance over S3 and is more suitable to the case where multiple disc operations are required. Instance storage is attached to a particular EC2 instance, can only be accessed by that particular EC2 and will be lost as soon as the EC2 instance stops. The Elastic Block Storage (EBS) provides block storage for EC2 but is independent of a particular instance and can be shared between EC2 instances.

EC2 provides the Elastic Load Balancer which as the name suggests automatically balances the load across multiple servers. The load balancer also scales the number of servers up or down depending on the requirements of the particular load.

5.10.5 Amazon Elastic Beanstalk

AWS Elastic Beanstalk is currently in beta but promises to provide 'an even easier way for you to quickly deploy and manage applications in the AWS cloud'. The developer need only upload their applications, and the Elastic Beanstalk will handle the deployment details, load balancing and scaling. In some ways this makes the product more like a PaaS offering although in this case the developer can control the underlying infrastructure if required (Beanstalk will use resources such as EC2 and S3 when deploying applications). Amazon clearly states that the aim is to offer the developer the best of both the PaaS and IaaS worlds.

The current release of Elastic Beanstalk is built for Java developers, and the Elastic beanstalk application should be packaged using the standard Java WAR structure. An AWS plug-in is available for Eclipse which also allows you to test and deploy your application to one or more EC2 instances running the Apache Tomcat web server.

5.10.6 FlexiScale

FlexiScale (http://www.flexiscale.com/) offers on-demand hosting and operates in a somewhat similar manner to Amazon EC2. FlexiScale supports both Windows and Linux servers and uses the Xen hypervisor.

5.10.7 GoGrid

GoGrid (http://www.gogrid.com/) allows users to utilise a range of premade windows and Linux images in a range of fixed instance sizes and also offers stacks on top for applications such as high-volume web applications, e-commerce and databases.

5.10.8 Eucalyptus ('Elastic Utility Computing Architecture
for Linking Your Programs to Useful Systems')

Eucalyptus (http://www.eucalyptus.com/) is an open source Linux-based software platform for creating cloud computing IaaS systems based on computer clusters. The project has an interface that can be connected to Amazon's compute and storage cloud system (EC2 and S3), and users can interact with Eucalyptus clouds using the same tools used on Amazon. Eucalyptus supports multiple hypervisor technologies within the same cloud and provides a range of cloud administration tools for system management and accounting. Eucalyptus is currently supported by most Linux distributions. Ubuntu enterprise cloud is a new initiative to make it easier to provide, deploy, configure and use cloud infrastructures based on Eucalyptus.

5.10.9 Rackspace

Rackspace (http://www.rackspace.com/) offers an IaaS solution fixed size instances in the cloud. Rackspace cloud servers offer a range of Linux-based premade images, and users can request different sized images.

5.11 Chapter Summary

In this chapter, we have looked at how using web services and service-oriented architectures has contributed to the rise of cloud computing. We have reviewed the SPI model and examined how it can be useful to view cloud computing as consisting of various layers which are most easily identified by considering the particular responsibilities of vendors, developers and end users. We should note that although the SPI model is extremely useful in categorising and understanding cloud-based systems, the layers are rather blurred as, for example, some SaaS offerings can be programmed and some PaaS products offer the developers the option of direct control of the underlying hardware.

5.11.1 End of Chapter Exercises

In this tutorial we are going to work with Google's cloud offering to create a simple web application. This choice is due partly to the availability of Google's free tier as we appreciate that many students of cloud computing may be put off by having to purchase cloud resources or supply credit card details.

Create a Google App Engine account (free) by clicking the Sign up link under Getting Started on http://code.google.com/appengine/ and follow the instructions. No credit card is required for the free tier, but you will need to be able to receive an SMS text message.

There are currently three programming languages which you can use on GAE, but we are going to use Java. One advantage of this is that we can use the GAE plug-in to the freely available eclipse IDE which we installed to our VM previously.

5.11.2 Task 1: Prepare Eclipse and Install GAE Plug-In

We need to install some add-ons to eclipse. Whilst the install takes place, you will need to agree to run unsigned content and agree to licence conditions. You will also need to restart eclipse when requested (if at any point you hit a problem, you should restart eclipse and try again).

1. Open your VM and go to the Ubuntu software centre. Type in eclipse and install.
2. Open eclipse and select the default Workspace location and then go to Help/ Install New Software. Click on the 'Available Software Sites' link and enable the entry whose location is http://download.eclipse.org/releases/helios
3. After the list populates (this may take some time depending on your Internet connection speed), in the text box below 'work with', type 'xml' to filter the entries and then select 'Eclipse XML Editors and Tools' which should be available in the 'programming languages'.
4. Select 'next' twice, agree the licence and 'finish' (again this may take some time to complete).
5. Restart eclipse when prompted.
6. You are now ready to install the plug-in for Google App Engine. Again, open eclipse and go to Help/Install New Software and enter this URL: http://dl.google. com/eclipse/plugin/3.7
7. Select the Google plug-in for eclipse and the SDKs as shown below.
8. Select 'next' twice, agree the licence and 'finish' (again this may take some time to complete) (Fig. 5.2).

5.11.3 Task 2: Create the First Web Application

1. Click on the Google icon and select 'new web application project' (Fig. 5.3). We are not going to use GWT (Google Web Toolkit), so make sure this option is unchecked. Fill in a project name and a package name and make sure the 'Use Google App Engine' is selected (Fig. 5.4).
2. You can then select 'Finish'. This will create a new eclipse project with a structure similar to that shown below (once you have expanded the elements) (Fig. 5.5). As you can see GAE uses a standard Java web archive folder (WAR).
3. Open the sample Java servlet code which has been generated for you (again you may need to expand by clicking the '+' sign) (Fig. 5.6). You can run the project locally by right clicking the project node in the package explorer (GAE_isbn) and then selecting 'run as' and then selecting 'web application'. If successful you will see the message appear in the console window:
   ```
   INFO: The server is running at
   http://localhost:8888/_ah/admin
   ```
4. Open a browser session and open http://localhost:8888/. Hopefully you will see a page similar to that shown below in Fig. 5.7.

If you click on the servlet, you should see the 'hello world' message returned by the sample servlet. Even if you are not familiar with Java, take a look at the code for the servlet and see if you can change the text of the message sent from the server.

We are now going to try and create a simple ISBN lookup service on GAE. This will be a limited application and really is only intended to give you a flavour of the type of thing you can do with app engine.

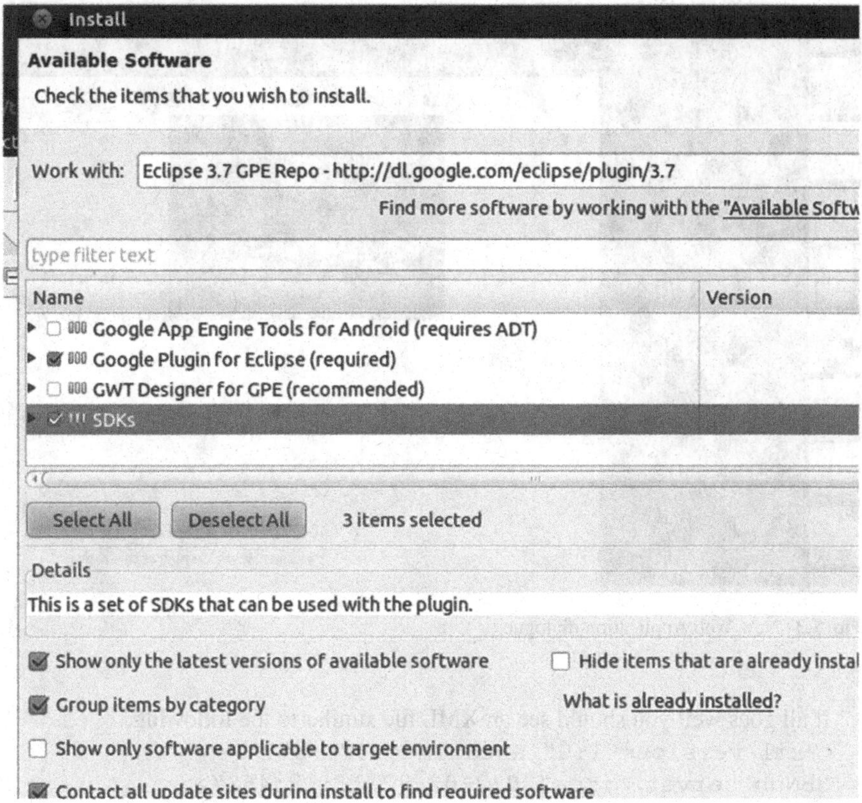

Fig. 5.2 GAE Install Dialogue

5.11.4 Task 3: ISBN App

Our GAE application is going to prompt the user for an ISBN number. Once the user submits the number, we will perform some very basic validation and then return the title, author and publisher of the book.

We are going to achieve this by composition. We will use the REST-based service offered by http://isbndb.com. The service is free, although you will need to complete the simple sign up procedure to obtain an access key. Once you have the key, you can test the service by pasting a URL similar to the following into your browser but replacing the value for key with your own key:

http://isbndb.com/api/books.xml?access_key=abc123&index1=isbn&value1=9 780045100606

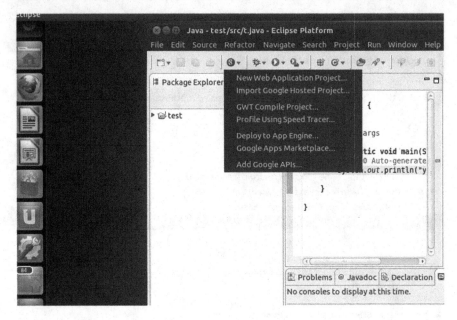

Fig. 5.3 New Web Application dialogue

If all goes well you should see an XML file similar to the following:

```
<?xml version="1.0" encoding="UTF-8"?>
<ISBNdb server_time="2012-02-22T13:19:46Z">
  <BookList total_results="1" shown_results="1">
   <BookData book_id="alan_turing_a04" isbn="0045100608"
isbn13="9780045100606">
    <Title>Alan Turing</Title>
    <TitleLong>Alan Turing: the enigma of intelli-gence</
TitleLong>
    <AuthorsText>Andrew Hodges</AuthorsText>
    <PublisherText publish-er_id="unwin_paperbacks">
London : Unwin Paperbacks, 1985.</PublisherText>
   </BookData>
  </BookList>
</ISBNdb>
```

Now return to eclipse and the GAE project you created earlier where we have
three updates to make:

1. We need to update the index.html file (in the WAR folder) which is the default
   starting place for the web application. Replace the existing contents with the
   following:

```
<html>
<head>
<script type="text/javascript">
  var xmlhttp;
```

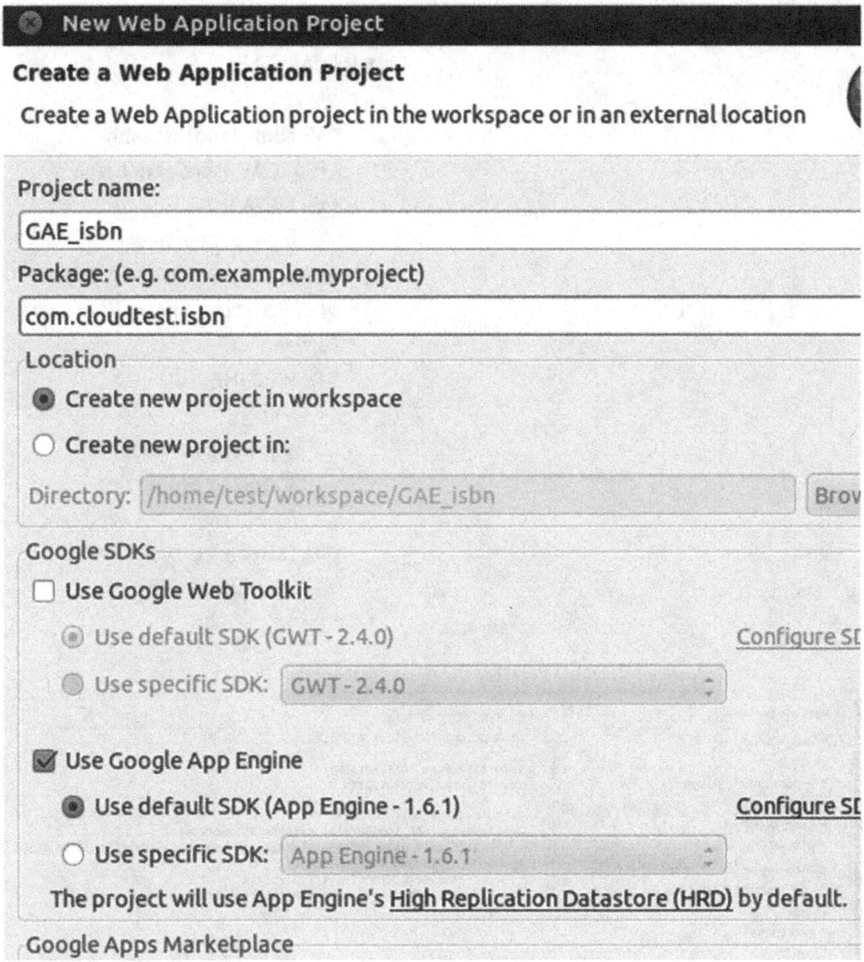

New Web Application Project

Create a Web Application Project

Create a Web Application project in the workspace or in an external location

Project name:

GAE_isbn

Package: (e.g. com.example.myproject)

com.cloudtest.isbn

Location

◉ Create new project in workspace

○ Create new project in:

Directory: /home/test/workspace/GAE_isbn   Brov

Google SDKs

☐ Use Google Web Toolkit

◉ Use default SDK (GWT - 2.4.0)   Configure SI

◉ Use specific SDK: GWT - 2.4.0

☑ Use Google App Engine

◉ Use default SDK (App Engine - 1.6.1)   Configure SI

○ Use specific SDK: App Engine - 1.6.1

The project will use App Engine's High Replication Datastore (HRD) by default.

Google Apps Marketplace

Fig. 5.4 New Web Application Project dialogue

```
function lookupISBN(isbn) {
 xmlhttp = null;
 if (window.XMLHttpRequest) {
  xmlhttp = new XMLHttpRequest();
 } else if (window.ActiveXObject){//code for IE6,IE5
   xmlhttp = new ActiveXObject("Microsoft.XMLHTTP");
 }
   if (xmlhttp != null) {
     xmlhttp.onreadystatechange = state_Change;
     var url = "/isbnservice?isbn=" + isbn;
     xmlhttp.open("GET", url, true);
     xmlhttp.send(null);
```

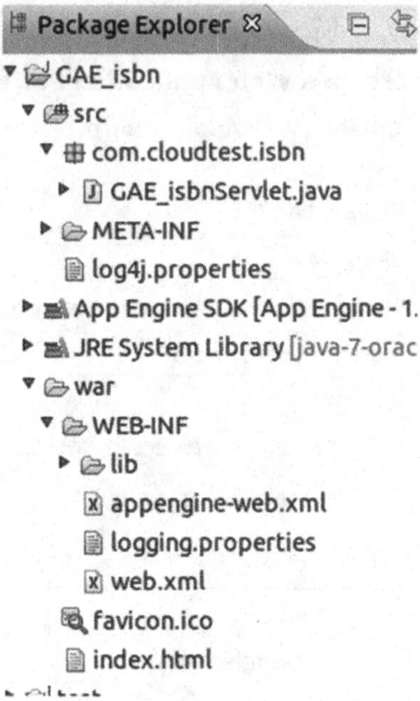

Fig. 5.5 Eclipse Package
Explorer

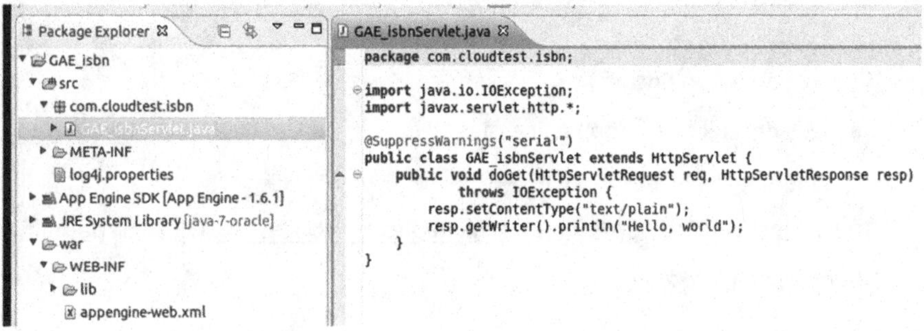

Package Explorer ☒

▼ 🗁 GAE_isbn
  ▼ 📁 src
    ▼ ⊞ com.cloudtest.isbn
      ▶ 🗋 GAE_isbnServlet.java
    ▶ 🗁 META-INF
      📄 log4j.properties
  ▶ 🗟 App Engine SDK [App Engine - 1.
  ▶ 🗟 JRE System Library [java-7-orac
  ▼ 🗁 war
    ▼ 🗁 WEB-INF
      ▶ 🗁 lib
        ⊠ appengine-web.xml
        📄 logging.properties
        ⊠ web.xml
      🗔 favicon.ico
      📄 index.html

Package Explorer ☒   │ 🗋 GAE_isbnServlet.java ☒

▼ 🗁 GAE_isbn
  ▼ 📁 src
    ▼ ⊞ com.cloudtest.isbn
      ▶ 🗋 GAE_isbnServlet.java
    ▶ 🗁 META-INF
      📄 log4j.properties
  ▶ 🗟 App Engine SDK [App Engine - 1.6.1]
  ▶ 🗟 JRE System Library [java-7-oracle]
  ▼ 🗁 war
    ▼ 🗁 WEB-INF
      ▶ 🗁 lib
        ⊠ appengine-web.xml

```java
package com.cloudtest.isbn;

import java.io.IOException;
import javax.servlet.http.*;

@SuppressWarnings("serial")
public class GAE_isbnServlet extends HttpServlet {
    public void doGet(HttpServletRequest req, HttpServletResponse resp)
            throws IOException {
        resp.setContentType("text/plain");
        resp.getWriter().println("Hello, world");
    }
}
```

Fig. 5.6 Servlet code

```
      } else {
    alert("Your browser does not support XMLHTTP.");
  }
}
  function state_Change() {
   if (xmlhttp.readyState == 4) {// 4 = "loaded"
    if (xmlhttp.status == 200) {// 200 = "OK"
  docment.getElementById(
    'ISBNServiceResponse').innerHTML =
        xmlhttp.responseText;
    } else {
```

Fig. 5.7 Hello App Engine

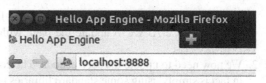

```
      alert("Problem looking up ISBN Service :" +
          xmlhttp.statusText);
      }
    }
    }
</script>
</head>
<title>ISBN Lookup</title>
<body>
  <h2>ISBN Lookup</h2>
  <hr />
  <h4>
      (Powered by ISBNdb
<a href="http://isbndb.com/">ISBN Service</a>)
</h4>
<hr />
<p>
    <b>Lookup ISBN:</b><input type="text"
        id="isbn"></input>
</p>
<p>
    <b>Book details :</b> <br />
    <span id="ISBNServiceResponse"></span>
</p>
<button onclick="lookupISBN(isbn.value)">
      Lookup ISBN</button>
</body>
</html>
```

The above includes html and JavaScript. The JavaScript function called look-upISBN will use AJAX to update the page with the information returned by the isbnservice.

2. We now need to update the servlet code. The code below might look complex but in fact is simply using some standard libraries to make a call to the ISBNdb URL, navigate the XML returned and write out the data from the selected elements. Update the servlet code with the following:

```
package com.cloudtest.isbn;
import java.io.BufferedReader;
import java.io.IOException;
import java.io.InputStreamReader;
import java.io.StringReader;
import java.net.URL;
import javax.servlet.ServletException;
import javax.servlet.http.HttpServlet;
import javax.servlet.http.HttpServletRequest;
import javax.servlet.http.HttpServletResponse;
import javax.xml.parsers.DocumentBuilder;
import javax.xml.parsers.DocumentBuilderFactory;
import org.w3c.dom.Document;
import org.w3c.dom.Element;
import org.w3c.dom.Node;
import org.w3c.dom.NodeList;
import org.xml.sax.InputSource;
@SuppressWarnings("serial")
public class ISBNService extends HttpServlet {
public void doGet(HttpServletRequest req,
   HttpServletResponse resp)
     throws IOException {
  String strCallResult = "";
  resp.setContentType("text/plain");
  try {
// Extract out the user entered ISBN number
  String strISBN = req.getParameter("isbn");
// Do basic validation - could be much more thorough
  if (strISBN == null)
    throw new Exception("ISBN field cannot be empty.");
// Trim
  strISBN = strISBN.trim();
  if (strISBN.length() == 0)
    throw new Exception("ISBN field empty.");
  String strISBNServiceCall =
    "http://isbndb.com/api/books.xml?access_key=123&index1=
isbn&value1=";
strISBNServiceCall += strISBN;
```

```
URL url = new URL(strISBNServiceCall);
BufferedReader reader =
    new BufferedReader(new InputStreamReader(
    url.openStream()));
StringBuffer response = new StringBuffer();
String line;
  while ((line = reader.readLine()) != null) {
   response.append(line);
  }
  reader.close();
  strCallResult = response.toString();
  DocumentBuilderFactory builderFactory =
   DocumentBuilderFactory.newInstance();
  DocumentBuilder builder =
   builderFactory.newDocumentBuilder();
  Document doc =
   builder.parse(new InputSource(new StringReader(
    strCallResult.toString())));
  doc.getDocumentElement().normalize();
  NodeList nList =
   doc.getElementsByTagName("BookData");
  if (nList.getLength() < 1)
   throw new Exception("no books: check the ISBN.");
  for (int temp = 0; temp < nList.getLength(); temp++)
{
  Node nNode = nList.item(temp);
  if (nNode.getNodeType() == Node.ELEMENT_NODE) {
   Element eElement = (Element) nNode;
   resp.getWriter().println(
    "<br />Title : "+
    getTagValue("TitleLong", eElement));
    resp.getWriter().println("<br />Author : " +
    getTagValue("AuthorsText", eElement));
    resp.getWriter().println("<br />Publisher : "+
    getTagValue("PublisherText", eElement));
  }
  resp.getWriter().println(strCallResult);
  }
  } catch (Exception ex) {
  strCallResult = "Error: " + ex.getMessage();
  resp.getWriter().println(strCallResult);
  }
}
@Override
public void doPost(HttpServletRequest req,
```

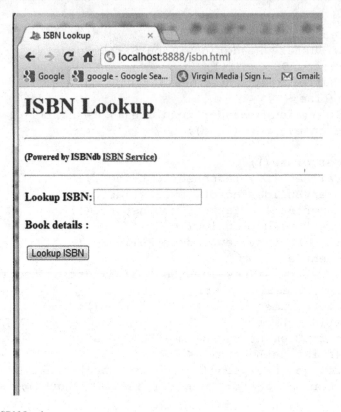

Fig. 5.8 ISBN Lookup

```
  HttpServletResponse resp)
   throws ServletException, IOException {
    doGet(req, resp);
  }
private static String getTagValue(String sTag,
  Element eElement) {
   NodeList nlList =
          eEle-ment.getElementsByTagName(sTag).item(0).
getChildNodes();
    Node nValue = (Node) nlList.item(0);
    return nValue.getNodeValue();
  }
}
```

3. Change the package statement (if required) at the top so that it reflects the name
   of the package you created when setting up your GAE project.
4. Update the value of the string for the strISBNServiceCall so that your access
   code for isbndb.com is used.

5. Finally, you need to update the web.xml (also in the WAR folder) file such that it
   includes the following:

```
<servlet>
<servlet-name>ISBNService</servlet-name>
 <servlet-class>com.cloudtest.isbn.ISBNService</
servlet-class>
</servlet>
<servlet-mapping>
 <servlet-name>ISBNService</servlet-name>
 <url-pattern>/isbnservice</url-pattern>
</servlet-mapping>
```

You need to ensure that the packages specified for the servlet-class matches your
own package. Once you have saved these updates, you can test the application
locally. Run the web application and open in the browser. Hopefully now the page
will look something like that shown below in Fig. 5.8.

Test the application by entering ISBN numbers (e.g. 1884133320).

Finally, we are ready to deploy the application. Click on the Google icon in
eclipse and select the deploy option. You will need to give a name for your application that has not been used before. Once deployed you should be able to open and
test the application in your browser using a URL such as http://lazaruscloud.appspot.
com/isbn.html

References

Chu-Carrol C.: Code in the Cloud: Programming Google App Engine. Pragmatic Programmers
    (2011)
Marcel, C.B., Marcel, K., Mimis, J., Tai, S.: Cloud Computing: Web-based Dynamic IT Services.
    Springer, Heidelberg (2011)

Data in the Cloud

6

What the reader will learn:

- That there are many types of data storage available, meeting different needs
- That the web and cloud provide special challenges to database users but also provide opportunities to design data-centric solutions that are not just relational
- Some hands-on experience of using NoSQL databases and understanding of the business needs addressed by each solution
- An appreciation of the other data-centric uses the cloud can help with, such as backup and recovery and disaster recovery

6.1 Historic Review of Database Storage Methods

These days we tend to think only of computer-based databases, but databases have been with us for centuries. The ancient Egyptians stored data on stone tables in columns and rows. More recently, libraries used a card index system to allow users to retrieve an ISBN number from an indexed drawer, full of cards.

The key attributes of a database could be seen as:

- They contain data (though not necessarily information).
- They allow the data to be read and can allow data to be updated, deleted and inserted.
- There are often mechanisms to (rapidly) search for data items.

In the modern era, the first universally accepted standard model was that of the hierarchical database. They stored data in a tree-like hierarchy. When querying the data, you navigated down the hierarchy to get to the record you needed (see Fig. 6.1).

Users of current relational databases may recognise the idea as very similar to that of a B-tree index, which is usually the default form of index storage in current Relational Database Management System (RDBMS). This is not accidental. The speed with which you get to an item of data is potentially much faster than other search algorithms and is always a known, manageable number of data reads.

R. Hill et al., *Guide to Cloud Computing: Principles and Practice*, Computer
Communications and Networks, DOI 10.1007/978-1-4471-4603-2_6,
© Springer-Verlag London 2013

Hierarchical Model

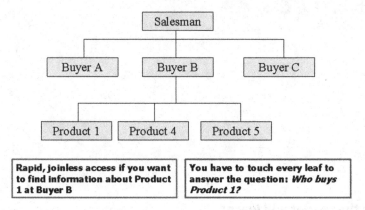

Fig. 6.1   The hierarchical data storage model

6.2   Relational Is the New Hoover

Rapid though certain queries can be in hierarchical databases, they do have some significant downsides. Especially from the perspective of today when we have extremely flexible RDBMS available, the rigidity of the hierarchy means that accessing data in any other way than through the tree structure is very resource costly and slow.

Unlike today, at the time when these databases were in common use, hard disk space was very expensive. The only way to provide some alternative routes through the data was effectively to duplicate the data within different trees. This was very costly.

Ad hoc queries of the type we take for granted now were not easy either. In the example in Fig. 6.1, we could probably already guess that we would have a product, buyer and salesman table in a relational schema for the same data. Once stored, we can select our required data at will, by forming joins between tables.

At a time when hard disk drives were expensive and managers wanting to understand the data in the system would often have to wait days, or even weeks, for the query to be coded, punched and run, it is not surprising that Codd's seminal works on the relational model in the 1970s caused such an upheaval in the database world.

SQL, the standardised language which comes with relational databases, is, provided the database is designed properly, extremely flexible in what it allows a user to query. The query language itself, whilst it can challenge a newcomer, is a far cry from the difficult alternative of writing your own data access mechanisms in a programming language. Its near-English nature means that many managers became free of the constraints of having to use programmers to get the data they needed to understand their businesses better.

Note: It is the change in the way which we store the data that changes the way we can access it. No one storage model is perfect. Hierarchical still works well if you only ever query data using a known tree structure. Other models have coexisted with relational over the last couple of decades. Object and object relational are perhaps still the most common, for example. It is the change in storage brought about by web and cloud technologies that have now generated a number of alternative 'NoSQL' databases that we explore later in this chapter.

6.3　Database as a Service

In previous chapters, we have described a variety of cloud service models. One that is important in terms of this chapter is the idea of databases being available as a service.

Cloud computing provides opportunities for efficient data management where users define, update and query a database which is running in the cloud environment. As with the other 'as-a-service' services, it has the familiar characteristics of pay-per-use and an on-demand model. Instead of having the necessary resources for deploying a database management system, companies may prefer to employ DaaS mainly for flexibility and costs.

Many organisations have invested heavily in client–server-based database systems over the last two decades. Names like Oracle, SQL Server and DB2 are in everyday parlance for most corporate data professionals. However, some heavy investment has been made to open up the pay-for-use approach to storing data. The big players include Amazon RDS and Microsoft Azure, although most vendors now include cloud versions of their RDBMS. There are new players in the smaller-scale database field too, such as Amazon's SimpleDb.com.

6.4　Data Storage in the Cloud

The cloud has not only enabled database management systems to become pay-as-you-go; it has also provided organisations with the opportunity to store their raw data, or perhaps copies of it, off-site. By storing multiple copies of the data on several servers, these sites have built in 'redundancy', that is, the objects you store in them are replicated. This means a single point of failure will not cause the loss of any data overall. Organisations can use services such as Amazon's S3 or more specialist backup and disaster recovery vendors like Backup Technology to keep copies of data in the cloud, rather than having an expensive second, standby server on-site.

6.5　Backup or Disaster Recovery?

It is to be hoped that the computer-using reader will understand the concept of backing up their valuable data! Hard drives do go wrong, and when they do, they can destroy information. For many organisations, this information is vital to their livelihood. Losing it would not be a minor inconvenience but could actually put them out of business.

In database systems, it is normal for database administrators (DBA) to be responsible for ensuring no data is ever lost. The difference between backup and DR can be seen as a matter of scale. We can describe a backup strategy as an approach to ensuring no data is permanently lost. At its simplest, this means taking copies of the changes that are made to the database over a certain period (a week for example) and storing those changes externally to the database. Should data go missing, as a result of some disk failure, for example, a recovery mechanism comes into play to allow the DBA to 'replay' the changes to the database since a point in time when the entire database was consistent. Depending upon how much data is lost and which parts of the database are effected, this can be a relatively simple process or can mean retrieving the last full backup copy of the database and then replaying all changes since that backup.

Backup and recovery normally works on the premise that the server and DBMS are up and running and that what needs repairing are holes in the database itself. Disaster recovery is focused on how to keep a business's critical systems available when calamities happen: earthquakes, fires, floods, accidental deletion of tables or other user mistake—things that can affect the very fabric of our IT systems.

DR often requires the duplication of systems so that if the master system goes down, a parallel system in a different site kicks in, allowing users to continue using the system. This is, of course, costly, as it means duplicating expensive IT equipment. The speed with which a system becomes available again is measured as the Mean Time to Recovery (MTTR). Better MTTR will normally require expensive solutions. Parallel systems connected by high-speed networks mean that the system out time could be measured in seconds but do mean virtually doubling the hardware and maintenance costs of an organisation's IT systems.

Less costly alternatives exist. A standby server can, for example, be separate from the active system but has a complete backup of the database stored on it and has changes applied to it on a regular basis, often overnight.

Now cloud brings other alternatives and is causing organisations to rethink their backup and DR strategies. Traditional backup and recovery methods have largely been based around magnetic tape as a medium for storing data. The advantage of this medium is that it is relatively cheap. The disadvantage is that it is slow to access and can be quite labour intensive. Systems where the user simply clicks a button to send their backup information to one of several servers somewhere in the cloud are fast pressuring the traditional approach.

However, there are issues, real and perceived, about the security of storing your data in the cloud. Many decision-makers are just more comfortable with knowing where their data is physically stored and putting in place a security mechanism to protect that data. Putting data in the cloud, they fear, makes it open to hacking.

Of course, data on your own server is not necessarily always safe. Encrypting data before it is passed into the backup environment is one way to add extra layers of protection around the data. True though these facts may be, to the frustration of the providers of disk in the cloud, the perception is still sometimes that you are safer having control of your own data on your own servers. We cover security and governance in the cloud in more detail in Chap. 10.

6.6   If You Only Have a Hammer – Or Why Relational May Not Always Be the Right Answer

Relational databases (RDBMS) have dramatically changed the way we deal with organisational data. They allow nonprogrammers to access data relatively easily on an ad hoc basis. They are also very safe, and it is given that the data you look at when you query the database is correct, valid and current. This is no accident. RDBMS are designed around the ACID characteristics; that is, data held in them have:

- *Atomicity.* All changes must be 'all or nothing' to allow transactions to work (see below).
- *Consistency.* All data must always follow the rules as defined in the schema.
- *Isolation.* Any data being affected by one transaction must not be used by another transaction until the first is complete.
- *Durability.* Once a transaction is committed, it should become permanent and unalterable by machine failure of any type.

The business need addressed by an RDBMS is often based around the concept of a transaction as opposed to a process. As a simple example, if I was to want to transfer £100 from my account to Richard's to settle a debt, we can see two basic processes:

1. Reduce my account by £100
2. Increase Richard's account by £100

Once both processes have completed, the transaction is complete, and we can say the changes have been committed to the database. However, should the database crash after step (1), but before step (2), the transaction is not complete. If we were only dealing with successful processes, then my account would be £100 lighter, but Richard would still think that I owed him £100.

Both in the world of work and on university courses, the ACID model is often taken for granted as a requirement for any database. We can lose sight of the fact that sometimes our data needs are not transactionally focused, and therefore, sometimes, the relational model isn't the most appropriate for what we need to do with the data we are storing. This statement may come as a shock to people for whom a database is a relational database!

6.7   Business Drivers for the Adoption of Different Data Models

Relational databases have been at the centre of most business systems for decades. For large organisations, with large volumes of data, they are essential. However, as web-driven systems began to expand, it became clear that the relational model is not good at everything. Google eventually took the decision to write their own database system to support their global requirement for information searching, for example.

The story behind BigTable is well documented, especially by Chang et al. (2008). Its basic data model is not relational, as that model did not allow Google to provide rapid text-based searches across the vast volumes of data stored in the web. It is rather a sparse, distributed multidimensional database. Although it is Google's own product and not openly available, other such databases do exist. HBase is an open source database that claims to have a similar data model to that of BigTable, for example.

Why would Google feel it is necessary to put so much effort and resource to create their own database? Simply because relational databases, with their large processing overhead in terms of maintaining the ACID attributes of the data they store and their reliance on potentially processor hungry joins, is not the right tool for the task they had before them: quickly finding relevant data from terabytes of unstructured data (web content) which may be stored across thousands of geographically desperate nodes. In short, they found that relational does not scale well for this type of data.

6.8   You Can't Have Everything

DBAs have long had to balance a number of business drivers. And DBAs have long realised that there are balances to be found between competing drivers. Availability (the fact that the database and systems using it should ideally be always ready to accept work) is one such driver, for example. A bit like grandma's apple pie, everyone wants their database to be five 9s (99.999%) available. But that sort of availability costs both money and time. Moreover, particularly in an ACID environment, built-in redundancy (having multiple copies of the data in case one node fails) is also likely to slow performance (another key driver for a DBA) as more writes are required to keep the system consistent.

As we have alluded to already, some of today's data processing tasks involve data which is duplicated (for redundancy and performance reasons) across potentially many different nodes in the web. This can be when RDBMS start to struggle, especially with large volumes of such distributed data.

The DBA of such an RDBMS may start by examining ways that he or she can speed retrieval up by using secondary indexing. The problem is that whilst this may speed a read operation, it is also likely to slow every write operation. Further, they may find that the RDBMS, in a quest to maintain ACID properties, struggles with keeping every node consistent.

There have been some interesting papers published which attempt to justify the NoSQL approach by referring to CAP theorem. Brewer (2012) makes the point that there is a three-way pull when designing distributed systems in general and for the web in particular. The three forces competing are the needs for the data to be:

- Consistent
- Available
- Partition tolerant (coping with breaks in physical network connections)

Most traditional RDBMS would guarantee that all the values in all our nodes are identical before it allows another user to read the values. But as we have seen, that is at a significant cost in terms of performance.

6.9 Basically Available, Soft State, Eventually Consistent (BASE)

BASE is the NoSQL operating premise, in the same way that traditional transactionally focused databases use ACID. You will note that we move from a world of certainty in terms of data consistency to a world where all we are promised is that all copies of the data will, at some point, be the same.

Even here there is no single approach. The eventual state of consistency can be provided as a result of a read-repair, where any outdated data is refreshed with the latest version of the data as a result of the system detecting stale data during a read operation. Another approach is that of weak consistency. In this case, the read operation will return the first value found, not checking for staleness. Any stale nodes discovered are simply marked for updating at some stage in the future. This is a performance-focused approach but has the associated risk that data retrieved may not be the most current.

Again, some people used to traditional RDBMS environments will find it hard to handle the last sentence! In some applications, however, it is not critical for every user to have identical data at all times. Think, for example, of a discussion board application:

In a thread, let's say 100 answers exist as a result of a user, A, asking a question. User B decides to add comment 101. A user C, logging on to review the threads after user B has committed their comment, should expect to see 101 answers. But if one node (node N) fails to get rapidly updated and user C retrieves their data from N, they will only see 100 answers. But does this really matter? User C is in the same position as if they had viewed the thread a minute ago. It's easy to say it does matter, but if we give you the option of free access to an uncertain number of answers or charge you £10 to access a guaranteed up-to-date list, you may start to think it matters less!

6.10 So What Alternative Ways to Store Data Are There?

As we have seen, the ACID requirements that have guided relational database designers for decades are not sacrosanct. Moreover, implementing the procedures needed to ensure that the ACID properties can be guaranteed is a large overhead on the DBMS—an overhead that costs in terms of performance.

There may, for example, be occasions when the database user would be willing to forgo a guarantee that every user sees the same version of the data (consistency) eventually for a rule that everyone can see a version of the data immediately. Techniques used to ensure consistency in RDBMS environments typically include storing old values in an undo area and preventing other users seeing data by locking rows, or even tables, whilst transactions happen. For the locked-out user, this seems like the database is performing poorly or, worse, is not functioning properly.

6.11   Column Oriented

We have become very used to thinking of rows of data. Many of the database professionals' standard tools force this way of looking at data upon us. Not only do tables hold rows, but it can be exported as a CSV (comma-separated value) or fixed length text file. For many applications, this model is entirely appropriate.

However, in some circumstances, the majority of activity against the data happens in a column-focused way. Often in data analysis, for example, we will be taking averages, looking for high and low values or looking for trends in one particular column.

In those circumstances, it is rather inefficient (in terms of disk reads and CPU usage) to have to find each row, locate the column concerned, check if it contains data and then read the value. Many high-end RDBMS have invented methods for speeding this read-and-search process, but, nonetheless, it is wasteful if all you want to do is read the same attribute from each row. We should remember that reading from disk is a slow process and limiting disk reads is an important aspect of any DBMS optimisation process.

The column-oriented approach improves read efficiency (though not necessarily write efficiency) by not having any row identifier and packing data to allow compression schemes to reduce the volume of disk storage required. This allows for more rapid analysis of those column values but does mean that full tuples (or records) have to be recreated by using positional information to look up the other data items from a row, and that is inefficient. Column based is therefore better suited to implementations where analysis of one column is needed.

Moreover, because the best performance, in terms of compression, will happen when similar values are adjacent to each other, the values of a column should ideally be known at the outset, so they can be written down to disk in the most efficient way. One insert could result in many rewrites as the data is shuffled round to accommodate the new value, making low data volatility essential.

Examples include Ingres Vectorwise, Apache HBase and Cassandra. We will be using the latter as an example of the type for you to experiment with later in this chapter.

6.12   Document Oriented

Relational database design techniques all work on the assumption that the data you wish to store is predefinable and will always contain the same type of data. But in life, we sometimes collect data which is less well structured.

Take as an example the following contact information from a CRM database:

```
FirstName = "George", Surname="Smith" ,
Pets=[{Type:"Dog",   Name:"Flint",Age:5},   {Type:"Cat",
Name:"Jade",Age:7}], Tel="0111223344".
   FirstName = "Mary", Surname="Songo" ,
Pets=[{Type:"Dog", Name:"Ajax",Age:2}],
Mob="077777777", Tel="0211225555".
```

Both of these are entirely realistic data about the customer, but the data items are not identical. Whilst a relational database would have a schema which included columns to store all potential data items, document-oriented databases have the flexibility to allow you to store this sort of semi-structured data in a *schema-less* environment.

Many of the document-centric databases don't allow data to be locked in the way that is required for atomic transactions in RDBMS. Since locking is a significant performance overhead, this enables them to claim performance advantages over traditional databases. The downside, of course, is that some applications absolutely require secure transactional locking mechanisms. Document oriented is probably not the right vehicle for highly structured data in a transaction-dependent environment, as occurs in many OLTP systems.

The performance advantages that accrue from document-centric implementations mean that they are often used when there are large volumes of semi-structured data, such as web page content, comment storage and event logging. They may well also support sharding (spreading a table's rows) of data across multiple nodes, again as a performance device.

Examples include CouchDb and MongoDB. We will be using the latter as an example of the type for you to experiment with later in this chapter.

6.13   Key–Value Stores (K–V Store)

In some situations, the database user needs are even more basic than either of the two examples above. Sometimes you just want to store some information against a particular key (or index). If you always know the key value when you want to get data out from the store and you don't need the rule enforcement that comes with an RDBMS, then a K–V store will probably be the fastest option. See the section about MapReduce in Chap. 5.

Because of their light footprints, such databases can often be built into applications, removing the need for any DBMS.

As with all the data storage options mentioned here, the real driver for the move from RDBMS being the single answer to all database needs has been the web and latterly the cloud. The enormous amounts of data for applications like Facebook and Twitter will be stored in data centres across many different geographic locations.

Horizontal scaling is the process of having that data spread across many nodes, and many of these newer, NoSQL-type database systems are designed from the start to be able to cope with this physical aspect of the data store. RDBMS on the other hand, with query responses typically created by joining data from two or more tables, can struggle with managing distributed data that is spread across many nodes.

Examples include Voldemort and Redis.

6.14   When to Use Which Type of Data Storage?

The first point to make is that the various types of database need not be mutually exclusive. This is not, as some websites argue, a great battle to the death for the future of databases. Relational databases certainly handle transactional data well, and, for the foreseeable future, especially given the huge levels of investment in RDBMS made by most organisations, they will remain the most frequently used type of database.

When data professionals are looking at querying large datasets that may be distributed across the web, however, some other tools have entered their armoury. In undertaking the tutorials later this chapter, you will be able to gauge for yourself what the relative strengths and weaknesses are. And it is important to say that every application will be different, but as a rule of thumb, we can say:

1. Column-based databases allow for rapid location and return of data from one particular attribute. They are potentially very slow with writing, however, since data may need to be shuffled around to allow a new data item to be inserted. As a rough guide then, traditional transactionally orientated databases will probably fair better in an RDBMS. Column based will probably thrive in areas where speed of access to non-volatile data is important, for example, in some decision support applications. You only need to review marketing material from commercial contenders, like Ingres Vectorwise, to see that business analytics is seen as the key market and speed of data access the main product differentiator.

2. Document-centric databases are good where the data is difficult to structure. Web pages and blog entries are two oft-quoted examples. Unlike RDBMS, which impose structure by their very nature, document-centric databases allow free-form data to be stored. The onus is then on the data retriever to make sense of the data that is stored.

3. If you do not need large and complex data structures and can always access your data using a known key, then key–value stores have a performance advantage over most RDBMS. Oracle has a feature within their RDBMS that allows you to define a table at an index-organised table (IOT), and this works in a similar way. However, you do still have the overhead of consistency checking, and these IOTs are often just a small part of a larger schema. RDBMS have a reputation for poor scaling in distributed systems, and this is where key/value stores can be a distinct advantage.

6.15   Summary

In the previous chapters in this part two, we have looked at cloud from the application perspective. In this chapter, we have seen that there are many different data storage methods available for a database. The decision as to which is the right one is driven by the task at hand. How we estimate the potential benefits of a move to cloud is covered in more detail in Chap. 8.

We have also seen how cloud can help with typical database tasks such as backup and recovery and disaster recovery whilst reviewing the business drivers that would come into play for using the cloud for these tasks.

This chapter is different to the others in that the following tutorials are longer. Many readers will have had some experience of the relational model and SQL already, but we felt that readers need to appreciate the different approaches on offer. In the following tutorials, therefore, we concentrate on two of the more modern approaches—one column based and one document based.

6.16   Further Reading

The tutorials that follow provide pointers to more resources about the Cassandra and MongoDB.

"Transforming relational database into HBase: a case study" by Chongxin Li is an interesting discussion of the complexities of mapping relation to Hbase. Chongxin Li: Transforming relational database into HBase: a case study. 2010 IEEE International Conference on Software Engineering and Service Sciences (ICSESS), pp. 683–687 (16–18 July 2010). doi: 10.1109/ICSESS.2010.5552465 (Chang et al. 2008).

6.17   Tutorials

In this section, we ask you to try examples of NoSQL databases. The business case for these trials is given below, and sample datasets with further work can be downloaded from our book website.

6.18   BookCo

In this case study, we are looking at data from a chain of booksellers called BookCo. You are the chief information officer of this company that sells books and other related products via the Internet. You have many information needs to address, but you feel you need to assess some new tools which may help with some of those tasks. BookCo has already invested heavily in a leading client/server database solution, and that will remain at the centre of most transactional business needs. However, there are two areas that you feel are worthy of further investigation:

1. One task that has been problematic in the past has been the statistical analysis of the sales data. In particular, you need to increase the speed at which the analysts get data back on trends and averages. You decide to investigate column-based approach as you have heard that this can dramatically increase query performance.
2. You capture communications from customers from a variety of sources. As the BookCo chain is international, the different sources may well be generated anywhere in the world. You need to investigate if it would be useful to allow this data to be stored using a document-centric data store, rather than an RDBMS.

6.19   The Column-Based Approach

There are a number of column-based solutions available. To get a feel for the approach, you have decided to give Cassandra a try. It is an open source solution, so there are no costs for this experiment.

6.20   Cassandra Tutorial

6.20.1   Installation and Configuration

The tutorial demonstrates the use of Cassandra on Ubuntu Linux. Cassandra will also run on other Linux servers and can be installed on Windows.

This guide was created using Ubuntu Linux 11.10. As at April 2012, the current stable release is 1.0.9. It is expected that basic Unix commands are known in order to install the system. If you are unsure, there are many web-based Linux command guides. If you don't mind being called 'clueless', this is a good starting point: http://www.unixguide.net/linux/linuxshortcuts.shtml

The first step is to download the latest version of Cassandra. (http://cassandra.apache.org/download/). Make sure it is the latest stable version. Once you have the download page in your browser:
- Select to download the latest bin version. As at April 2012, the current version is apache-cassandra-1.0.9-bin.tar.gz
- Save the binary to preferred location, for example, your desktop.
- Open a Linux terminal window and navigate to the folder where the file was saved.
- Decompress the .gz file using the following process.

```
#Assuming that the file was saved in folder Desktop
$called Desktop
$tar xzf apache-cassandra-1.0.9-bin.tar.gz
```

#where 1.0.9 is the version should be changed to the version you have downloaded
Cassandra needs you to install the JRE dependency if you don't already have it. Use the following command:

```
$sudo apt-get install openjdk-6-jre
#wait for the download and installation process to finish
```

Moreover, it is required to create some directories for Cassandra to store data and logs. Appropriate permissions should be granted to users. This task is a once-only task. Open a terminal session and perform the following operations. (Replace USERNAME with the OS authentication username.)

```
$sudo mkdir -p /var/log/cassandra
$sudo chown -R USERNAME /var/log/cassandra
$sudo mkdir -p /var/lib/cassandra
$sudo chown -R USERNAME /var/lib/cassandra
```

The next step is to run the server. This has to be done through a terminal session. This step must be repeated each time you reboot your OS.

Navigate again to the folder into which you have extracted Cassandra. Then, navigate to the bin directory.

To start the server, use the 'cassandra' command.

```
$cd apache-cassandra-0.8.4
$cd bin
$./cassandra
```

Note: It is important not to close this terminal.

Now that the server is running, the client interface should be started. Open a new terminal session and execute the command below, after navigating to the bin folder as before:

```
$cd apache-cassandra-0.8.4
$cd bin
$./cassandra-cli
Welcome to the Cassandra CLI.
Type 'help;' or '?' for help.
Type 'quit;' or 'exit;' to quit.
[default@unknown]
```

Once the client interface is open, we need to connect to the local server you started earlier by using the connect/command. By default, the port is 9160, and notice that commands should end with a semicolon ';'. By default, the system will connect the 'test' cluster/keyspace.

```
[default@unknown] connect localhost/9160 ;
Connected to: "Test Cluster" on localhost/9160
```

To recap, we have downloaded and installed Cassandra. We then started the Cassandra server in a terminal session. In a separate session, we then started the client. Finally, we used the client to connect to our default 'test cluster' using port 9160.

Note: There are alternative graphical user interface (GUI) tools you could use with Cassandra instead of the Cassandra CLI. However, the CLI makes the technical underpinning far more visible and therefore gives the new user a better insight into how Cassandra works.

6.20.2 Data Model and Types

Before we get our hands dirty with our new toy, we need to understand some of Cassandra's basic concepts.

A *keyspace* in Cassandra can be seen as the equivalent to a database schema in a relational DBMS, and it is a group of related column families. With an attribute called placement_strategy, you can determine how you will distribute replicas around the nodes you will be using.

A *column family* is very broadly equivalent to a table in an RDBMS. Each such family is stored in a separate file. The file itself is sorted into key order. It is therefore important, in terms of reducing disk reads and therefore improving performance, that columns which are regularly accessed together should be kept together, within the same column family, and that data types within a family should ideally be the same.

A *column* is the smallest unit of storage in Cassandra. A standard column is composed of the tuple of a unique name (key), value and a timestamp. The key identifies a row in a column family. The timestamp corresponds to the last update time.

A *supercolumn* is a list of columns used to store multiple items of a similar type. Supercolumns do not have timestamps.

Put another way, the building blocks we will be reviewing in Cassandra are:

- A column, which is a key–value pair.
- A supercolumn which is a collection of associated columns that are sorted.
- A column family, which is a container for columns which are sorted. These columns can be referenced through a row id.

Examples may help clarify the difference between standard and supercolumns. This is an example of a standard column in use:

```
{
"example" :
{
column : "emailaddress"
value : "example@example.com"
timestamp: 123456
}
}
And here is an example of a Super-Column in use:
{
name: "homeaddress"
value: {
  street : {name: "street" , value : "Oxford", time-stamp
: 12345},
   postcode: {name: "postcode", value: "SO234", time-
stamp : 123456}
  }
}
```

Note how there are a variety of values in the supercolumn but one, and only one, value in the column.

Now we have Cassandra installed, we should get used to the basic commands. One of the first useful commands to learn is the show command. If we get into the situation where we forget which cluster we are working on, we can ask Cassandra by using the 'show cluster name;' command.

And if we need to know which keyspaces there are, we again use show:

```
[default@unknown] show cluster name;
Test Cluster
[default@unknown]show keyspaces;
Keyspace: system:
....other names would appear here
```

6.20.3   Working with Keyspaces

The output of the last command displays various information about the 'system' keyspace. This is used mainly for system tasks and is not dissimilar to the system tablespace in Oracle, for example. Once a new keyspace is created, it would also be displayed as an output of the command.

Initially, a new keyspace (analogous to a relational database) has to be created using the ' create keyspace KeyspaceName [with att1="value1"] [and att2="value2"] ' where KeyspaceName corresponds to the name you want to give to the keyspace. Two attributes can be added to keyspace:

1. The replication
2. Replica placement strategy

Until we get a feel for Cassandra, however, these are not required as we are using Cassandra locally instead of on many machines. But don't lose sight of the fact that one of the main reasons that Cassandra was invented was to be able to cope with large volumes of data in a distributed, replicated environment.

After creation, to connect to a keyspace, we use the use Keyspacename where the Keyspacename is the name given to the created keyspace.

For the BookCo sales records, we are going to create a keyspace with the name sales. When doing this, we will see that Cassandra will respond with a unique UUID number:

```
[default@unknown] create keyspace sales;
89478600-c772-11e0-0000-242d50cf1fbf #UUID
Waiting for schema agreement…
… schemas agree across the cluster
[default@unknown] use sales;
Authenticated to keyspace: sales
Working with Column Families
```

To create a column family (analogous to a relational table), we should provide a name and a comparator. The comparator is required by Cassandra because it needs to know the order in which to store data, and the comparator is responsible for this sorting of the columns within the column family. Once any new column is added, it is compared with others and is sorted accordingly—during the insert. This is important as it is not possible to sort results during a query. One way of dealing with the lightweight query facility is to have multiple column families, one for each expected query return type.

Columns in Cassandra are sorted based on their name. So the comparator can be used to tell Cassandra how to order columns inside their row and, in extent, how the columns will be sorted when they are returned. The comparator can also be used in subcolumns (of supercolumns). These are the comparators that are available out of box:

Type	Explanation
BytesType	It is the default type that sorts based on bytes. If it is not required for validation process, then choose instead of UTF8Type
AsciiType	Sorting by using the character encoding
UTF8Type	Sorting based on a string that uses UTF-8 as character encoder. It gives the advantage to allow data validation
LongType	Sorting based on 64-bit long numbers
TimeUUIDType	Sorting based on a 16-byte timestamp

Advanced users can, if this list doesn't cover an application's needs, write their own comparators using Java. The comparator is a required element for a valid column family. However, the other column metadata is optional:

- *Data validation.* Remember, validation is a costly overhead, but we may need, for some applications, to test the data being entered. The types are the same as in the table above but are used for validation purposes instead of sorting. Predefinition is not required, but if you are aware of the columns that need validation, such rules should be implemented at family creation time. The 'schema' is flexible so new columns can be added later, if required.
- *Index keys.* This is another optional attribute. With it, you can create indexing keys which allow search queries against the indexed values. If no indexes exist, querying based on certain values will not be possible. An example of creating a primary index key will be demonstrated later in these notes. More than one column can be indexed in a column family, and these are called secondary indexes. Secondary indexes are recommended for columns with low cardinality because rewriting the indexes is a very costly overhead, and so, where possible, we avoid indexing volatile data.

The command for creating a column family is

```
create column family ColumnFamilyName with comparator =
'Type' and column_metadata = [ {column_name: Col-
umnName, validation_class: 'Type', index_type: KEYS },
...];
```

Note: When referring to types, look at the types table and add them without the single quotes. As mentioned before, the column_metadata is optional.

For the BookCo sales, we should create a 'sale' standard column family by using the UTF8Type and then again this type for validation class, without indexing any key at the moment.

```
[default@sales] create column family sale with compara-
tor = UTF8Type
... AND column_metadata =
... [ {column_name: sale_id, validation_class: UTF8Type},
... {column_name: book_id, validation_class: UTF8Type},
... {column_name: seller, validation_class: UTF8Type},
... {column_name: buyer, validation_class: UTF8Type},
... {column_name: price, validation_class: UTF8Type},
...    {column_name:  payment_method,  validation_class:
UTF8Type},
... {column_name: date , validation_class:UTF8Type}];
8760e289-c84f-11e0-9aeb-e700f669bcfc
Waiting for schema agreement...
... schemas agree across the cluster
```

Now we are going to create another column family about novelratings and recommendations.

To do so, we should create a new `SuperColumn` column family using the `create column family ColumnFamilyName with comparator = 'Type' AND column_type='Super' AND subcomparator= 'Type' [AND column_metadata = [{ column_name : Col-umnName , validation_class: 'Type' , index_type: KEYS }, … ];` command. Everything after the subcomparator attribute could have been omitted.

You should notice the 'column_type=Super' attribute and 'subcomparator= Type' which refers to the comparator used for the subcolumns of this type of column family.

```
[default@sales] create column family Novelrating with
comparator = 'UTF8Type'
… AND column_type='Super' AND subcomparator= 'UTF8Type'
AND column_metadata =
… [{column_name : author , validation_class : UTF8Type
},
… {column_name : comment , validation_class : UTF8Type
},
… {column_name : rate , validation_class : UTF8Type }];
c12796d9-c8f3-11e0-af3e-e700f669bcfc
Waiting for schema agreement...
… schemas agree across the cluster
```

A very important operation with column families is Update. We may need to update a column family with the specified attribute(s) and value(s) or even add index keys (see previous paragraphs).

To do so, we use the `update column family ColumnFamilyName with comparator = 'Type' AND column_metadata = [{ column_name : ColumnName , validation_class: 'Type'}, index_type : KEYS …];` command. This is similar to the Create command but with the changed attributes and values.

If, for example, we want to create an index key on the `sale_id`. Follow the example on how to use the update command:

```
[default@sales] update column family sale with com-
parator =update column family sale with comparator =
'UTF8Type' and default_validation_class=UTF8Type and
key_validation_class=UTF8Type and column_metadata=
[ {column_name: sale_id, validation_class: UTF8Type,
index_type: KEYS},
{column_name: book_id, validation_class: UTF8Type},
{column_name: seller, validation_class: UTF8Type},
{column_name: buyer, validation_class: UTF8Type},
{column_name: price, validation_class: UTF8Type},
{column_name:    payment_method,    validation_class:
UTF8Type},
```

```
{column_name: date , validation_class:UTF8Type}];
58f6aa1b-c9a2-11e0-af3e-e700f669bcfc
Waiting for schema agreement...
... schemas agree across the cluster
```

6.20.4   Working with Columns

6.20.4.1   Inserting and Updating Values

As we pointed out above, the column is the base storage unit in Cassandra. We will find ourselves inserting to, deleting from, updating and creating columns extensively as we build our applications.

To add or update data in a column, use the `ColumnFamilyName['key']` `['ColumnName'] = 'value';` command. (cf = column family name)

We mentioned that a column also has a timestamp associated with it. This is added or updated automatically by Cassandra.

The key refers to the row key. An example of this command being used is below. We are going to create a new entry for `sale1`:

```
[default@sales] set sale['sale1']['sale_id'] = '1';
Value inserted.
[default@sales] set sale['sale1']['book_id'] = '123';
Value inserted.
[default@sales] set sale['sale1']['seller'] = 'mike';
Value inserted.
[default@sales] set sale['sale1']['buyer'] = 'john';
Value inserted.
[default@sales] set sale['sale1']['price'] = '15';
Value inserted.
[default@sales]  set  sale['sale1']['payment_method']  =
'PayPal';
Value inserted.
[default@sales]      set      sale['sale1']['date']      =
'10Aug2011';
```

The column family, as it stands at the moment, is shown in below.

Now we will populate the sale column family with more data. You can use these examples, but do try to add more of your own:

```
#Creating a new row for sale 2
set sale['sale2']['sale_id'] = '2';
set sale['sale2']['book_id'] = '143';
set sale['sale2']['seller'] = 'peter';
set sale['sale2']['buyer'] = 'john';
set sale['sale2']['price'] = '25';
set sale['sale2']['payment_method'] = 'PayPal';
set sale['sale2']['date'] = '12Aug2011';
```

```
#Creating a new row for sale 3
set sale['sale3']['sale_id'] = '3';
set sale['sale3']['book_id'] = '144';
set sale['sale3']['seller'] = 'paul';
set sale['sale3']['buyer'] = 'peter';
set sale['sale3']['price'] = '43';
set sale['sale3']['payment_method'] = 'Visa';
set sale['sale3']['date'] = '13Aug2011';
#Creating a new row for sale 4
set sale['sale4']['sale_id'] = '4';
set sale['sale4']['book_id'] = '127';
set sale['sale4']['seller'] = 'josh';
set sale['sale4']['buyer'] = 'alex';
set sale['sale4']['price'] = '45';
set sale['sale4']['payment_method'] = 'Visa';
set sale['sale4']['date'] = '12Aug2011';
```

To add data in a supercolumn and its subcolumns, use the set ColumnFamily Name['key']['superColumnName']['col'] = 'value'; The key refers to the row key. The example here adds for a novel called 'Alpha Mike'.

```
[default@sales] set Novelrating['Alpha Mike']['entry1']
['author'] = 'Peter Pond';
Value inserted.
[default@sales] set Novelrating ['Alpha Mike']['entry1']
['comment'] = 'Alpha Mike is a very good novel';
Value inserted.
[default@sales] set Novelrating ['Alpha Mike']['entry1']
['rate'] = '5/5';
[default@sales] set Novelrating ['Alpha Mike']['entry2']
['author'] = 'Jason Stream';
Value inserted.
[default@sales] set Novelrating ['Alpha Mike']['entry2']
['comment'] = 'Good storyline';
Value inserted.
[default@sales] set Novelrating ['Alpha Mike']['entry2']
['rate'] = '4/5';
Value inserted.
```

Now we will populate the novelrating column family with more data. You can use these examples, but do try to add more of your own:

```
#Some more recommendations for Mike.
set  Novelrating['Alpha  Mike']['entry3']['author']  =
'Phil Nastis';
set  Novelrating['Alpha  Mike']['entry3']['comment']  =
'Excellent thriller';
```

```
set    Novelrating['Alpha    Mike']['entry3']['rate']    =
'5/5';
#Creating a new row for a Novel called Catch 22 and add-
ing 2 entries for recommendations
set    Novelrating['Catch    22']['entry1']['author']    =
'Heller';
set    Novelrating['Catch    22']['entry1']['comment']    =
'Brilliant book';
set Novelrating['Catch 22']['entry1']['rate'] = '5/5';
set    Novelrating['Catch    22']['entry2']['author']    =
'Heller';
set    Novelrating['Catch    22']['entry2']['comment']    =
'Dated,but still good';
set Novelrating['Catch 22']['entry2']['rate'] = '4/5';
1.
```

6.20.4.2   Reading Data from Column Values

There are different ways to retrieve data from an existing keyspace. Initially, we can use the count `ColumnFamilyName['key'];` command to count the number of columns stored in the key.

To do the same thing for subcolumns of the supercolumn, use the `count ColumnFamilyName['key']['superColumnName'];`.

Note: The `sale1` is the row key and not the column. In the second command, `Alpha Mike` is the key and the supercolumn is `entry1`.

```
[default@sales] count sale['sale1'];
7 columns
[default@sales] count Novelrating['mike']['entry1'];
3 columns
#Try to retrieve a key that does not exist
[default@sales] count sale['sale10'];
0 columns
```

To retrieve all the information about `sale1`, use the get `ColumnFamilyName['key'];` command. Notice that the records have an added 'timestamp' value that is automatically added or updated when the record is added or updated:

```
[default@sales] get sale['sale1'];
 => (column=book_id, value=123,
time-stamp=1313532897200000)
 => (column=buyer, value=john,
time-stamp=1313532920840000)
 => (column=date, value=10Aug2011,
 time-stamp=1313532967504000)
 => (column=payment_method, value=PayPal,
time-stamp=1313532956880000)
```

```
 => (column=price, value=15,
time-stamp=1313532931944000)
 => (column=sale_id, value=1,
time-stamp=1313532878948000)
 => (column=seller, value=mike,
time-stamp=1313532909544000)
 Returned 7 results.
 [default@sales]
```

Now we could try to retrieve the information from the supercolumns we have created previously. To retrieve all the information, the command is the same as above. Try the command for yourself to see the full output:

```
[default@sales] get Novelrating['Alpha Mike'];
 => (super_column=entry1,
 (column=author, value=Peter Pond,
time-stamp=1313601352679000)
 (column=comment, value=Alpha Mike is a very good Novel,
timestamp=1313601369614000)
 (column=rate, value=5/5, timestamp=1313601388350000))
 => …. And so on …..
```

We can also retrieve only the value of a column by using the `get ColumnFamilyName ['key'] ['columnName']` command.

To retrieve a value from a subcolumn of a supercolumn, we use the `get ColumnFamilyName ['key'] ['superColumnName'] ['column-Name']` command. Examples are

```
[default@sales] get sale['sale1']['book_id'];
 => (column=book_id, value=123,
time-stamp=1313532897200000)
[default@sales] get Novelrating['Alpha Mike']['entry1']
['rate'];
 => (column=rate, value=5/5,
time-stamp=1313601388350000)
```

We can put conditions on our queries, just like a where in an SQL command. However, in order to use this command properly, we need to add indexes to support specific queries. For example, to retrieve data based on the index created for the `sale_id`, we would use the get CF where `column= 'value'` [and `column= 'value'` and …] command.

To help understand why indexing key is important, let us initially retrieve data based on `book_id` which was not previously indexed.

```
[default@sales] get sale where book_id = '143';
```

No indexed columns present in index clause with operator EQ.

The system responds that the book_id column is not indexed. Now try with the sale_id column which was indexed previously during the update command demonstration:

```
[default@sales] get sale where sale_id = '1';
-------------------
RowKey: sale1
=>      (column=book_id,      value=123,      time-stamp=
1313532897200000)
..........
1 Row Returned.
```

To allow the retrieval of books information using the book_id, we can update the column family to add a secondary index as shown below. We will also add an index on the price column:

```
[default@sales] update column family sale with compa-
rator = 'UTF8Type' and column_metadata=
… [ {column_name: sale_id, validation_class: UTF8Type,
index_type: KEYS},
… {column_name: book_id, validation_class: UTF8Type,
index_type: KEYS},
… {column_name: seller, validation_class: UTF8Type},
… {column_name: buyer, validation_class: UTF8Type},
… {column_name: price, validation_class: UTF8Type, index_
type: KEYS},
…     {column_name:  payment_method,  validation_class:
UTF8Type},
… {column_name: date , validation_class:UTF8Type}];
b6cee09c-c9a6-11e0-af3e-e700f669bcfc
Waiting for schema agreement…
… schemas agree across the cluster
```

Now we can try to retrieve information based on the book_id again. Then, we will use price and then combine both. Just as with SQL, with the price column, we can use comparison operators such as greater or smaller than:

```
[default@sales] get sale where book_id='143';
-------------------
RowKey: sale2
=>      (column=book_id,      value=143,      time-stamp=
1313673572425000)
..........
1 Row Returned.
[default@sales] get sale where price = 15;
-------------------
RowKey: sale1
```

```
=>        (column=book_id,      value=123,      time-stamp=
1313532897200000)
..........
1 Row Returned.
[default@sales] get sale where book_id='143' and price >
25;
0 Row Returned.
[default@sales] get sale where book_id='143' and price <
35;
-------------------
RowKey: sale2
=>        (column=book_id,      value=143,      time-stamp=
1313673572425000)
..........
1 Row Returned.
```

Another way to retrieve all the rows in a column family is the list ColumnFamilyName; command:

```
[default@sales] list Novelrating;
```

Before you try this, imagine what the output might be like to make sure you understand the data being stored. Once you run it, did you get the data back you expected?

List can also be used with the limit condition to control the number of records that will be retrieved. The returned results indicate that random records are returned instead of ordered.

```
[default@sales] list sale LIMIT 2;
-------------------
RowKey: sale3
=>        (column=book_id,      value=144,      time-stamp=
1313673579083000)
...............
-------------------
RowKey: sale2
=>        (column=book_id,      value=143,      time-stamp=
1313673572425000)
...............
2 Rows Returned.
```

6.20.4.3   Deleting Rows and Columns

In keeping our data current, we may need to delete a column from a row. For example, to delete the 'date' column from 'sale1', we would use the del ColumnFamilyName['key']['col']; command.

To delete the entire row of 'sale1' we would use the del ColumnFamilyName['key']; command.

To delete a supercolumn, we would use the del ColumnFamilyName['key'] ['super']; command.

To delete a subcolumn, we would use the del ColumnFamilyName['key'] ['super']['col']; command.

Examples of all these are given below:

```
[default@sales] del sale['sale1']['date'];
column removed.
[default@sales] get sale['sale1']['date'];
Value was not found
[default@sales] del sale['sale1'];
row removed.
[default@sales] get sale['sale1'];
Return 0 results.
[default@sales]    del    Novelrating['mike']['entry1']
['rate'];
column removed.
[default@sales] del Novelrating['mike']['entry1'];
column removed.
[default@sales] get Novelrating['mike']['entry1'];
Returned 0 results.
```

6.20.4.4   Drop Column Families and Keyspace

To drop a column family, we use the drop column family; command.

To drop a Cassandra keyspace, we use drop keyspace keyspacename; command.

```
[default@sales] drop column family sale;
ade3bc44-236f-11e0-8410-56547f39a44b
#To drop the keyspace follow the example
[default@sales] drop keyspace sales;
4eb7c292-c841-11e0-9aeb-e700f669bcfc
Waiting for schema agreement...
... schemas agree across the cluster
```

6.20.5   Shutdown

At the end of our busy day, we may need to bring down the Cassandra client. To do this, we simply use the quit; or exit; command from the client terminal session.

If we also want to shutdown the Cassandra server, we use the Ctrl + C keys.

6.20.6   Using a Command-Line Script

You can build scripts which create column families and insert data. This is very useful in the prototyping phase when we typically need to keep recreating elements. In the example below, we are going to create a new family called tsale in the sales keyspace; don't forget to have your authentication as the first line.

Open a new editor page and add this into it:

```
use sales ;
create column family tsale with comparator = 'UTF8Type'
and default_validation_class=UTF8Type and key_valida-
tion_class=UTF8Type and column_metadata=
[ {column_name: sale_id, validation_class: UTF8Type,
index_type: KEYS},
{column_name: book_id, validation_class: UTF8Type},
{column_name: Novel, validation_class: UTF8Type},
{column_name: buyer, validation_class: UTF8Type},
{column_name: price, validation_class: UTF8Type},
{column_name: payment_method, validation_class: UTF8Type},
{column_name: date , validation_class:UTF8Type}];
set tsale['sale1']['sale_id'] = '1';
set tsale['sale1']['book_id'] = '123';
set tsale['sale1']['Novel'] = 'mike';
set tsale['sale1']['buyer'] = 'john';
set tsale['sale1']['price'] = '15';
set tsale['sale1']['payment_method'] = 'PayPal';
set tsale['sale1']['date'] = '10Aug2011';
```

Now save this as cass.txt into your Cassandra\bin directory directory.

Open a new terminal session and CD to the Cassandra\bin directory. Do not run cassandra-cli at this stage. Instead, type

```
./cassandra-cli -host localhost -port 9160 -f cass.txt
```

This will, if it can, run the content of the script file called cass.txt that you have just created.

6.20.7 Useful Extra Resources

We have only just got started with Cassandra with these notes. We hope that there is enough here to give you an understanding of the key principles and to help identify how Cassandra is different to an RDBMS.

If you wish to find out more, some useful resources include:

- This book's website (link). There are a bigger dataset and some more detailed queries to give you practice in using the product.
- Hewitt, E. (2010) Cassandra: The Definitive Guide, published by O'Reilly Media.
- Apache Cassandra (2011) Official Site. Last accessed on 1 Sept 2011 at http://cassandra.apache.org
- Apache Wiki (2011) Wiki Frontpage. Last accessed on 1 Sept 2011 at http://wiki.apache.org/cassandra/

- DataStax (2011) Official Portal. Last accessed on 1 Sept 2011 at http://www. datastax.com/

6.20.8   The Document-Based Approach

There are a number of document-based solutions available. To get a feel for the approach, you have decided to give MongoDb a try. It is an open source solution, so there are no costs for this experiment.

6.21   MongoDB Tutorial

6.21.1   Installation and Configuration

This guide was made and tested with Ubuntu Linux 11.10. Several Linux systems include package managers that can help to install MongoDB. As at the time of writing, packages are available for Ubuntu, Debian, CentOS, Fedora and Red Hat. It is expected that basic Unix commands are known. If you are unsure, there are many web-based Linux command guides. If you don't mind being called 'clueless', this is a good starting point: http://www.unixguide.net/linux/linuxshortcuts.shtml

Follow the following steps:

1. Go to MongoDB downloads page (http://www.mongodb.org/downloads) and select the Linux 32-bit or Linux 64-bit product version.
2. Save the binary to preferred location.
3. Open a terminal window and navigate to the folder where the file was saved.
4. Decompress the .tgz file using the following process:

```
#Assuming that the file was saved in folder Desktop
$called Desktop
$tar zxf mongodb-linux-i686-2.0.4.tgz
#where 2.0.4 is the current version
$cd mongodb-linux-i686-2.0.4
```

Important tip: By default, MongoDB stores data in data/db directory. However, this has to be created manually but only once. To do so, in a terminal type:

```
$sudo mkdir -p /data/db/
#We have to grant access for the directory to our
username
# Where USERNAME is the Operating System Username
$sudo chown username /data/db
```

The next step is to run the server. This has to be done through a terminal window. This step is essential each time you reboot your OS:

```
#In a terminal, navigate to the previously extracted
mongodb folder. For this example it is on the Desktop
$cd Desktop
$cd mongodb-linux-i686-2.0.4
#Remember that the version number may vary
#Navigate to BIN directory and start the mongod server
$cd bin
$./mongod
```

You should see a series of feedback lines. If you receive any errors indicating that the binary cannot be executed properly, you probably downloaded a 64-bit version which is not supported by your OS, or vice versa. Repeat the process by downloading the correct version.

Do not close the current terminal window. Finally, in a new terminal window, start the MongoDB shell:

```
#Navigate again in the BIN directory and start the
shell
$cd Desktop/mongodb-linux-i686-2.0.4/bin
$./mongo
```

By default, MongoDB each time connects to the 'test' database. This will be explained in the next section.

6.21.2 Documents, Data Types and Basic Commands

To recap, MongoDB as a document-oriented storage system replaces tables, rows and columns with documents. Each document includes one or more key–value pairs. Each document is part of a collection, and in a database, more than one collection can exist. A collection can be seen as similar to a table in an RDBMS.

Below is an example of the key–value pairs that constitute the documents. A document can have any structure as we can see in the example below.

```
{"key" : "value"}
{"name" : "George"}
#The previous example shows a single key "name" with the
value of "George". A document may include multiple key/
value pairs as below
{"name" : "George", "surname": "James"}
{"name" : "John", "surname": "King","email": "example@
example.com"}
#Example documents of a collection with different fields
```

6.21.3   Data Types

Many data types can be part of a document in a MongoDB database, and some of them are listed below:

Data type	Explanation and examples
Boolean	`{"x" : true}`. A boolean value can be either true or false
Null	`{"x" : null}`. It can be used to express a null value
Numbers	`{"x" : 3.14} {"x" : 3}`
String	`{"x" : "George"}`. Any string can be used with this type
Date	`{"x" : new Date()}`. Dates stored as milliseconds
Array	`{"x" : ["1","2","3"]}`. Lists of values can be stored as an array
Embedded document	`{"x": {"name" : "George"}}`. Documents can contain embedded documents in them, a document inside another document

6.21.4   Embedding and Referencing

By embedding a document, it is meant that a document is embedded within another document as explained in the table above. Referencing refers to storing the data in a separate collection (say collection A) and referencing it in another collection (say collection B). However, the MongoDB manual suggests that embedding documents inside a document is preferred of the two approaches. The usage of references requires extra queries to retrieve data from other collections, slowing the query.

Any of these data types can be used in a document. As there is no schema in a document, data types do not have to be predefined. Examples will be shown later.

Having started the database server and the shell, we can now start using the database. But first, here are some general navigational tips to start with:

1. Commands related to collections have the syntax of `db.COLLECTION_NAME.COMMAND()`. The db variable is the currently used database.
2. To switch between databases, we use the command `use Name_of_Database`.
3. To see which database is currently in use, execute the `db` command.
4. The database is automatically created upon the creation of the first document.
5. To identify which collections are in the a database, we can use `db.getCollectionNames()`.
6. To see a list of useful database commands, type 'help' in the shell script.

Review examples of these commands below and then execute them for yourself in your terminal session. First of all, switch to the 'products' database, which will be used for our case study.

Note: In all the examples, commands typed in the shell are indicated by '>'. Responses from the system do not include that sign.

```
cloud@project:~/Desktop/mongodb-linux-i686-2.0.4/bin$
./mongo
MongoDB shell version: 2.0.4
connecting to: test
> db
test
> use products
switched to db products
> db
products
> db.getCollectionNames();
[ ]
```

Note: The last command returns an empty array as at the moment no collection exists in the database.

As with most databases, there are four basic types of operation we will need to complete. They are often described as CRUDing: create, read, update and delete. We will use MongoDB to do each of these tasks.

6.21.4.1 Create

This operation adds a new document to a collection. To enter some new components in the database, we can create a local variable (one for each new document) and then insert it in the collection.

As the shell is using JavaScript objects, we are going to use a variable to represent the document. In this example, we need to create two documents corresponding to two books that the company sells.

To create a variable, use this syntax:

```
book1 = {"isbn" : "123" , "type": "fictional", "price"
: "50", "description" : "A fictional book"} .
```

In the figure below, the shell returns the details of the variable once it is created. For this example, create the two variables as shown below. Then, use the
db.COLLECTION_NAME.insert(variable) command to store it as a document in a collection.

Note: Data can also be inserted directly through the shell without defining the document as a variable. This will be covered later in the more advanced command section. (Note: Depending on your terminal settings, when you paste this in, you can only see the end of the line in the terminal.)

```
# Creating variable for book1
> book1 = {"isbn" : "123" , "type": "fictional", "price"
: "50", "description" : "A fictional book"}
#System response indicating that variable has been
created
{
"isbn" : "123",
```

```
"type" : "fictional",
"price" : "50",
"description" : "A fictional book"
}
# Creating variable for component_two
> book2 = {"isbn" : "124" , "type": "tech", "price" :
"40", "description" : "Book for tech", "pages" : "150"}
#System response indicating that variable has been
created
{
"isbn" : "124",
"type" : "tech",
"price" : "40",
"description" : "Book for tech"
"pages" : "150",
}
# Inserting variables as documents in a collection // The
collection will be automatically created once the first
insert occurs
> db.products.insert(book1);
> db.products.insert(book2);
```

At the moment, we have created two documents in the product collection that was created as a result of the first insert. You may have noticed that the schema-free feature of MongoDB allows us to use different data elements in each document. The first document does not have the 'page' element which exists in the second document, for example.

6.21.4.2   Read

To start with, let's use the count operation to see how many documents are in a collection. The command is db.COLLECTION_NAME.count(). To retrieve the documents themselves, we can use 'db.COLLECTION_NAME.find()'. This command returns all the documents in a collection. db.COLLECTION_NAME.findOne() returns only one document from a collection.

We can also filter our results by specifying selectors as parameters to find. The parameter can be expressed in the form of {x : x} which means 'where x == x'. This will be shown in more depth later in this tutorial.

```
#Counting the number of documents in a collection
> db.products.count();
2
#Retrieving all the documents in a collection
> db.products.find();
{ "_id" : ObjectId("4e2c2a88ae1a6bc450311480"), "isbn" :
"123" , "type": "fictional", "price" : "50", "description" :
"A fictional book" }
```

```
{ "_id" : ObjectId("4e2c2a99ae1a6bc450311481"), "isbn" :
"124" , "type": "tech", "price" : "40", "description" :
"Book for tech", "pages" : "150" }
#Retrieving    the    first    document    in    a    collection.
Alternativelly , we can use parameters to specify the
result and remove "We will see it later".
> db.products.findOne();
{
"_id" : ObjectId("4e2c2a88ae1a6bc450311480"),
"isbn" : "123",
"type" : "fictional",
"price" : "50",
"description" : "A fictional book"
}
#Retrieving the document in a collection with isbn equals 123
> db.products.find({"isbn" : "123"});
{ "_id" : ObjectId("4e2c2a88ae1a6bc450311480"), "isbn" :
"123" , "type": "fictional", "price" : "50", "description" :
"A fictional book" }
```

As you can see, the document has an added field _id. This is automatically generated by the system once a document is inserted in the database to ensure that each
document has a unique identity similar to a primary key in relational databases. If
we wish, we can define that object id manually, but for the moment, we will make
do with the system-generated version.

6.21.4.3 Update

Of course we may need to update the product details in our database at some time.
For example, the company buyer may wish to add stock quantity information for a
book. Using the update operation, we need to pass two parameters:

(i)   The document to update
(ii) The changes to be made

The command is db.COLLECTION_NAME.update({documentToChange},
newVariable)

Initially, we have to use an object as before. We can use the same one (book1) or
a new one which will include the same information.

Review the example below and execute the same commands for yourself. Then,
try some for changes of your own.

```
#Here we add a new element in the document with the key
'quantity' and value '3'.
> book1.quantity=3
3
#Now we have to update the document which has 'serial'
123 with the updated object
```

```
# db.COLLECTION_NAME.update({parameter1},parameter2)
> db.products.update({"isbn":"123"},book1)
#Use the find command to query the changed document. In
this example we are using a selector to filter our results.
Further explanation will be given later.
> db.products.find({isbn:"123"});                            •
{
"_id" : ObjectId("4e2c2a88ae1a6bc450311480"),
"isbn" : "123",
"type" : "fictional",
"price" : "50",
"description" : "A finctional book"
"quantity" : 3
}
# the document has been successfully updated
```

6.21.4.4 Delete

We may need to remove documents from a collection. For this, we use db. COLLECTION_NAME.remove(). Parameters may be passed to specify the document to be deleted or (CAUTION!) without parameters to remove all the documents within a collection. We can also use the drop operation to remove a collection.

Follow the sequence of the commands:

```
#Removing the document with isbn 123
> db.products.remove({isbn:"123"});
#Query the collection to define whether the document has
been removed
> db.products.findOne({isbn:"123"});
null
#As there is no entry for the document with isbn '123',
the shell returns a null value.
#Now check the collections that are currently in the
database and then drop the "products".
> db.getCollectionNames();
[ "products", "system.indexes" ]
> db.products.drop();
#System confirmation of the action
true
> db.getCollectionNames();
[ "system.indexes" ]
```

6.21.5 Advanced Commands and Queries

This section contains examples of more advanced usage of the MongoDB command set. From the case study, we will try to implement these requirements:

Each product has its own ISBN, description, author and other characteristics as well as a number of available sellers for it. Moreover, each book may be associated to a number of tags for easier searching. User reviews and comments are available. Finally, users should be able to find a book based on its characteristics, prices and other filtering options.

6.21.6 More CRUDing

We have dropped the collection, so a new one has to be created. Moreover, we need to create at least 20 new documents to represent books. This tutorial gives 20 examples that can be used, but it is recommended that you create your own documents in order to familiarise yourself with the concept.

At this stage, data will be inserted directly in the shell without defining the document as an object. You may still create objects and insert them in the 'products' collection if you wish.

An example of how the different data types are used is shown below. Then, ten documents are listed after the code box.

```
{
"isbn":123,
"title":"Book1",
"author":"Mike",
"coathor":"Jessy",
"description":"A fictional book",
"pages" : 150,
"publicationdate" : new Date('10-06-2010'), #Date
"publisher" : { "name": "Willeyy", "location": "UK" },
#Embedded Document
"tag-category": ["fictional","science"], #Array
"sellers" : [ #Array of Documents
{"sellername": "bookstore" , "price" : 50},
{"sellername": "seller4523" ,"price" : 60} ],
"comments": [
{"email": "test@example.com", "comment" : " test test"}
]
}
#Now Insert it in the collection following the
in-structions below. The insert command is in red:
db.product.insert({"isbn" : 123 , "title": "Book 1",
"author" : "Mike","coathor" : "Jessy", "description" :
"A fictional book","pages" : 150, "publicationdate" : new
```

Date('10-06-2010'), "publisher" : { "name": "Springer",
"location":"UK"},"tag-category": ["fiction-al","science"],
"sellers" : [{"sellername": "bookstore" , "price" :
50},{"sellername": "seller4523", "price" : 60}],
"comments": [{"email": "test@example.com", "com-ment" :
"test test"}]});

6.21.7   Sample Data Set

Insert these data sets in your MongoDB collection. You should then create at least
another ten similar documents for yourself. We are using the book ISBN as the primary key.

Book 1 = db.product.insert({"isbn" : 123 , "title":
"Book 1", "author" : "Mike","coathor" : "Jessy",
"description" : "A fictional book","pages" : 150,
"publicationdate" : new Date('10-06-2010'), "publisher"
: { "name": "Willeyy", "location": "UK"},"tag-category":
["fictional","science"], "sellers" : [{"sellername":
"bookstore" , "price" : 50},{"sellername": "seller4523"
,"price" : 60}], "comments": [{"email": "test@example.
com", "comment" : " test test"}]});
Book 2 = db.product.insert({"isbn" : 124 , "title":
"Book 2", "author" : "George", "description" : "Comedy
book about","pages" : 120, "publicationdate" : new
Date('12-06-2010'), "publisher" : { "name": "Wil",
"location": "USA"},"tag-category": ["comedy","family"],
"sellers" : [{"sellername": "bookstore" , "price" : 50}],
"comments": [{"email": "test1@example.com", "comment" :
"test test"}]});
Book 3 = db.product.insert({"isbn" : 125 , "title":
"Book 3", "author" : ["Tony","James"], "description" :
"geographic","pages" : 80, "publicationdate" : new
Date('14-07-2010'), "publisher" : { "name": "Wil",
"location": "USA"},"tag-category": ["geographic"],
"sellers" : [{"sellername": "John" , "price" : 45},
{"sellername": "Joe" , "price" : 55}], "comments":
[{"email": "test1@example.com", "comment" : " test
test"},{"email": "bookreviewer@example.com", "comment"
: "very good book"}]});
Book 4 = db.product.insert({"isbn" : 128 , "title":
"Book 4", "author" : ["Mike","Jack"], "description" : "A
physics book","pages" : 150, "publicationdate" : new
Date('10-06-2010'), "publisher" : { "name": "Mike",
"location": "CHINA"},"tag-category": ["physics",

```
"science"], "sellers" : [{"sellername": "Mikee" , "price"
: 30},{"sellername": "jackk", "price" : 10}]});
   Book 5 = db.product.insert({"isbn" : 133 , "title":
"Book 5", "author" : "Bob","description" : "chemistry",
"pages" : 100, "publicationdate" : new Date('2006-05-
01'), "publisher" : { "name": "Jason", "location":
"India"},"tag-category":  ["chemistry"], "sellers" :
[{"sellername": "take" , "price" : 80}]});
   Book 6 = db.product.insert({"isbn" : 137 , "title":
"Book 6", "author" : ["Chuck","Paul"],"description" :
"Mathematics  Computer  Science",  "pages"  :  430,
"publicationdate" : new Date('3-04-2001'), "publisher" :
{ "name": "Willey", "location": "UK"},"tag-category":
["mathematics","computers","science"],    "sellers"    :
[{"sellername": "pricess" , "price" : 20}], "comments":
[ {"email": "test1@example.com", "comment" : "not good"},
{"email": "test2@example.com", "comment" : "this book is
great"}]});
   Book 7 = db.product.insert({"isbn" : 136, "title": "Book
7", "author" : "George", "description" : "Crime" ,"pages"
:  120,  "publicationdate"  :  new  Date('20-05-2000'),
"publisher" : { "name": "Willey", "location": "UK"},
"tag-category": ["crime","action"], "sellers" : [{"sellername":
"bookstore3" , "price" : 40},{"sellername": "book1231" ,
"price" : 50}], "comments": [ {"email": "test1@example.
com", "comment" : "good book"}]});
   Book 8 = db.product.insert({"isbn" : 138, "title":
"Book 8", "author" : ["Tony","Jack"], "description" :
"Drama","pages" : 80, "publicationdate" : new Date
('24-07-2010'), "publisher" : { "name": "John", "location":
"Canada"},"tag-category": ["drama","thriller"], "sellers"
: [{"sellername": "John" , "price" : 55},{"sellername":
"Joesw" , "price" : 65}], "comments": [ {"email":
"tasdfas1@example.com", "comment" : " test is good"},
{"email": "bookreviewer@example.com", "comment" : "very
good book"}]});
   Book 9 = db.product.insert({"isbn" : 140 , "title":
"Book 9", "author" : ["Mike","George"], "description" :
"Architect","pages" : 150, "publicationdate" : new
Date('10-06-2010'), "publisher" : { "name": "Take",
"location": "CHINA"},"tag-category": ["architecture",
"science"], "sellers" : [{"sellername": "Mike" , "price"
: 30},{"sellername": "jack" ,"price" : 10}]});
   Book 10 = db.product.insert({"isbn" : 141 , "title":
"Book 10", "author" : "Bob","description" : "English",
"pages" : 100, "publicationdate" : new Date('2006-05-01'),
```

```
"publisher" : { "name": "Mikes", "location": "Sweden"},
"tag-category":  ["English","language"],  "sellers"  :
[{"sellername": "Paul" , "price" : 60}]});
```

6.21.8   More on Deleting Documents

It is important to understand that once data is removed, there is no undo of the action or recovery of the removed documents.

An example we could use from the case study is that the books of the author "Tony" have been suspended and are not available for sale anymore. This example will delete any documents from the product collection where the author is "Tony". If you have inspected the data set above, you should have noticed that two documents include this author: books 3 and 8.

```
>db.produ     ct.count();
10
>db.product.remove({"author": "Tony"});
>db.product.count();
8
```

At the beginning of the process, there were ten documents in the collection. After removing those where the value of the author was "Tony", only eight documents were left in the collection. Despite that the authors were listed inside an array, so the query mechanism worked efficiently.

Over to you: To familiarise yourself with the process, use any other criteria to remove documents. Once finished, reinsert the removed documents.

6.21.9   More on Updating Documents

A document that is stored in the database can be changed anytime. As previously explained, the update method requires two parameters: There are many ways to replace a document, and these are explained in this section:
- The simplest way to update a document was illustrated in the basic commands. That method was useful as it was necessary to make changes to the schema of the document.
- The second way is to use modifiers in cases where only specific parts of the document will be updated. This section presents the most important modifiers.

6.21.10   The Modifiers

6.21.10.1 $set/$unset
These are used to set the value of a key, and if the key does not exist, it is created automatically. Unset is used to delete a given field. Let us see some examples:

```
" db.COLLECTION_NAME.update({"documentToChange"}, { "$set"
{"values..."})"
```

```
"db.COLLECTION_NAME.update({"documentToChange"}, { "$unset"
: {fieldToRemove : 1});"
```

Note: Number 1 in the fieldToRemove is required as a positive action.

When a book is sold, appropriate actions should be taken. Consider the need for an update where one stock item is sold. For this, we can use $set. Moreover, "$set" can be used to change the type of a value, for instance, changing a string to an array. We can use "$unset" to delete the comment field just for demonstration purposes.

```
>db.product.find({"isbn" : 128});
{ "_id" : ObjectId("4e302e849d72be29a7d749e9"), "isbn" :
128, "title" : "Book 4", "author" : [ "Mike", "Jack" ],
"description"  :  "A  physics  book",  "pages"  :  150,
"publicationdate"   :   ISODate("1970-01-01T00:00:00Z"),
"publisher" : { "name" : "Mike", "location" : "CHINA" },
"tag-category" : [ "physics", "science" ], "sellers" :
[ { "sellername" : "Mikee", "price" : 30 }, { "sellername"
: "jackk", "price" : 10 } ] }
#The document with isbn 128 has two sellers at the
beginning
#Once a book is sold the associated entry should be
removed like as illustrated below
>db.product.update({"isbn" : 128}, {"$set" : {"sellers"
: [ { "sellername" : "Mikee", "price" : 30 }]}});
>db.product.find({"isbn" : 128});
{     "isbn"     :     128,     "_id"     :     Objec-tId
("4e302e849d72be29a7d749e9"), "author" : [ "Mike", "Jack"
], "description" : "A physics book", "pages" : 150,
"publicationdate"   :   ISODate("1970-01-01T00:00:00Z"),
"publisher" : { "name" : "Mike", "location" : "CHINA" },
"sellers" : [ { "sellername" : "Mikee", "price" : 30 }
], "tag-category" : [ "physics", "science" ], "title" :
"Book 4" }
#The query returns the updated and correct document
#Now we will remove the comments field from another docu-
ment with $unset command. First retrieve the docu-ment
to see that the comments field exists and then use the
$unset command
> db.product.find({"isbn" : 124})
{"isbn" : 124 , "title": "Book 2", "author" : "George",
"description"  :  "Comedy  book  about","pages"  :  120,
"publicationdate" : new Date('12-06-2010'), "publisher"
: { "name": "Wil", "location": "USA"},"tag-category":
["comedy","family"],    "sellers"    :    [{"sellername":
"bookstore" , "price" : 50}], "comments": [ {"email":
"test1@example.com", "comment" : " test test"}]}
```

```
> db.product.update({"isbn" : 124},{"$unset" : {comments
:1}});
> db.product.find({"isbn" : 124})
{      "isbn"      :      124,      "_id"      :      ObjectId
("4e30801e9889f6cdcf761296"),      "author"   :   "George",
"description"  :  "Comedy  book  about",  "pages"  :  120,
"publicationdate"    :    ISODate("1970-01-01T00:00:00Z"),
"publisher"  :  {  "name"  :  "Wil",  "location"  :  "USA"  },
"sellers" : [ { "sellername" : "bookstore", "price" : 50
} ], "tag-category" : [ "comedy", "family" ], "title" :
"Book 2" }
# The comments field was completely removed from the
document
```

Try to update at least two more documents by modifying (adding/removing) the different sellers or changing the names of author(s) or others.

6.21.10.2 $inc

It is similar to $set, but it is strictly used only for numbers. It increases an existing number by adding to it a given number .It is regularly used for analytics such as the update visitor counter of a website. The case study does not refer to these issues, but a suitable example could be to change the pages of a book:

```
#Using the update query to increment the pages of a
particular book. The pages were 150 (see the previous
query) and now incrementing by 205
>  db.product.update({"isbn"  :  128},{"$inc"  :  {pages
:205}});
> db.product.find({"isbn":128});
{      "isbn"      :      128,      "_id"      :      ObjectId
("4e302e849d72be29a7d749e9"), "author" : [ "Mike", "Jack"
], "description" : "A physics book", "pages" : 355,
"publicationdate"    :    ISODate("1970-01-01T00:00:00Z"),
"publisher" : { "name" : "Mike", "location" : "CHINA" },
"sellers" : [ { "sellername" : "Mikee", "price" : 30 }
], "tag-category" : [ "physics", "science" ], "title" :
"Book 4" }
#The update was successful and the pages currently are
355
```

6.21.11 Querying Documents

The find method is used to search for documents in a collection. It is possible to define more than one key/value pair as a parameter to search. For instance, a customer wants to find all the books that are in the 'science' category and then one of them which was written by George. Moreover, we can specify which keys will be returned. For this example, we will return only the title, ISBN and author(s) of the book(s).

The command we will use is db.COLLECTION_NAME.find({"condition"});
For specifying which keys to return, use the extended command:

" db.COLLECTION_NAME.find({"condition"},{"key" : 1});

Number 1 is a true/false setting used to define that a key should be returned; number 0 is used to define that a key should not be returned.

```
# In this query we want to find science books, and present
only their isbn,author and title
> db.product.find({"tag-category" : "science"},{"isbn" :
1 , "author" : 1 , "title" : 1, "_id": 0});
{ "isbn" : 123, "title" : "Book 1", "author" : "Mike" }
{ "isbn" : 128, "title" : "Book 4", "author" : [ "Mike",
"Jack" ] }
{ "isbn" : 137, "title" : "Book 6", "author" : [ "Chuck",
"Paul" ] }
{ "isbn" : 140, "title" : "Book 9", "author" : [ "Mike",
"George" ] }
# Then we are using another condition for querying the
books in science category and those written by George.
In this example we don't want to return the "_id" key.
> db.product.find({"tag-category" : "science", "author" :
"George"},{"isbn" : 1 , "author" : 1 , "title" : 1 ,
"_id" : 0});
{ "isbn" : 140, "title" : "Book 9", "author" : [ "Mike",
"George" ] }
```

6.21.11.1 Query Criteria and Operators

Query Condition		Explanation
$lt	< ,	less than
$lte	<= ,	less than or equal
$gt	> ,	greater than
$gte	>= ,	greater than or equal
$ne		not equal
$in		in between
$or		one or other condition

Using the query criteria and operators (or combinations) in the table above, examples are presented below to demonstrate their usage. All the examples relate to the case study, whilst customers use the search engine based on different criteria to define their books.

```
#Using $lte and $gte to look for book price greater and
equal to 20 , and less than and equal to 80. Also specifying
what to return.
```

```
>  db.product.find({"pages"   :   {"$gte"   :   20,   "$lte":
80}},{"isbn" : 1, "_id": 0});
{ "isbn" : 125 }
{ "isbn" : 138 }
#Create a variable with time and use it to find the books
published before that date
> thedate = new Date("01/01/2009");
ISODate("2009-01-01T00:00:00Z")
>db.product.find({"publicationdate"      :      {"$lt"      :
thedate}})
#Using $in to match pages of books with books
>db.product.find({"pages"   :   {"$in"   :[80,100]}},{"isbn"
:1,"_id" : 0}); {"isbn" : 125 }
{ "isbn" : 133 }
{ "isbn" : 138 }
{ "isbn" : 141 }
#Using $or to find books that are written from Tony or are
science category
>db.product.find({"$or":[{"author":"Tony"},{"tag-
category":"science"}]},{"isbn" :1,"_id":0});
{ "isbn" : 123 }
{ "isbn" : 125 }
{ "isbn" : 128 }
{ "isbn" : 137 }
{ "isbn" : 138 }
{ "isbn" : 140 }
```

Limits, Skips and Sorting

To extend the query options, this section presents limits, skips and sorting on the returned results of a query.

Limit sets the maximum number of results that will be obtained.

Skip skips the given number of results and then returns the rest of the results. If the collection has fewer documents than the given number, then nothing will be returned.

Sort sorts documents in given ascending (1) or descending (−1) order.

See the examples below and then try some similar queries for yourself:

```
#Requiring all results (therefore the {}) from the
collection and limit to 3
>db.product.find({},{"isbn":1, "_id":0}).limit(3);
{ "isbn" : 123 }
{ "isbn" : 128 }
{ "isbn" : 140 }
#Requiring all results from the collection and skipping
the first 5 while returning the rest in the collection
> db.product.find({},{"isbn":1, "_id":0}).skip(5);
{ "isbn" : 137 }
```

```
{ "isbn" : 136 }
{ "isbn" : 141 }
{ "isbn" : 125 }
{ "isbn" : 138 }
#Requiring  all  results  (therefore  the  {})  from  the
collection sorted by book title descending and number of
pages ascending
>   db.product.find({},{"title":1,"pages":1,   "_id":0}).
sort({pages: -1});
{ "title" : "Book 6", "pages" : 430 }
{ "title" : "Book 1", "pages" : 150 }
{ "title" : "Book 4", "pages" : 150 }
{ "title" : "Book 9", "pages" : 150 }
.........
{ "title" : "Book 3", "pages" : 80 }
{ "title" : "Book 8", "pages" : 80 }
#Finally,  we  will  combine  all  the  query  options
to-gether
>   db.product.find({},{"title":1,"pages":1,   "_id":0}).
sort({pages: -1}).limit(3).skip(2);
{ "title" : "Book 4", "pages" : 150 }
{ "title" : "Book 9", "pages" : 150 }
{ "title" : "Book 2", "pages" : 120 }
```

Shutdown

To shutdown MongoDB client, use the 'exit;' command.

To shutdown the MongoDB server, use the Ctrl + C keys.

6.21.11.2   Useful Extra Resources

We have only just got started with MongoDB with these notes. We hope that there is enough here to give you an understanding of the key principles and to help identify how MongoDB is different to an RDBMS.

If you wish to find out more, some useful resources include:

- Chodorow, K. and Dirolf, M.: MongoDB: The Definitive Guide Powerful and Scalable Data Storage. O'Reilly Media, Sebastopol (2010)
- MongoDB: MongoDB Official Website. http://www.mongodb.org/ (2011). Accessed 1 Sept 2011
- MongoDB(2011b) Quickstart Unix. Available at http://www.mongodb.org/display/DOCS/Quickstart+Unix

6.22   Review Questions

The answers to these questions can be found in the text of this chapter.

- What does ACID stand for, and how sacrosanct are each of the elements in NoSQL databases?

- What was Cassandra designed for in terms of the types of data it stores?
- What is meant by horizontal scaling?
- How might the cloud be used as part of a disaster recovery strategy?
- What types of data are ideal for MongoDB, and what for Cassandra?

6.23   Group Work Research Activities

These activities require you to research beyond the contents of the book and can be tackled individually or as a discussion group.

6.24   Discussion Topic 1

Once you have become conversant with one or other of the databases in the tutorials of this chapter, attempt to draw up a SWOT analysis to see what the strengths and weaknesses, threats and opportunities there may be from adopting the database in an organisation.

6.25   Discussion Topic 2

Try to think of useful criteria for comparing different types of database to help you decide which might be the most appropriate for a given application. Two examples of criteria might be scalability and performance which we have already referred to in the text above.

Acknowledgements Much of the tutorial material was initially created by Antonis Petrou as an output from his MSc dissertation at Sheffield Hallam University. He was an excellent student to supervise and achieved an excellent final mark for his work. I am grateful for his permission to use portions of his work. Peter Lake

References

Cassandra: The Definitive Guide By: Eben Hewitt Publisher:O'Reilly Media, Print: November (2010). Ebook: November 2010, Print ISBN:978-1-4493-9041-9   ISBN 10:1-4493-9041-2, Ebook ISBN:978-1-4493-9042-6 | ISBN 10:1-4493-9042-0

Chang, F., Dean, J., Ghemawat, S., Hsieh, W.C., Wallach, D.A., Burrows, M., Chandra, T., Fikes, A., Gruber, R.E.: Bigtable: a distributed storage system for structured data. ACM Trans. Comput. Syst. **26**(2), 26 (2008). doi:10.1145/1365815.1365816. http://doi.acm.org/10.1145/1365815.1365816, Article 4 (June 2008)

Brewer, E.: Pushing the CAP: strategies for consistency and availability. Computer **45**(2), 23–29 (2012). doi:10.1109/MC.2012.37. URL: http://ieeexplore.ieee.org/stamp/stamp.jsp?tp=&arnu mber=6133253&isnumber=6155638

Intelligence in the Cloud

7

What the reader will learn:
- The importance of search in web and cloud technology
- The challenges and potential of unstructured text data
- How collective intelligence is being used to enhance a variety of new applications
- An introduction to text visualisation
- An introduction to web crawling

7.1   Introduction

We have seen how web and cloud technology allow us to easily store and process vast amounts of information, and as we saw in Chap. 6, there are many different data storage models used in the cloud. This chapter looks at how we can start to unlock the hidden potential of that data, to find the 'golden nuggets' of truly useful information contained in the overwhelming mass of irrelevant or useless junk and to discover new knowledge via the intelligent analysis of the data. Many of the intelligent tools and techniques discussed here originated well before cloud computing. However, the nature of cloud data, its scalable access to huge resources and the sheer size of the available data means that the advantages of these tools are much more obvious. We have now reached a place where many common web-based tasks would not be possible without them.

Much of this new information is coming directly from users. The art of tapping into both the data created by users and the interaction of users with web and cloud-based applications brings us to the field of collective intelligence and 'crowd sourcing'. Collective intelligence has roots predating the web in diverse fields including biology and sociology. The application of collective intelligence techniques to web-based data has rightly been receiving a lot of attention in recent years, and it has become clear that, particularly with the rapid expansion of cloud systems, this is a fruitful area for developing new ways of intelligently accessing, synthesising and analysing our data. It has been suggested that the eventual result will be Web 3.0.

R. Hill et al., *Guide to Cloud Computing*: *Principles and Practice*, Computer Communications and Networks, DOI 10.1007/978-1-4471-4603-2_7, © Springer-Verlag London 2013

We will start this chapter with a brief overview of the kind of data we are dealing with and the techniques that are already being employed to extract intelligence from user data, interaction and collaborations. We will then look in some detail at the process of searching including an appraisal of the challenges of dealing with textual data and an overview of the procedures underlying a search engine. We then move to the field of collective intelligence and what it can offer web and cloud applications. We will finish by looking at the power of visualisation. At the end of this chapter, the exercises will use open source libraries to perform some of the stages of extracting and analysing online text.

7.2   Web 2.0

Ten years ago the majority of websites had the feel of a lecture: The static information flowed one way from the site to the user. Most sites are now dynamic and interactive, and the result is better described as a conversation. We should perhaps remember that HTTP itself is designed to work in a conversational manner. Web 2.0 is all about allowing and encouraging users to interact with websites. As the interaction increases, so does the amount of data. In this chapter, we will look at some of the tools we can employ to get more out of user-generated content. Often the process of using this content effectively to improve our site leads to increased interest and further activity thus creating a virtuous circle.

7.3   Relational Databases

Relational database technology is mature and well known by most software developers and benefits from the compact and powerful SQL language. Data stored in relational databases has a number of distinct advantages when it comes to information retrieval including:
- Data is stored in labelled fields.
- The fields (or columns) have a predetermined data type and size attributes.
- We can specify constraints on the fielded data, for example, 'all entered values must be unique', 'null values are not accepted' or 'entered data must fall within a particular set or range of values'.
- The well-understood normalisation technique can be applied which has been shown to reduce redundancy and provide an easy to understand logical to physical storage mapping.

7.4   Text Data

Despite the benefits listed above, it has been estimated that approximately 80% of an organisations data is in an unstructured format. The data is of course multimedia, but text data has attracted the huge interest as the primary source for web mining

Table 7.1 Example synonyms

Synonyms	
Physician	Doctor
Maize	Corn

Table 7.2 Example homonyms

Homonyms	
Java (country)	Java (programming language)
Board (board of directors)	Board (wooden board)

although in recent years attention is shifting towards other formats, particularly images and video where significant advances have been occurring.

Unstructured text data has the useful property of being both human and machine readable, even if it makes no 'sense' to a machine. The rules for text data are very different to those of relational databases. Text data may or may not be validated and is often duplicated many times. It may have some structure, such as in an academic article, or little or no structure, for example, in the case of blogs and email. In some cases, spellings and grammar are checked very carefully, but in others many mistakes, misspellings, slang words, abbreviations and acronyms are common. There is a notorious many to many relationship between words and meaning. In text data we frequently find synonyms that are different words with the same meaning and homonyms that are words with the same spelling but with distinct meanings. Examples are shown in Tables 7.1 and 7.2.

Text also has many examples of multi-word units such as 'information retrieval' where more than one word is referring to a single concept, new words are constantly appearing, there are many examples of multinational crossover and the meaning of words can vary over time. For these reasons extracting useful information from textual data is in many ways a harder problem than with data stored in relational databases. Typical examples of text likely to be targeted for intelligent analysis are articles, white papers, product information, reviews, blogs, wikis and message boards. One effect of Web 2.0 has been to greatly increase the amount of online text data. The cloud is providing easy access to scalable computing power with which to process this data in innovative and fruitful ways. The web itself can be thought of as one huge data store. We will look at the tools and techniques which have been developed to maximise the potential of this fantastic resource at humanity's fingertips.

7.5 Natural Language Processing

Natural language processing is a broad set of techniques used to process written and spoken human languages. Natural language processing tasks often involve categorising the type of word occurring in text. A particularly useful type of data refers to things like countries, organisations and individual people. The process of automatically identifying these is known as entity extraction. A second common task is to identify the 'part of speech' of particular words so that, for example, nouns, adjectives and adverbs can be automatically identified. GATE (http://gate.ac.uk/) is a freely available open source tool written in Java which performs the above tasks together with many more related to text processing. Natural language processing has made great advances in areas such as automatic translation, speech recognition and grammar checking. One of the long-term goals of natural language processing is to enable machines to actually understand human text, but there are still huge challenges to overcome, and we should be circumspect in the case of claims that this goal has been achieved by an existing system or that a solution is very close.

7.6 Searching

Searching was one of the first applications to which we might attach the term 'cloud', and searching remains, for most users, the most important tool on the web. Search engines such as Google, Bing and Yahoo are well-known examples of mature cloud applications and also give a good introduction to many important concepts relating to cloud data along with text engineering and collective intelligence.

It is therefore worth a brief look 'under the hood' to get an introduction to the inner workings of search engines. As well as providing an insight into one of the key tools for web and cloud data, our investigation will bring to light a number of important themes and concepts that are very relevant to web and cloud intelligence and make the most of noisy, unstructured data commonly found on the web. Of course, the commercial search engine market is a big business, and vendors keep the exact working of their systems well hidden. Nonetheless, there are a number of freely available open source libraries available, and at the end of this chapter, we build our own search engine. We will be using the widely used and much praised Apache Lucene index together with related Apache projects Nutch, Tika and Solr. It is worth noting that Nutch is specifically designed to run on Apache Hadoop's implementation of MapReduce which we investigated in Chap. 4.

7.6.1 Search Engine Overview

Search engines have three major components as shown in Fig. 7.1:
1. Crawler
2. Indexer
3. Web interface

7.6.2 The Crawler

The web is unlike any other database previously encountered and has many unique features requiring new tools as well as the adaptation of existing tools. Whereas previous environments such as relational databases suggested that searching should cover

Fig. 7.1 Search engine components

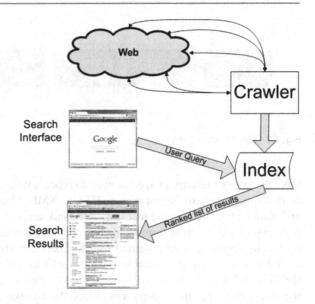

the entire database in a precise and predictable manner, this is simply not possible when we scale to web magnitudes. Web crawlers (often called spiders or bots) browse the web in a methodical manner often with the aim of covering a significant fraction of the publicly available part of the entire web.

To start the crawl, a good set of seed pages is needed. A common way to do this is to obtain the seeds from a project such as the Open Directory Project (http://www.dmoz.org/). Once the list of seed pages has been obtained, the crawler essentially works by performing a series of HTTP GET (see Chap. 4) commands. Hyperlinks found in any page are stored and added to a list of sites to be fetched. Of course, there are many complications such as scheduling of the crawl, parallelisation, prioritisation, politeness (avoiding overwhelming particular sites by respecting their policy regarding crawling) and the handling of duplicates and dead links. There are a number of open source libraries which can be used for crawling ranging from the fairly simple and easy to use HTTP Track (http://www.httrack.com/) to Apache Nutch (http://nutch.apache.org/) which can be used to build a whole web search engine. We look at these in our end of chapter tutorials. Crawling the whole web is a major undertaking requiring massive resources in terms of storage, computation and management. In most cases organisations will be performing a crawl of their own data or perhaps a focused or intelligent web crawl on a particular topic area.

7.6.3 The Indexer

Instead of trying to answer the question 'what words are contained in a particular document?', which you could answer by simply reading the document, an indexer aims to provide a quick answer to the question 'which documents contain this particular word?', and for this reason the index is referred to as an 'inverted index'.

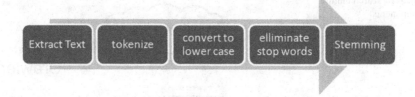

Fig. 7.2 Text processing steps

Once the crawler returns a page, we need to process it in some way. The page could be in a wide variety of format such as HTML, XML, Microsoft Word, Adobe PDF and plain text. Generally, the first task of the indexer will be to extract the text data from any of the different formats likely to be encountered. This is a complex task but luckily open source tools such as Apache Tika (http://tika.apache.org/) are freely available. Once the text is extracted, we can start to build the index by processing the stream of text. A number of processes are normally carried out before we build the index. Note that these steps will reduce the number of words stored which is likely to be helpful when extracting intelligence from text data (Fig. 7.2).

7.6.3.1 Tokenisation
The task of the tokeniser is to break the stream of characters into words. In English or most European languages, this is fairly straightforward as the space character can be used to separate words. Often punctuation is removed during this stage. In languages such as Chinese where there is no direct equivalent of the space character, this is a much more challenging task.

7.6.3.2 Set to Lower Case
When computer programs read text data, the upper- and lower-case forms of individual characters are given separate codes, and therefore, two words such as 'cloud' and 'Cloud' would be identified as separate words. It is generally useful to set all the characters to a standard form so that the same word is counted whether, for example, it is at the start or middle of a sentence although some semantic information may be lost.

7.6.3.3 Stop Word Removal
It is often useful to remove words which are very frequent in text but which carry low semantic value. For example, the Apache Lucene (http://lucene.apache.org) indexing system contains the following default list of stop words:

'a', 'an', 'and', 'are', 'as', 'at', 'be', 'but', 'by', 'for', 'if', 'in', 'into', 'is', 'it', 'no', 'not', 'of', 'on', 'or', 'such', 'that', 'the', 'their', 'then', 'there', 'these', 'they', 'this', 'to', 'was', 'will', 'with'

Including, even this small set·of stop words can greatly reduce the total numbers of words which are stored in the index.

7.6.3.4 Stemming

Stemming allows us to present various word forms using a single word. For example, if the text contains the words 'process', 'processing' and 'processes', we would consider these as the same word for indexing purposes. Again, this could also greatly reduce the total number of words stored. Various methods for stemming have been proposed; the most widely used is the Porter stemming algorithm (Lucene contains classes to perform Porter stemming). However, there are some disadvantages to stemming, and some search engines do not use stemming as part of the indexing. If stemming is used when creating an index, the same process must be applied to the words that the user types into the search interface.

7.6.4 Indexing

Once the words have been extracted, tokenised, filtered and possibly stemmed, they can be added to an index. The index will be used to find documents relevant to users' search queries as entered into the search interface. An index will typically be able to quickly return a list of documents which contain a particular word together with other information such as the frequency or importance of that word in a particular document. Many search engines allow the user to simply enter one or more keywords. Alternatively they may build more complex queries, for example, requiring that two words must appear before a document is returned or that a particular word does not occur. Lucene has a wide range of query types available.

7.6.5 Ranking

A search engine which indexes a collection of hundreds of documents belonging to an organisation might produce acceptable results for most searches, especially if users gain expertise in more advanced query types. However, even in this case some queries might return too many documents to be useful. In the case of the web, the numbers become overwhelming, and the situation is only made worse by the fact that the web has no central authority to accept, categorise and manage documents; anyone can publish on the web and data is not always trustworthy. One of the most straightforward and widely used solutions is to place the results of a query in order, such that the pages or documents most likely to meet the user's requirements are at the top of the list. There are a number of ways to do this.

7.7 Vector Space Model

The vector space model (VSM) originally developed by Salton in the 1970s is a powerful way of placing documents in order of relevance to a particular query. Each word or term remaining after stop word removal and stemming is considered to be a 'dimension', and each dimension is given a weight. The model takes no account of the order of words in a document and is sometimes called a 'bag of words' model. The weight value (*W*) is related to the frequency of each term in a document (the term frequency) and is stored in the form of a vector. A vector is a useful way of recording the magnitude and the direction. The weight of each term should represent the relative importance of the term in a document. Both documents (*d*) and queries (*q*) can be stored this way:

$$dj = \left(w1, j, w2, j, \ldots, wt, j\right)$$

$$q = \left(w1, q, w2, q, \ldots, wt, q\right)$$

The two vectors can then be compared in a multidimensional space allowing for a ranked list of documents to be returned based on their proximity to a particular query.

We could simply store a binary value indicating the presence or absence of a word in a document or perhaps the word frequency as the weight value in the vector. However, a popular and generally more effective way of computing the values to store against each term is known as *tf-idf* weighting (term frequency–inverse document frequency) which is based on two empirical observations regarding collections of text:

1. The more times a word occurs in a document, the more relevant it is to the topic of the document.
2. The more times the word occurs throughout the documents in the collection, the more poorly it discriminates between documents.

It is useful to combine the term frequency (*tf*) and the inverse of the number of documents (*idf*) in the collection in which the term occurs at least once to create a weight.

tf-idf weighting assigns the weight to a word in a document in proportion to the number of occurrences of the word in the document and in inverse proportion to the number of documents in the collection for which the word occurs at least once, that is,

$$w\left(i, j\right) = tf\left(i.j\right) * \log\left(N / df(i)\right)$$

The weight of the term *i* in document *j* is the frequency of the term *i* in document *j* multiplied by the log of the total number of documents (*N*). The log is used as a way of 'squashing' or reducing the differences and could be omitted but has been found to improve effectiveness. Perhaps it is easier to follow with an example.

Assume we have 500 documents in our collection and the word 'cloud' appears in 60 of these. Consider a particular document wherein the word 'cloud' appears 11 times.

To calculate the *tf-idf* for that document:

The term frequency (*tf*) for 'cloud' is 11.

The inverse document frequency (*idf*) is log(500/60)=0.92.

The *tf-idf* score that is the product of these quantities is $11 \times 0.92 = 10.12$.

We could then repeat this calculation across all the documents and insert the *tf-idf* values into the term vectors.

There are many variations of the above formula which take account of other factors such as the length of each document. Many indexing systems, such as Apache Lucene, will store the term vector using some form of *tf-idf* weighting. Documents (or web pages) can then be quickly returned in order depending on the comparison of the term vectors of the query and documents from the index. Inverted indexes, such as that created by Apache Lucene, are essentially a compact data structure in which the term vector representation of documents is stored.

7.8   Classification

We find classifications in all areas of human endeavour. Classification is used as a means of organising and structuring and generally making data of all kinds accessible and manageable. Unsurprisingly, classification has been the subject of intensive research in computer science for decades and has emerged as an essential component of intelligent systems.

In relation to unstructured text data, the ability to provide automatic classification has numerous advantages including:

- Labelling search results as they appear
- Restricting searches to a particular category (reducing errors and ambiguities)
- An aid to site navigation allowing users to quickly find relevant sections
- Identifying similar documents/products/users as part of a recommendation engine (see below)
- Improving communication and planning by providing a common language (referred to as an 'ontology')

Classification is used extensively in enterprise search such as that provided by Autonomy (http://www.autonomy.com/), and many tools such as spam filters are built on the principles of classification.

The term vector representation of a document makes it relatively easy to compare two or more documents. Classifiers need to be supplied with a set of example training documents where the category of each document is identified. Once the classifier has built a model based on the training documents, the model can then be used to automatically classify new documents. Generation of the model is usually performed by a machine learning algorithm such as naive Bayes, neural networks, support vector machines (SVM) or an evolutionary algorithm. Each of the different methods has its own strengths and weaknesses and may be more applicable to particular domains. Commonly different methods of classifiers are combined.

7.9   Measuring Retrieval Performance

The aim of a search query is to retrieve all the documents which are relevant to the query and return no irrelevant documents. However, for a real world data set above a minimum size and complexity, the situation is more likely to be similar to that shown

Fig. 7.3 Search query results

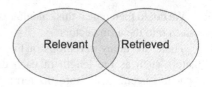

in Fig. 7.3 where many relevant documents are missed and many of the documents retrieved are not relevant to the query.

When testing a search or classification engine, it is important to be able to give some measure of effectiveness. Recall measures how well the search system finds relevant documents and precision measures how well the system filters out the irrelevant documents. We can only obtain values for recall and precision when a set of documents relevant to a particular query is already known.

The F1 measure is a commonly used way of combining the two complementary measures to give an overall effectiveness number and has the advantage of giving equal weight to precision and recall. The actual accuracy achieved will depend on a number of factors such as the learning algorithm used and the size and quality of the training documents. We should note that the accuracy is ultimately down to a human judgement. Even using a human classifier will not achieve 100% accuracy as in most domains two humans are likely to disagree about the category labels for some documents in a collection of reasonable size and complexity. An impressive result of machine learning technology lies in the fact that with a good set of example documents, it has been reported that automatic classifiers can achieve accuracy close to that of human experts as measured using F1 or similar.

7.10 Clustering

Clustering is another useful task, especially when performed automatically. In this case no labelled training documents are given, and the clustering algorithm is required to discover 'natural categories' and group the documents accordingly. Some algorithms such as the widely used k-means require that the number of categories be supplied in advance, but otherwise no prior knowledge of the collection is assumed. Again, the term vectors of documents are compared, and groups of documents created based on similarity.

By organising a collection into clusters, a number of tasks such as browsing can become more efficient. As with classification, clustering the description of products/blogs/users/documents or other Web 2.0 data can help to improve the user experience. Automatic identification of similar items is an important component in a number of other tools such as recommendation engines (see below).

Classification is referred to as a 'supervised learning' task and is generally more accurate than clustering which is 'unsupervised' and does not benefit from the set of labelled training documents. A good example of clustering is http://search.yippy.com/ (formerly clusty.com). Go to the site and search for 'java'. Another example is provided by Google News (http://news.google.com/) which

Fig. 7.4 Link graph

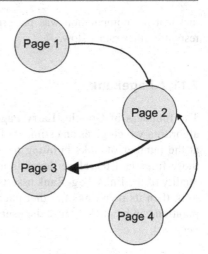

automatically collects thousands of news articles and then organises them by subject, subtopic and region and can be made to display the results in a personalised manner. Commonly, clustering is used in conjunction with other tools (e.g. classification rules) to produce the final result.

7.11 Web Structure Mining

A fundamental component of the web is of course the hyperlink. The way pages link together can be used for more than just navigation in a browser, and a good deal of research has gone into investigating the topology of hyperlinks. We can consider web pages to be nodes on a directed graph (put simply where lines between nodes on a graph indicate a direction), and where there is a link from a particular page (p) to another page (q), we can consider this to be a directed edge. So for any page, we can assign it a value based on the number of links pointing to and from that page. The out degree of a node p is the number of nodes to which it links, and the in degree of p is the number of nodes that have links to p. Thus, in Fig. 7.4 page 1 has an out degree of 1, and page 2 has an in degree of 2. The link from page 2 to page 3 is considered more important than the other links shown because of the higher in degree of page 2.

In web structure mining, we look at the topology of the web and the links between pages rather than at just the content of web pages. Hyperlinks from one page to another can be considered as endorsements or recommendations.

7.11.1 HITS

In 1998 Kleinberg created the HITS algorithm which was a method of using the link structure to assign an importance value to a web page which could be factored into the ranking of query results. The algorithm had some disadvantages including the fact that the computation was performed after the query was submitted making response times rather slow.

7.11.2 PageRank

The founders of Google (Larry Page and Sergey Brin) created the PageRank algorithm which gives an estimate of the importance of a page. PageRank looks at the number of links pointing to a web page and the relative importance of those links and therefore depends not just on the number of links but on the quality of the links. PageRank asserts that if a page has important links pointing to it, then its own links to other pages are also important. The PageRank computation can be made before the user enters the query so that response times are very fast.

7.12   Enterprise Search

Searching is not limited to whole web search, and there is a huge market for focused searching or searching with a particular domain or enterprise. Companies such as Autonomy and Recommind (http://www.recommind.com/) use artificial intelligence combined with advanced search technology to improve user productivity. One of the key challenges lies in the fact that much of an organisation's data may exist in disparate repositories or database systems which have their own unique search facility. More recently it has been noted that with the provision of cloud-based systems such as Google Docs and Microsoft Live Office, people are naturally storing vital information outside the organisations networks. The provision of a federated search capability where one search interface can access the maximum amount of relevant data, possibly including data stored in external cloud sites, has become critical. Technology used by whole web search engines such as PageRank is not always applicable to the enterprise case where links between documents may be minimal or non-existent.

7.13   Multimedia Search

There has been increasing interest and huge investment in the development of new technology for searching audio and visual content. In its simplest form, this is a case of giving special consideration to the text in HTML tags for multimedia data. However, many vendors have gone beyond this and now provide a 'deep' search' of multimedia data including facilities such as searching with images rather than text. The ability to automatically cluster or classify multimedia data has also made major advances.

7.14   Collective Intelligence

Collective intelligence is an active field of research but is not itself a new phenomenon, and examples are cited in biology (e.g. evolutionary processes), social science and economics. In this chapter, we are using collective intelligence to refer to the kind of intelligence that emerges from group collaboration in web- and cloud-based systems. Collective intelligence like 'cloud' is a term where an exact definition has not been agreed although it is mostly obvious when collective intelligence is being harnessed. The Center for Collective Intelligence at the Massachusetts Institute of Technology (http://cci.mit.edu/) provides a nice description by posing the question that tools based on collective intelligence might answer:

> How can people and computers be connected so that collectively they act more intelligently than any individuals, groups, or computers have ever done before?

The rise of the web and Web 2.0 has led to huge amounts of user-generated content. Users no longer need any special skills to add their own web content, and indeed Web 2.0 applications actively invite users to interact and collaborate. Cloud computing has accelerated the process as ease of access, storage availability, improved efficiency, scalability and reduced cost have all increased the attractiveness of storing information on the web and also made it easier and simpler for new innovative applications seeking to exploit collective intelligence to be developed.

There are many examples of collective intelligence where systems leverage the power of the user community. We list a few below to give a flavour of the topic:

1. Wikipedia is an outstanding result of a huge collaboration, and each article is effectively maintained by a large collection of individuals.
2. Many sites, such as reddit.com, allow users to provide content and then decide through voting 'what's good and what's junk'.
3. Google Suggest provides a list of sites as soon the user begins typing. The suggestions are based on a number of factors, but a key one is the previous searches that individuals have entered (see Fig. 7.4).
4. Genius Mixes from iTunes automatically suggests songs that should go well with those already in a users' library.
5. Facebook and other social networks provide systems for 'finding friends' based on factors such as the links already existing between friends.
6. Online stores such as Amazon will provide recommendations based on previous purchases.
7. Image tagging together with advanced software such as face recognition can be used to automatically label untagged images.
8. The algorithms used by movie rental site Netflix to recommend films to users are now responsible for 60% of rentals from the site.
9. Google+ social network allow users to +1 any site as a means of recommendation.
10. Mail systems such as Gmail will suggest people to include when sending an email (Fig. 7.5)

In his book, Wisdom of the Crowds, James Surowiecki, suggests that 'groups are remarkably intelligent, and are often smarter than the smartest people in them'.

Fig. 7.5 Google suggest

He goes on to argue that under the right circumstances, simply adding more people will get better results which can often be better than those produced by a small group of 'experts'. A number of conditions are suggested for 'wise crowds':

1. Diversity: the crowd consists of individuals with diverse opinions.
2. Independence: the individuals feel free to express their opinions.
3. Decentralisation: people are able to specialise.
4. Aggregation: there is some mechanism to aggregate that information and use it to support decision-making.

Note that we are not talking about consensus building or compromise but rather a competition between heterogeneous views; indeed certain parallels have been drawn with Darwinian evolution.

The PageRank algorithm discussed above is actually an example of collective intelligence as the ordering is partly the result of a kind of voting occurring in the form of links between websites, and we can see how it easily meets all four criteria set out above. The web is a hugely diverse environment, and independent individuals are free to add links to any other page from their own pages. The underlying system is famously decentralised and aggregation is central to the PageRank algorithm. Real search engines actually use a complex mix of mathematically based algorithms, text mining and machine learning techniques together with something similar to PageRank. Let's take a look at some more examples of 'Collective Intelligence in Action'.

7.14.1 Tagging

Tagging is a process akin to classification whereby items such as products, web pages and documents are given a label. In the case of automatic text classification, we saw that both a predefined set of categories and a set of labelled example documents were required to build a classifier. In this case people with some expertise in the domain would be required to give each example document the appropriate category labels. One approach to tagging is to use professionals to label items, although this could take up significant resources and could become infeasible, for example, where there is a large amount of user-generated content.

A second approach is to produce tags automatically either via clustering or classification as described above or by analysing the text. Again we can use the term vector to obtain the relative weights of terms found in the text which can be presented to the user in various visual formats (see below). A third option, which has proved increasingly popular in recent years and indeed has become ubiquitous on the web, is to allow users to create their own tags, either by selecting tags from a predefined list or by using whatever words or phrases they choose to label items.

This approach, sometimes referred to as a 'folksonomy' (a combination of 'folk' and 'taxonomy'), can be much cheaper than developing a controlled taxonomy and allows users to choose the terms which they find the most relevant. In a folksonomy users are creating their own classification, and as they do collective intelligence tools can gather information about the items being tagged and about the users who are creating the tags. Once a reasonable number of items have been tagged, we can then use those items as examples for a classifier which can then automatically find similar items. Tags can help with finding users with similar tagged items, finding items which are similar to the one tagged and creating a dynamic, user-centric vocabulary for analysis and collaboration in a particular domain.

7.14.2 Recommendation Engines

Recommendation engines are a prime example of 'Collective Intelligence in Action'. In 2006, Netflix held the first Netflix Prize find a program to better predict user preferences and beat its existing Netflix movie recommendation system by at least 10%. The prize of $1 million was won in 2009, and the recommendation engine is now reported to contribute to a large fraction of the overall profits. Perhaps the best known recommendation engine comes from Amazon. If we select the book 'Lucene in Action', we get the screen shown in Fig. 7.6 where two sets of suggestions are shown.

In fact if you click on some of the suggestions you will soon pick up most of the recommended reading for this chapter. As is indicated on the page, the information is obtained largely by analysing customers' previous procurement patterns. Many other features can be factored into the recommendations such as similarity of the items analysed, similarity between users and similarity between users and items.

7.14.3 Collective Intelligence in the Enterprise

In large organisations, employees can waste significant time in trying to locate documents from their searches. Enterprise search companies such as Recommind (http://www.recommind.com/) encourage users to tag and rate items. The information is aggregated and then fed into the search engines so that other users can quickly get a feel for the particular topic from the tags and the usefulness derived from the classifications and recommendations of others. This also allows for the option of removing or reducing the ranking of poorly rated items, a process sometimes referred to as collaborative filtering.

7.14.4 User Ratings

Many e-commerce sites give users the option of registering their opinion regarding a product, often in the form of a simple star system. The ratings of users can be

Fig. 7.6 Amazon recommendation engine

aggregated and reported to prospective buyers. Often the users are also able to write a review which other customers can then read and many sites now offer links to social network sites such as Facebook and Twitter where products can be discussed. The ratings of a particular user can also be evaluated by comparing with those given by other users.

Recently there has been significant interest in tools which can automatically mine textual reviews and identify the sentiment or opinion being expressed, particularly in the case of social network data. The software may not be completely accurate due to the challenges of natural language text mentioned above but as a recurring theme in collective intelligence, if the accuracy is reasonable and the number of reviews being mined above a minimal threshold there may still be great value in using the tool.

7.14.5 Personalisation

Personalisation services can help in the fight against information overload. Information presented to the user can be automatically filtered and adapted without the explicit intervention of a user. Personalisation is normally based on a user profile which may be partly or completely machine generated. Both the structure and content of websites can be dynamically adapted to users based on their profile. A successful system must be able to identify users, gather knowledge about their preferences and then make the appropriate personalisation. Of course, a degree of confidence in the system is required, and it would be much better to skip personalisation functions rather than make changes based on incorrect assumptions leading to a detrimental user experience and reduced effectiveness of the site.

We have already looked at web content mining, at least in terms of textual data and web structure mining in terms of PageRank. Users also provide valuable information via interacting with websites. Sometimes the information is quite explicit as in the case of purchasing, rating, bookmarking or voting. In e-commerce, products and services can be recommended to users based not only on the purchasing actions of other users but depending on specific needs and preferences relating to a profile. Web usage mining which deals with data gathered from user visits to a site is especially useful for developing personalisation systems. Data such as frequency of visits, pages visited, time spent on each page and the route navigated through a site can be used for pattern discovery, often with the aid of machine learning algorithms, which can then be fed into the personalisation engine.

7.14.6 Crowd Sourcing

Many of the systems for harnessing collective intelligence require minimal or no additional input from the users. However, directly asking customers or interested parties to help with projects has proved a success in a number of areas. One of the earliest and most famous examples dates from 2000 when NASA started its ClickWorker study which used public volunteers to help with the identification of craters. There are a number of systems springing up such as IdeaExchange from Salesforce.com (http://success.salesforce.com/) where customers can propose new product solutions and provide evaluations of existing products. Amazon Mechanical Turk (https://www.mturk.com/mturk/welcome) uses crowdsourcing to solve a variety of problems requiring human intelligence.

7.15   Text Visualisation

We finish this chapter with a brief introduction to the field of text visualisation. It has long been known that where there is a huge amount of information to digest, visualisation can be a huge aid to users of that data. Recent years have seen a growing set of tools to automatically visualise the textual content of documents and web pages.

Tag clouds are simple visualisations that display word frequency information via font size and colour that have been in use on the web since 1997. Users have found the visualisations useful in providing an overview of the context of text documents and websites. Whereas many systems are formed using user-provided tags, there has been significant interest in 'word clouds' or 'text tags' which are automatically generated using the text found in documents or websites. For example, the popular tool Wordle has seen a steady increase in usage, and Wordle or similar diagrams are commonly seen as part of a website to give users a quick view of the important topics.

Generally the word clouds are based on frequency information after stop word removal and possibly stemming. If stemming is used, it is important to display a recognisable word (often the most frequently occurring form) rather than the stemmed form which may be confusing to users. We can think of the diagrams as a visual representation of the term vector for a document and as in the term vector representation, it is based on a 'bag of words', and word proximity is generally not taken into account when generating the word cloud.

If you go to the Wordle site (http://www.wordle.net/), you can see examples or you can create your own word clouds by pasting in text or pointing to resources containing text. The system selects the most frequent words and then presents them using various techniques to adjust font, colour, size and position, in a way that is pleasing and useful to the user.

An experimental alternative is available at http://txt2vz.appspot.com/ Txt2vz is similar to Wordle but also shows how words are linked in the text and has some of the features of a mind map. Two formats of the txt2vz word cloud are available and examples generated from the text of this chapter are shown below (Figs. 7.7 and 7.8).

Word clouds are simple and are commonly presented on websites with little or no explanation of how they should be used or interpreted. Often the words presented are made clickable as a means to provide a dynamic navigation tool which adjusts in real time as users add content.

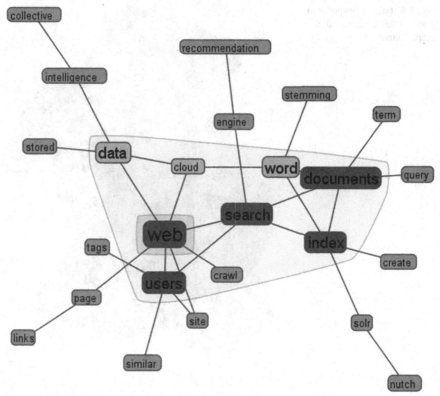

Fig. 7.7 txt2vz.appspot.com graph of this chapter, simple graph format

7.16   Chapter Summary

In this chapter, we have taken an overview of the various ways in which we can get the most out of web- and cloud-based systems. In particular we have looked at Web 2.0 applications and the exciting possibilities of using intelligent tools to gain valuable information and to enhance the user experience.

7.17   End of Chapter Exercise

7.17.1 Task 1: Explore Visualisations

We begin by a brief look at some examples of the many freely available visualisation tools.

1. Wordle http://www.wordle.net/ is probably the most popular of the tools and a good starting point for the exercise. Experiment with the different clouds and create your own Wordle by pasting in plain text.

Fig. 7.8 txt2vz.appspot.com
graph of this chapter, radial
graph format

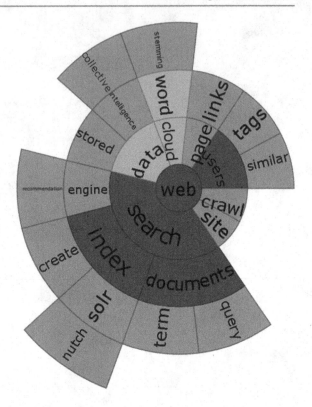

2. Visit the many eye sites (http://www-958.ibm.com/software/data/cognos/manyeyes/)
   and look at the various visualisations and try creating your own visualisations.
3. Explore the tree cloud site (http://www2.lirmm.fr/~gambette/treecloud/) and
   create a tree cloud using the same text you used for Wordle. Explore the different
   options.
4. Try txt2vz (http://txt2vz.appspot.com/). Use the same text again and notice any
   similarities or differences from the other tools. Try the adjustments to find the
   best setting for your document.

7.17.2 Task 2: Extracting Text with Apache Tika

Online text is stored in a wide variety of formats such as HTML, XML, Microsoft
Office, Open Office, PDF and RTF. For most applications trying to extract useful
information from documents, the first step is the extraction of the plain text from the
various formats.

Text extraction is a challenging task but can be rendered quite straightforward
via the freely available Tika Java library from the Apache Software Foundation:
http://tika.apache.org/. Tika can smoothly handle a wide range of file formats and
even extract text from multimedia data. In this tutorial we will begin by downloading

Tika and writing a short Java program to extract text. It would certainly help if you have some Java knowledge before you try this tutorial and you can learn the basics of Java at http://docs.oracle.com/javase/tutorial/. However, you can run this tutorial without Java knowledge by just carefully following each of the steps below:

1. Open your Ubuntu VM.
2. Create a new folder on your VM under 'home' called 'dist'.
3. Go to the Tika site http://tika.apache.org/ and locate the latest download http://tika.apache.org/download.html
4. Download the latest version of the jar file (e.g. http://www.apache.org/dyn/closer.cgi/tika/tika-app-1.1.jar) to the dist folder.
5. Open eclipse, select File/New/Project, select 'Java Project' and select 'next'.
6. Give your project a name such as 'Text Analysis', leave all the other options and select 'next'.
7. Click on the 'libraries' tab and select 'Add External JARs'.
8. Locate the 'dist' folder you created above and select the Tika jar file and then select 'finish'.
9. If you are asked if you would like to switch to the Java perspective, select 'yes'.
10. In the package explorer on the left, expand your project, right click on the 'src' folder and select 'New/Class'.
11. In the name field, call the class 'TikaTest' and select 'finish'.
12. Paste in the following code replacing and code stubs automatically generated by eclipse. Change 'testDoc.docx' with file of your choice, ensuring that the path to the document is correct on your VM.

```java
import java.io.File;
import java.io.IOException;
import org.apache.tika.Tika;
import org.apache.tika.exception.TikaException;
public class TikaTest {
  public static void main(String[] args) {
    TikaTest tikatest1 = new TikaTest();
    File f = new File("/home/hirsch/testDoc.docx");
    try {
      String s = tikatest1.getText(f, 1000);
      System.out.println(s);
    } catch (IOException e) {
      e.printStackTrace();
    } catch (TikaException e) {
      e.printStackTrace();
    }
  }
}
public String getText(File f, int maxSize) throws
IOException, TikaException
{
    Tika tika = new Tika();
    Ntika.setMaxStringLength(maxSize);
```

```
try {
    return tika.parseToString(f);
    catch (IOException e) {
     return " Error: "+e;
    }
   }
  }
```

13. Click on the save icon and then right click on the 'TikaTest.java' in the package explorer and select 'Run as' and then 'Java Application'. If all is well, you will see the first part of the text of your document appear in the console window. Test the code with several different file formats such as docx, doc, rtf, pdf, odt, html and xml.
14. If you are reasonably confident with Java, try to modify the program so that stop words are removed. You can search the web for a suitable set or use the following set:
'a', 'an', 'and', 'are', 'as', 'at', 'be', 'but', 'by', 'for', 'if', 'in', 'into', 'is', 'it', 'no', 'not', 'of', 'on', 'or', 'such', 'that', 'the', 'their', 'then', 'there', 'these', 'they', 'this', 'to', 'was', 'will', 'with'

7.17.3 Advanced Task 3: Web Crawling with Nutch and Solr

Nutch is an open source library for web crawling and again uses Lucene index for storing the crawled data. This task will take some time and effort and is probably for more experienced users. At the end of it, you will be able to perform a small crawl of the web, create a Lucene index and search that index.

Go to the Nutch page and examine the documentation (http://nutch.apache.org/) and follow the tutorial (http://wiki.apache.org/nutch/NutchTutorial). Try and run a small crawl on your virtual machine. The tutorial shows you how you can combine a web crawl with Apache Solr. Solr provides a server based solution with projects based around Lucene indexes and will allow you to view and search the results of your crawl.

References

Alag, S.: Collective Intelligence in Action. Manning, Greenwich (2009)
Langille, A.A.: Google's PageRank and Beyond. Princeton University Press, Princeton (2006)
Lingras, R.A.: Building an Intelligent Web Theory and Practice. Jones and Bartlett, Sudbury (2008)
Marmanis, H., Babenko, D.: Algorithms of the Intelligent Web. Manning, Greenwich (2009)
McCandless, M., Hatcher, E., Gospodnetic, O.: Lucene in Action. Manning, Greenwich (2010)
Segaran, T.: Programming Collective Intelligence. O'Reilly Media, Sebastopol (2007)
Surowiecki, J.: The Wisdom of Crowds: Why the Many are Smarter than the Few and How Collective Wisdom Shapes Business, Economies, Societies, and Nations. Anchor, Port Moody (2005)

Part III

Business Context

Cloud Economics

8

What the reader will learn:

- The strategic context of cloud investment
- Key economic drivers for cloud computing
- How to apply and evaluate some key financial techniques commonly used in investment appraisals
- How to justify investment choices in relation to cloud adoption
- How to develop a business case for cloud adoption

8.1 Introduction

The majority of academic and industry literature focuses predominantly on the technical benefits of cloud computing. Where a discussion of business value exists, the technical benefits of cloud computing tend to be espoused:

- *Cloud elasticity* gives rise to auto-scaling of computing resources, resulting in an on-demand service that can be scaled up or down, with near instant service availability (resource pooling). Also, it is a lot easier to predict traffic patterns, hence forward planning forecast can be done more effectively.
- *Rapid deployment* is a result of a more efficient development life cycle, since production systems can easily be cloned as development or testing environments.
- *Abstraction of infrastructure* and simplicity of application access make service provisioning independent of devices or locations. This permits faster provisioning and integration of services through web interfaces at much lower risk and administrative overhead.
- *Multi-tenancy* makes it possible to run a single application instance for multiple users simultaneously, resulting in economies of scale both on the supply and demand sites. Full or partial multi-tenancy means that the cost of maintenance, updates and upgrades of services and applications are shared and distributed over

R. Hill et al., *Guide to Cloud Computing: Principles and Practice*, Computer Communications and Networks, DOI 10.1007/978-1-4471-4603-2_8,
© Springer-Verlag London 2013

a large number of customers. This drives down the cost per customer, to a negligible amount resulting in a meaningful reduction in total costs. This is especially true in the case of public cloud deployment models.

- *Cloud quality of service* (*QoS*) ensures the operational uptime delivered (service reliability) is that which is promised, through effective utilisation of redundant resources. Service availability and scalability is achieved through data replication, distribution and load balancing to give consumers the appearance of a seamless and transparent experience.

These properties offer considerable technical performance improvements, through more efficient resource utilisation and significant cost efficiencies by lowering cost impact of over or under provisioning, lowering entry cost structure and reducing the time taken to realise value. Having said that, it very much depends on the deployment model and scale; the economic effect of the cloud may not surface or in fact make it more expensive to run. For instance, the only way for SMEs or business units to reap the benefits at scale from cloud computing is by moving to a public cloud. This is because a small installed base of servers makes private clouds too expensive compared to public clouds, for the same unit of service, due to the combined effects of scale, demand diversification and multi-tenancy. This is in addition to upfront investment that increases the overall cost of deployment and business risk, offering little comparative benefit.

It is also important to consider some of the key business drivers that are linked to creating value beyond cost efficiencies and business scalability:

- Cloud computing enables *business agility* by enabling the business to respond faster to the demanding needs of the market; by facilitating access, prototyping and rapid provisioning, organisations can adjust processes and services to meet the changing needs of the markets. Faster, and easier, prototyping and experimentation can also serve as a platform for innovation. This allows shorter development cycles and faster time to products and value.
- *Virtualisation* offers a tangible benefit of abstracting away the operational system complexity, resulting in better user experience and productivity. This, in turn, can significantly reduce maintenance and upgrade costs, whilst at the same time provide flexibility for innovative enhancements and developments in the background.
- Expanded computing power and capacity allows cloud computing to offer simple, yet context-driven, variability. It can improve user experience and increase product relevance by allowing a more enhanced, and subtle customisation of products and services, and personalised experience.

Perhaps one of the most important offerings of the cloud is how it is creating an ecosystem of partners, vendors, service providers, users, etc. The drive to deliver and consume effective, efficient and reliable cloud technologies, products, services, marketplaces, security, standards, models, frameworks and best practices has created a unique and dynamic platform for collaboration and co-innovation. As the ecosystems mature, the network effect will contribute to increasingly intelligent and interactive environments and generate, collectively, tremendous value.

It is true that cloud computing and associated technologies have given rise to emerging and innovative business models, but the rush to tap into potential benefits tends to ignore the significance of due diligence in strategic planning for cloud adoption, as one component in the wider IT portfolio of organisations. This is the case for both SMEs and larger enterprises alike.

Most approaches build a business case for cloud that is predominantly viewed through operational efficiencies, focusing on cost optimisations that are evaluated using cost-based calculations linked to resource utilisation. The metrics often used (especially by SMEs) are linked to cost efficiencies achieved as a result of a perceived shift from CAPEX (capital expenditure) to OPEX (operating expenditure), TCO (total cost of ownership), and at best, looking at ROI (return on investment) and NPV (net present value) of cloud investment.

The application of financial techniques addresses some of the complex economic context of cloud computing, rather than the broader scope of cloud *value*. The latter requires a fuller scope, a strategic framework and a holistic perspective to capture the essence of cloud business value. This, in itself has been one of the key inhibitors of cloud computing adoption to date. As the technology has been maturing, greater management emphasis is being placed on the need to realise business benefits from cloud investment. The pace of technology maturity and cloud ecosystem push needs to match the market demand/pull to increase the adoption rate. There will be a shift in how vendors supply their cloud technology and solutions, and how cloud consumers build on new business models through the technology enhancements offered by cloud.

Investment in cloud computing should be more than a business enabler and cost reduction exercise, but capability building leveraged to drive the business, with increased adaptability, agility, flexibility, scalability and mobility across the enterprise system landscape. On balance, there are the challenges of new risks that steepen the learning curve across the entire cloud marketplace.

As technology and business models mature, IT will continue on its path to commoditisation. 'Outsourcing' of non-core IT assets and competencies thus becomes cost effective and a predictable operational entity.

8.2 The Historical Context

It would be useful for us to have a quick overview of how we have got to what we know as cloud computing. However, in contrast to Chap. 1, this will not be a technology standpoint but instead a business model view, to put some of the discussions in this section in perspective.

8.2.1 Traditional Model

Over the years, vendors produced hardware and software applications and organisations purchased them to run their businesses. The traditional on-premise approach as we know it, has been costly. It is important to note that the key cost element for the users has been tied in, not in purchasing hardware and software licences, but the required consulting, change management, education, maintenance and enhancements and significant management overheads to ensure service availability, security, performance, etc. At the heart of this there is the cost of labour and expertise.

Taking into account this potentially massive cost to the user organisation topped with opportunity-loss due to up-front capital expenditure, vendor lock-in, inflexibility and operational costs, the overall cost impact is incredibly high. This has changed the attitude towards IT decisions and budgets to become more strategic, giving rise to a whole new discipline of IS/IT strategic planning and benefits realisation to ensure that IT budgets are effective.

8.2.2   Open Source

The open source paradigm challenged some of the key tenets of this traditional model, by offering commercial grade software for 'free'. The revenue model has been built around delivering support services. The attractiveness of the open source model has not only been a potential for reduced total cost of ownership (TCO) of high quality products, but also the fact that it opened up new innovation pathways, that could enhance the overall user experience and even result in new business models. The intrinsic value offering of open source though, has been as much, if not more, about instilling change, transformation and innovation in communities of practice, than it can be about cost savings.

The economics of open source has created new industries and new markets, though these open source providers have, in many cases, struggled to monetise their services easily.

8.2.3   Outsourced and Managed Services

The need to increase IT service reliability and availability, yet reducing the costs coupled with the increasing need for flexibility, systems integration, standardisation and specialisation, has meant that consolidating their services, vendors and service providers could tap into the repeatable and scalable expertise that they had developed to offer outsourcing, managed and on-demand service models. This simplified some aspects of IT cost structure by creating a hybrid costing/revenue model, where customers are charged in a number of ways for software/applications; a one-off, upfront payment, followed by service and management charges per user per period (month/year) for example. This provides the companies with choice at reduced cost.

On-demand solutions overlap with the software as a service (SaaS) model of cloud computing in that they tap into the power of the web to deliver services.

Developments in service orientation and other enabling technologies to scale and exponential decreasing cost of hardware following Moore's Law mean that there is significant cost advantage for IT as utility. Economies of scale, standardisation and automation help service providers significantly reduce their operational costs yet deliver reliable and repeatable services.

8.2.4 Services in the Cloud

Recent enterprise acquisitions to consolidate the software market and vendor portfolios preserve licensing and maintenance revenues and continue to provide a one-stop shop to deliver an integrated user experience. Although there are common-alities, the cloud provision has challenged the traditional software model, paving the way for emerging utility models. The basic premise of the shift is often linked to the *elasticity* property of cloud, making it possible to plan and provision IT assets flexibly and on demand. This way, companies can avoid significant capital expendi-ture on fixed assets and the associated costs of licensing, maintenance and upgrade, in favour of pay-for-unit-used models, with minimal or no setup cost and risk of vendor lock-in. Although still at its early stage of life cycle, vendors are enabling clouds of enterprise capability, through federated applications and infrastructure capability. Large enterprise vendors and pure cloud players such as Salesforce.com (http://salesforce.com) have successfully been delivering on-demand managed ser-vices in the cloud. This has been extended by full cloud-based ERP provisions such as SAP Business ByDesign (http://www.sap.com/solutions/sme/businessbydesign).

The issue with the cloud cost is that although the overall cost per month for con-sumption of service is low in comparison, organisations need to standardise their business processes to be able to take advantage of cloud choice. Whereas this has been accounted for in previous models, business process change and management are typically absent from cloud costings. One reason, therefore, is that the cloud offer costs less due to the much higher degree of provider standardisation and service simplification.

However, the trends in mobility, social media and collaboration, powered by Internet infrastructures and cloud computing, offer a real game-changing value opportunity in the marketplace that current models of managed services, outsourc-ing and on demand cannot easily fulfil.

8.3 Investment in the Cloud

The fast pace of technology innovation, and increasingly lower cost of processing power, coupled with unpredictable business environments, requires flexible and adaptive business models built upon agile IT platforms. Any new IT investment in cloud technologies or any emerging technology more than ever requires alignment and focus on the strategic business direction. Hence, a cloud investment strategy must build on a multifaceted business case that transcends evaluating technical fitness and cost efficiencies and assesses cloud readiness and implementation through the wider assessment of the current and future business value drivers, risks and governance, business processes, business and enterprise architectures with clear cloud transition vision.

Whereas more mature and successful organisations adopt a long-term focus towards future business opportunities through innovation and differentiation, as well as growth and shareholder economic value in their approach to their cloud valuation, smaller and less mature organisations tend to focus upon short-term profitability opportunities. In either case, companies need to develop and implement good practice techniques for planning their investment, governance and value realisation. Technology is often regarded as a key enabler of performance, requiring a business-driven change to maximise realisable value. Indeed, research shows that the value of IT is maximised when coupled with investment in new strategies, business models, business process transformation and new organisations (Brynjolfsson 1998). Therefore, cloud investment, just as any modern IT investment decision, needs to strike a balance between financial and organisational investment evaluation methods, with a view to project forward and evaluate the future, rather than the past and present states (Nokes 2000).

It is also important to qualify the discussion of moving to the cloud. As discussed earlier, companies need to think carefully about their total portfolios and decide what portion of their processes and supporting applications could be cloud driven and which ones are better off managed locally. Economics alone, as used often to justify cloud adoption, is not a suitable criterion for this purpose. This matters as much to SMEs as it does to larger organisations. Similarly, it affects the key business decisions by all players on the provider side of the equation. For them, cloud service provision needs to make sustainable economic sense, given the large capital expenditure they commit to.

We now consider some of the economic measures that are commonly used by organisations to appraise their investment option in projects. We will balance this by covering some of the more holistic approaches from an organisational perspective.

8.4 Key Performance Indicators and Metrics

Developing a robust business case that demonstrates the return on investment of cloud can benefit all parties in a cloud venture. The cloud customers and consumers can justify the investment in terms of costs and benefits of the key technology features and the new operating models. This exercise needs to identify any interdependencies and trade-offs. The output of this exercise will also serve as a key ingredient of the strategic planning process, which we will cover in the next chapter. It will also serve as a good performance benchmark tool and metric to monitor the investment effectiveness and determine if the cloud provision is delivering both the business and technology promises, whilst also identifying any potential scope for fine-tuning and improvement.

In this section we discuss some of the pertinent financial and accounting techniques that form an important aspect of measuring or appraising investment decisions.

It is important, however, to emphasise that no investment decision should be based purely on financial metrics. Organisations need to consider both financial and nonfinancial indicators to determine the value of cloud. Some contributing factors to this value will be qualitative and challenging to express in monetary value. As an example you would be able to measure the on-going monthly subscription, but would find it hard to quantify staff productivity or user experience. Having said that, there is some level of subjectivity in financial aspects too, for example, calculating the cost of service disruption and SLAs.

8.5   CAPEX Versus OPEX

Perhaps the economic justification of cloud computing starts with the assertion that the users can shift into the cloud with virtually a zero financial commitment and then pay as they go, which is classed as variable operational expenditure (OPEX). In contrast, for traditional IT, the organisations invest in infrastructure assets such as hardware and software code, which requires capital expenditure. Capital expenditure poses some risks:

- Capital is limited, especially in the case of public sector or SMEs.
- CAPEX raises the barrier for entry by making it difficult to access the latest technology, especially in the case of SMEs.
- Precious capital will be tied down in physical assets that rapidly depreciate, and there is the associated cost of maintenance and upgrade. This poses an opportunity cost as part of this capital that could be invested elsewhere to drive innovation.
- Large investment in physical IT hardware and software, especially in the case of large enterprises, risks vendor lock-in which reduces business flexibility and agility.
- For growth or scaling, in addition to the need for modernising old technology, substantial investment in the infrastructure, architecture and integration is needed.

In practice, many organisations prefer to shift their investments towards revenue-generating activities; hence, they lease assets where possible. Therefore, there is an option value in the alternative approach. One value proposition offered by cloud providers is the opportunity to reduce the IT capital expenditure and address the issues above. Instead, such larger capital investment is made by the providers themselves who require cloud computing platforms or private cloud users. In their case, they benefit from economies of scale through shared service models. Some other implications of using OPEX:

- There will be much faster rate of cost reduction using cloud.
- Cost of ownership will be transformed.
- Removal of upfront capital and release funds.
- Shift from balance sheet to operating statement.
- Cash flow implications where revenue generation and expenditure will be based on service usage.
- There will be a fresh focus on productivity and revenue generation whilst keeping capital costs down through greater efficiencies of working capital.
- Minimising upfront investment to drive improved asset usage ratios, average revenue per unit, average margin per user and cost of asset recovery.
- Maximising the use of capital by moving funding towards optimising capital investment leverage and risk management of sources of funding.

When the cost of capital is high, shifting CAPEX to OPEX may more easily be justified. However, this is not by any means the only scenario for a cloud business case. All the same, a business may still choose to invest in CAPEX for differentiated business processes, yet adopt a usage-based model to improve financial efficiency.

A caveat for OPEX to be beneficial is that there should be a reliable mechanism to measure and predict usage and tie this to business performance metrics or opt for a monthly or annual baseline fixed rate. Lack of ability to correlate system use with business performance can cause oversubscription, costing both the provider and the service users (The Open Group 2010).

To determine the cloud value proposition, it is imperative to account for the imputed value drivers and business benefits in wider business context (Golden 2009).

8.6   Total Cost of Ownership

One argument to justify the advantage of cloud computing over traditional IT has been the lower total cost of ownership (TCO) (Table 8.1). TCO is an accounting metric that takes all direct and indirect costs of technology acquisition and operation into account over the IT project life cycle. The costs include everything from initial investment in hardware and software acquisition to installation, administration, training, maintenance and upgrades, service and support, security and disaster recovery, power and any other associated costs.

In practice to derive value from TCO analysis, it should be included in the calculation of other measures such as return on investment (ROI), net present value (NPV), internal rate of return (IRR) or Economic Value Added (EVA). That way, value planning for cloud is not one-dimensionally cost focused, but it will take into account the quantified business benefits as well.

The typical cost components are broadly categorised as acquisition costs versus operational costs, each incurring administrative and management costs. A simple allocation of these costs is illustrated in Table 8.2.

Moving from traditional on-premise IT to on-demand cloud service requires a re-examination of the assumptions underlying TCO. The cloud environment tends to abstract asset virtualisation, obfuscate labour and deliver IT services at a contracted rate. In comparison, cloud services are supplied and metered on the

Table 8.1 Total cost of ownership (TCO)

Calculation	$TCO = \sum (Direct\ cost,\ Indirect\ cost,\ Overhead)$
Advantages	Accounts for all acquisition and operational costs, direct and indirect
	Reflects all costs to identify true investment viability
	Can be used as a simple comparison tool
	Can provide a picture of profitability over time
Disadvantages	Not holistic, only cost focused
	Does not account for business benefits and value
	A true analysis can be very complex (there is a complexity index to account for the complexity of the IT environment!)
	Challenging to assign indirect costs
Application	Primary method for investment justification

Table 8.2 Simple view of IT cost components. In practice, TCO analysis brings all of these costs components together

Direct costs	Indirect costs	Overheads
Server	Network	Facilities
Storage	Storage	Power
Software (application)	Software (infrastructure) labour (operational)	Bandwidth
Implementation	Maintenance and upgrades	Labour (admin)
	Support	
	Training	

resources consumed, and the cloud provider will typically have clear pricing models that cover the cost of the consumed resources. Hence, in cloud TCO calculations, there is an opportunity to consolidate and simplify some of the cost components, as the main infrastructure and upfront costs are displaced by service subscription and reassigned as operational costs. In the case of SaaS or PaaS, such costs are linked to readily identifiable and chunked infrastructure. The challenge is to identify the actual unit of deployment and all the cost components that make up the TCO.

In calculating TCO, both for traditional IT and cloud, it is important to consider the hidden costs. Whereas in-house provisioning incurs hidden costs such as additional administrative headcount, additional property and facilities requirements, inevitable over-provisioning costs and additional costs for ensuring redundancy, the cloud provision's hidden costs could come from potential costs such as service interruptions, inappropriate service scaling, mismanagement or a denial of service attack, extra security, and contingency disaster preparedness and recovery plan costs, as well as the initial cost of cloud-readiness including costs associated with setup, interfacing and integrating with discrete local infrastructure or resources and administrating the whole new operating system.

8.7   Categories of Cost Efficiencies

There are five key categories of cloud cost savings or gains in productivity that need to be accounted for when building the business case for the cloud. The degree to which they apply to the organisations depends on their cloud model (Mayo and Perng 2009). The first category to consider is *infrastructure*.

8.7.1   Infrastructure

Studies show that cost savings in infrastructure in terms of improved hardware utilisation and a decreased number of servers can significantly reduce the cost of hardware. In economic terms, less physical servers mean less depreciation expense, as well as less facility (floor space) and energy demands. Although the platform maturity may influence the equation, overall cost reductions are likely to be significant (between 30 and 70%). This is also valid in an outsourced scenario, reflected in the lower server management charges.

One significant payback on cloud infrastructure related to its automated provisioning which will reduce the amount of time required in deploying systems. This will improve the QoS and more efficient leverage of skilled resources. As the number of images increases due to standardisation and economies of scale, cost of testing, deployment, administration, maintenance upgrade and training significantly accelerates savings.

8.7.2 Software Application

In the case of public cloud, the software licence and implementation costs are replaced by pay-per-use model. For SMEs there is an immediate cost saving as there will be no/minimal upfront cost for software provision.

The case for in-house private cloud provision will be different in comparison, as there will be initial costs associated with virtualisation infrastructure setup. However, these costs will be fully or partially offset over time, by reduction in licence costs due to consolidation and enhancement in service management.

8.7.3 Productivity Improvements

Gains in productivity are evident in a number of places, especially where IT staff test, provision and manage systems as a result of considerably shorter cycle times. The effect of this productivity gain elsewhere in the organisation is felt by the users in reduced IT response time. The overall improvement in IT agility to meet business demand can be easily translated to business agility, faster time to value generation and innovation.

8.7.4 System Administration and Management

As mentioned earlier, the capability of more efficient management of virtual environments can result in significant cost savings. However, virtual systems can be more complex to administer which may lead to higher overheads; hence, effective and efficient management of the virtualised environments are a key tenet of cloud computing.

8.8 Things to Consider When Calculating Cloud TCO

The goal of TCO should be to balance accuracy in how computing resources are utilised, versus perfection, in terms of what cost advantage there is to unlock. In any calculations, it is common to evaluate multiple scenarios by carrying out a sensitivity analysis to understand how various patterns of usage influence cost derivers and overall TCO. It is then important to have a baseline cost advantage target (in %) to be able to benchmark the cloud deployment costs against it as follows (Golden 2011):

- *Identify all different cost streams both business and technical.* Some common sources of cost include amount of compute capacity, network traffic and storage. Certain services may be on pay-for-use basis but some costs such as static IP address for certain applications; in the same there are some service support and management costs, as well as cost of skills upgrade (offset by perhaps a leaner IT team), that need also be accounted for. By definition, cloud implies a dynamic service that assures optimal utilisation. This, on the other hand, means that fluctuations in service use could become challenging, unlike the static resources in a traditional IT environment that can be accounted for more easily.
- *Evaluate the application profiles and service mix.* Applications utilise computing resources at varying rates. Some are more compute intensive, whereas others do a small amount of processing across an enormous amount of data. This exercise helps to create a clearer TCO picture by assigning costs to the different cloud services, according to application profile.
- *Calculate the TCO under a number of different application topologies to understand costs under different loads.* Identify and cost the required compute instances according to application load variations. Technically speaking, study the horizontal and vertical scaling patterns of the applications. If the load on an application varies significantly, it will most likely require a larger deployment of multiple compute instances to reduce the application bottlenecks.
- *Evaluate the role of load variation.* It is important to identify the periods and patterns of application requiring or experience load variation, larger loads. A static pattern assumption is hardly useful to calculate cloud TCO. Carrying out a statistical (e.g. Monte Carlo) and scenario analysis to explicitly assess TCO under different load patterns can assist with more accurate estimation of TCO.

Although it is generally stated that the TCO of cloud computing is considerably lower than an on-premise equivalent, it is important to qualify this in the context of preferred or appropriate configuration model (i.e. combination of service and deployment models) and business maturity level of the organisation.

Organisations need to study the fully loaded costs in the light of the business benefits gained and the opportunity costs of not moving to the cloud. Often, it might be a case of paying a premium for much improved, optimised or secure IT provision. Hence, it is imperative to benchmark costs beyond an equivalent amount of internal server capability.

Depending on their level of maturity, organisations engage differently with cloud technology. In the case of many SMEs, reactive response to incident management, undocumented or unrepeatable processes, and unplanned implementations tend to increase the complexity and cost of any IT service regardless of the delivery mechanism.

8.9   Return on Capital Employed

Return on capital employed, also referred to as return on investment (ROI) and accounting rate of return (ARR), is a financial metric to determine and compare the net payback (profit or loss) from an investment in relation to the size of the capital dedicated to the (cloud) project (Table 8.3). It is typically described as an annual rate of return in percentage and is based on the past investment.

8.10   Payback Period

Payback period refers to the period of time (e.g. number of months or years) we expect to recover the original investment in the cloud. The shorter payback period is more desirable as it reduces the risk of longer term payouts. Although a popular investment appraisal method, payback period only qualifies as a first screening technique to initially appraise a project. Its scope is limited to the period the investment is recovered, hence it ignores potential benefits as a result of investment gains or shortfalls thereafter. Payback period is summarised in Table 8.4.

Table 8.3 Return on capital employed (ROCE)

Calculation	Average annual accounting profit × 100/investment
Advantages	Quick and easy calculation
	Simple indicator of return
	Good for first basic analysis
Disadvantages	Based on historic estimated data
	Cost of capital over time not accounted for
	Does not take into account the residual value of investment
	Ignores timing of profit/pattern of profit
	Ignores time value of money
	Not considering risk
Application	Early stage indicator for investment justification

Table 8.4 Payback

Calculation	The years when the accumulated net gain is equal to or greater than the initial investment
Advantages	Simple and easy to apply
	Quick indicator or investment recovery
	Quick indicator of risk if we accept that more distant cash flows are more uncertain and that increasing uncertainty is similar to increasing risk
	Uses cash flow rather than accounting profits, hence not prone to managerial preferences for particular accounting policies
Disadvantages	Ignores the time value of money
	Does not consider the investment as whole and ignores all cash flows outside the payback period
	Risk not accounted for
Application	Early indicator for investment justification

Table 8.5 Net present value (NPV)

Calculation	$$NPV = -I_0 + \sum C_n / (1+r)n$$
	where I_0 is the initial investment; C_n is project cash flows in years 1, 2,..., n; and r is the cost of capital or required rate of return
Advantages	Strong indicator of expected return over time
	Takes account of time value of money
	Uses cash flow rather than accounting profit
	Takes into account both the amount and timing of the project cash flows
	Takes into account all relevant cash flows over the life of the investment project
	Value creation of over cost of money
	Can used a good indicator of project comparison
Disadvantages	Does not take into account the lost opportunity form alternative investment
	Reliant on estimate cash flow model (a general issue for other methods too)
	Assumes that the cost of capital remain constant over the life of project
Application	NPV is a primary measure of investment appraisal
	Applied for shared infrastructure, systems and services investment
	Strategic investment

8.11 Net Present Value

Net present value (NPV), as illustrated in Table 8.5, is a capital investment measure to determine the value from contribution of investment, using discounted cash flow. It uses the cost of capital, or target rate of return, to discount all cash flows to their present value. It is a standard method of appraising longer term projects. The NPV decision rule is to accept all independent projects with a positive NPV as it indicates a return in excess of the cost of capital. A project with negative NPV value will be rejected.

8.12 Internal Rate of Return

Internal rate of return (IRR) is a capital investment measure that indicates how efficient an investment is (yield), using a compounded return rate. If the cost of capital used to discount future cash flows is increased, the NPV of the project will fall. As the cost of capital continues to increase, the net present value will become zero before it becomes negative (Fig. 8.1). The IRR is the cost of the capital (or a required rate of return) that produces a NPV of zero. Table 8.6 describes the constituent parts of the IRR calculation.

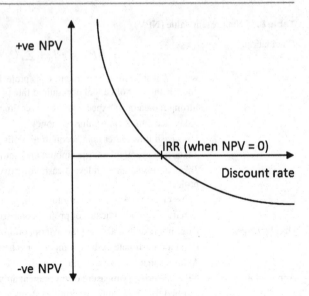

Fig. 8.1 The relationship between net present value (NPV) of a project and the discount rate. The internal rate of return (IRR) produces a net present value of zero

Table 8.6 Internal rate of return (IRR)

Calculation	$$NPV = -I_0 + \sum C_n / (1+r)n$$
	The *NPV* formula can be reinstated. *IRR* is *r* where *NPV* equals zero
Advantages	Strong indicator of expected return over time
	Gives the investment yield over cost of capital
	Uses cash flow rather than accounting profit
	Takes into account both the amount and timing of the project cash flows
	Takes into account all relevant cash flows over the life of the investment project
	IRR or yield is a popular measure amongst finance people
Disadvantages	Considers only a single discount rate over the life of the project
	Investment not fully accounted
	Not applicable for comparing mutually exclusive projects
Application	IRR is a primary measure of investment appraisal
	It is used as a hurdle rate (go/no-go decision)
	More applicable to shared infrastructure and systems investment

For the NPV method, we assume that the generated cash flows over the life of the project can be invested elsewhere, at a rate equal to the cost of capital, as the cost of capital represents an opportunity cost. The IRR, on the other hand, assumes that generated cash flows can be reinvested elsewhere at the internal rate of return. The larger the IRR in relation to the cost of capital, the less likely that the alternative returns can be realised; hence, the underlying investment assumption in the IRR method is a doubtful one, whereas for NPV, the reinvestment assumption seems more realistic. In the same way, NPV can accommodate conventional cash flows, whereas in comparison we may get multiple results through the IRR method.

8.13   Economic Value Added

Economic Value Added (EVA™), also known as economic profit, is a measure used to determine the company's financial performance based on the residual wealth created (Table 8.7). It depicts the investor or shareholder value creation above the required return or the opportunity cost of the capital. It measures the economic profit created when the return on the capital employed exceeds the cost of the capital. Reducing costs increases profits and economic value added. Unlike ROI, EVA takes into account the residual values for an investment.

Table 8.7 Economic Value Added (EVA)

Calculation	$EVA = NOPAT - (c.K)$
	or
	$EVA = (r - c)\,K$
	where
	$NOPAT$ is net operating profit after tax
	c is the amount of capital invested
	K is the (weighted) cost of the capital
	r is return on invested capital $r = NOPAT/K$
Advantages	EVA is a strong indicator of return over time
	Accounts for opportunity cost of the investment
	Provides the yield over the cost of capital
	Optimises the earnings for investors and/or shareholders
	Not prone to management accounting adjustments
	Increases long-term profitability
Disadvantages	Shareholder focused and does not necessarily consider all of the stakeholders
	Investment not fully accounted
	Cost of capital is subjective and difficult to estimate
	Offers little for capital budgeting as it only focuses on current earnings whereas in contrast NPV provides a richer analysis as it takes into account projections of all future cash flows
Application	Primary technique for investment justification
	Applied to shared infrastructure, systems and services
	Strategic investment

8.14   Key Performance Indicators

Once the organisations are in the cloud, they need to actively manage the service performance to make sure that the intended design benefits are realised. The monitoring process is key to service quality management and active benefits realisation management. A balanced scorecard approach, where business objectives and deliverables and relevant ratios and metrics are balanced against each other, is one such approach to managing key performance indicators (KPI).

Hayes and Wheelwright (1984) proposed that companies compete in the marketplace by virtue of a combination of what they termed 'competitive priorities'. Many authors and practitioners have added to and adapted this list over the years. In practice, each performance priority can be measured across multiple dimensions. Table 8.8 shows an example list of some of the KPIs that relate to key areas of cloud system performance.

Table 8.8 Key performance indicators from Hayes and Wheelwright (1984) that are applicable to cloud performance appraisal (Adapted from The Open Group 2010)

Quality	*Experiential*:	
	The quality of perceived user experience	
	The quality of User Interface (UI) design and interaction—ease of use	
	SLA response error rate:	
	Frequency of defective responses	
	Intelligent automation:	
	The level of automation response (agent)	
Time	*Timeliness*:	
	The degree of service responsiveness	
	An indicator of the type of service choice determination	
	Throughput:	
	The latency of transactions	
	The volume per unit of time throughput	
	An indicator of the workload efficiency	
	Periodicity:	
	The frequency of demand and supply activity	
	The amplitude of the demand and supply activity	
	Temporal:	
	The event frequency to real-time action and outcome result	
Benefits	*Revenue efficiencies*:	
	Ability to generate margin increase/budget efficiency per margin	
	Rate of annuity revenue	
	Market disruption rate:	
	Rate of revenue growth	
	Rate of new market acquisition	

(continued)

Table 8.8 (continued)

Speed of time reduction:
Compression of time reduction by cloud adoption
Rate of change of TCO reduction by cloud adoption
Optimising time to deliver/execution:
Increase in provisioning speed
Speed of multisourcing
Speed of cost reduction:
Compression of cost reduction by cloud adoption
Rate of change of TCO reduction by cloud adoption
Optimising cost of capacity:
Aligning cost with usage, CAPEX to OPEX utilisation pay-as-you-go savings from cloud adoption
Elastic scaling cost improvements
Optimising ownership use:
Portfolio TCO, licence cost reduction from cloud adoption
Open source adoption
SOA reuse adoption
Green costs of cloud:
Green sustainability
Optimising time to deliver/execution:
Increase in provisioning speed
Reduced supply chain costs
Speed of multisourcing
Flexibility/choice
Optimising margin:
Increase in revenue/profit margin from cloud adoption

8.15 Measuring Cloud ROI

As discussed already, it is imperative that we look beyond traditional methods and benefit models and focus upon value creation through cloud investment. Benefit is often associated with a 'discrete economic effect', whereas value has a broader scope, as to investment in the cloud will impact upon the business performance.

Information economics is an approach employed to capture and calculate the delivered value of an IT investment, both at the level of methodology and of process. Building on the critique of traditional approaches, it borrows the strengths and attempts to address the gaps. Using an information economics approach, it is possible to combine a range of concepts and techniques to assess the business value of cloud investments.

Cloud value, therefore, can be seen as a function of many factors which builds on and augments traditional cloud cost–benefit models to establish an enhanced return on investment model. The pertinent factors are illustrated in Fig. 8.2 and are as follows (adapted from Willcocks 2003):

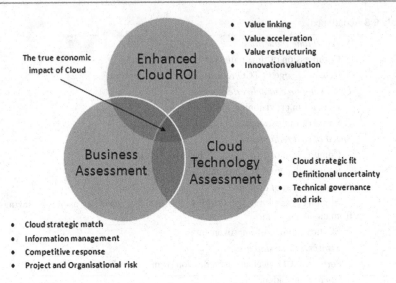

Fig. 8.2 Factors to be considered when calculating cloud cost–benefits

8.15.1   Enhanced Cloud ROI

- *Value linking*. Evaluating cloud costs and indirect benefits such as efficiencies through ripple and knock-on effects across the business value chain.
- *Value acceleration*. Evaluating additional benefits in the form of reduced time and scales for operations.
- *Value restructuring*. Evaluating the benefit of business and process change as a result of cloud adoption. This exercise helps to identify and measure the relationship to business performance.
- *Innovation valuation*. Evaluating the value of gaining and sustaining a competitive advantage whilst calculating the potential risks of cloud.

8.15.2   Business Domain Assessment

- *Cloud strategic match*: matching the business goals and cloud investment
- Competitive advantage: assessing the degree of competitive advantage gained and sustained by adopting cloud model
- *Information management*: assessing the information requirements across the value chain towards the more effective management information needs
- *Competitive response*: assessing the degree of risk and opportunity costs if the cloud option was not delivered
- *Project and organisational risk*: assessing the required competencies, infrastructure and degree of required business change to adopt and leverage cloud

8.15.3 Cloud Technology Assessment

- *Strategic fit*: assessing the degree to which cloud fits into the overall as-is information system architecture and the need to adapt and transition onto the new architecture
- *Definitional uncertainty*: assessing the potential complexities of the cloud venture and unanticipated change
- *Cloud infrastructure risk*: assessing dependencies on new or untried technologies, methodologies and capabilities

Perhaps it is also worth mentioning some of the shortcomings and criticisms of this approach:

- It can be time-consuming.
- Weighting and scoring may be subjective and difficult to justify.
- Results in a truncated risk assessment.

Earlier we explored some of the benefits of cloud such as achieving relative flexibility, cost efficiencies and reduced complexity across systems landscapes, though there are strategic pathways to develop capabilities that deliver the optimum business value. A 2012 study by IBM and Economist Intelligence Unit (Berman et al. 2012) identifies three categories of businesses in relation to their approach to leverage cloud computing for value advantage:

- *Optimisers* are organisations that tap into cloud to fine-tune and incrementally enhance their customer value propositions whilst building in and improving internal and external efficiencies.
- *Innovators* adopt cloud to significantly improve customer value resulting in new revenue streams or even changing their role within an existing industry ecosystem.
- *Disruptors* exploit the cloud to develop new business models and create radically different value propositions, generate new customer needs and segments and even new industry value chains.

These three categories also relate to the cloud investment. Organisations need to balance their investment, risks and return on three categories of investment: transactional investment (optimise the business), strategic investment (innovate and grow) and transformational investment (diversify).

8.16 Summing Up

Cloud computing offers some game-changing opportunities which we have discussed at several points in this text. However, identifying and exploiting the key business enablers to leverage the true value of cloud investment is still at its infancy for most managers.

Investment in cloud needs to be justified against the benefits and business value created. Traditional (financial) approaches to cloud investment appraisals do not fully encapsulate the potential business value that cloud has to offer. This is generally true in case of any IT/IS investment, and cloud technology is not unique from that perspective. There are many benefits management and value driven techniques that are commonly used. These perhaps demonstrate the diversity and complexity of value management and value realisation in the context of cloud investment.

Organisations need to carefully assess and determine how cloud can be leveraged to create sustainable business models for growth and profit. They need to assess the suitability of cloud in light of their core competencies and business value drivers. They need to determine the extent to which they can use the cloud to impact future growth through their differentiated company and industry value chains and customer value propositions. This requires careful consideration of as-is and to-be scenarios of business and technology portfolio as part of strategic planning. Next chapter will focus on strategic planning for cloud.

8.17   Review Questions

The answers to these questions can be found in the text of this chapter.
1. Which stakeholders should be involved in the cloud evaluation process?
2. What is the fundamental cost driver of outsourced software delivery? How might this cost be reduced? Research and list key tangible and intangible costs associated with cloud provision.
3. Critically discuss how CAPEX and OPEX may have a bearing on cloud business model and investment.
4. The value of cloud investments is often justified by understanding costs and using mainly notional figures for benefit realisation. Discuss the reasons for which appraising cloud investment and its contribution to true benefits realisation is so challenging.
5. Research and critically discuss the qualitative and quantitative aspects of a cloud investment business case. Evaluate traditional financial techniques, for example, NPV and ROI, and contrast with a benefits management/realisation approach to evaluating cloud as a business model.

8.18   Extended Study Activities

These activities require you to research beyond the contents of this book and can be approached individually for the purposes of self-study or used as the basis of group work:
1. Develop a holistic framework for investment appraisal of cloud computing. Why is it important to adopt a holistic value-driven investment approach towards cloud computing?
2. Using a spreadsheet, develop a ROI model for cloud investment appraisal that would appeal to an SME. What measurements and ratios would you consider? How would you take account of intangible and qualitative costs and benefits?
3. Develop a simple decision model to help CIO's and IT managers in determining their options for cloud adoption.

References

Berman, S. et al.: The power of cloud, driving business model innovation. IBM Global Business Services Executive Report. IBM Institute for Business Value, IBM Corporation (2012)

Brynjolfsson, E.: Beyond the productivity paradox. Commun. ACM **41**, 49–55 (1998)

Building Return on Investment from Cloud Computing. Cloud Business Artifacts Project, Cloud Computing Work Group, The Open Group www.opengroup.org/cloud/whitepapers/ccroi/ (2010)

Golden, B.: Capex vs. Opex: Most People Miss the Point About Cloud Economics. CXO Media, Inc., Framingham (2009). www.cio.com/article/print/484429. Accessed 15 Nov 2011

Golden, B.: Five Tips for Evaluating the TCO of a Cloud Application. www.techtarget.com; http://searchCloudcomputing.techtarget.com (2011). Accessed 15 Dec 2011

Hayes, R.H., Wheelwright, S.C.: Restoring our Competitive Edge: Competing Through Manufacturing. Wiley, New York (1984)

Mayo, R., Perng, C.: Cloud Computing Payback, An Explanation of Where the ROI Comes From. IBM, Greenford (2009)

Nokes, S.: Taking Control of IT Costs. Prentice Hall, Upper Saddle River (2000)

Willcocks, L.P.: Evaluating the Outcomes of Information Systems Plans, Managing Information Technology Evaluation Techniques and Processes. Butterworth–Heinemann, Oxford (2003)

Enterprise Cloud Computing

9

What the reader will learn:

- What is meant by 'Enterprise Cloud Computing'
- How service-oriented architecture informs cloud organisation
- What the business opportunities offered by a service-oriented enterprise are
- How to use enterprise architecture to leverage the service-oriented enterprise
- How to describe the Business Operations Platform in the context of Enterprise Cloud Computing

9.1   Just What Is Enterprise Cloud Computing?

Enterprise Cloud Computing is the use of cloud computing for competitive advantage. The competitive advantage goes beyond savings in the procurement, management and maintenance of infrastructure, by providing a model of utility computing that enables rapid agility and collaboration capabilities that support business innovation.

First of all, we should consider what 'rapid agility' and 'collaboration capabilities' mean to an enterprise:

1. *CapEx to OpEx.* Adoption of cloud computing enables enterprises to quickly shift fixed costs to variable costs that are tied more directly to usage. If you need more computing power, the cloud will automatically scale upwards and reduce back down when you don't need it any longer.
2. *Lower-risk start-ups.* Since you can draw extra computing resources on demand, you can afford to start innovating more. New business ideas can be tested without having to justify up-front capital expenditure (or losses), and if those ideas take off, you have confidence that the 'limitless' computing utility will not inhibit growth.
3. *Exploit and enhance collaboration.* Enterprises need to interact with other enterprises and customers to do business. The cloud offers easier access to mechanisms that promote collaboration, at ever-increasing levels of business intimacy.

R. Hill et al., *Guide to Cloud Computing: Principles and Practice*, Computer
Communications and Networks, DOI 10.1007/978-1-4471-4603-2_9,
© Springer-Verlag London 2013

Shared services allow a number of enterprises to collaborate and utilise optimised processes, driving down the costs incurred in a value chain, increasing competitive advantage. Indeed, enterprises may adopt a community cloud approach, where they all contribute something to a virtual enterprise; the customer 'sees' a homogeneous company that delivers value, and the individual enterprises that make up the virtual entity derive their own revenue from the part they play.

Clearly, the headline rhetoric of cloud computing promises much, and as we have seen in previous chapters, the way in which existing technologies are orchestrated into a fully functioning cloud is crucial to the successful realisation of added value. What is challenging for the typical enterprise is not the first foray into the cloud; most IT departments will dabble with a noncritical system to test the new capabilities and explore any potential limitations. But it is the next step, when the business case has been made, that an enterprise will face more fundamental questions about how to truly embrace the cloud. What is particularly interesting is that a business case for cloud adoption is fundamentally about business improvement. The repackaging of established technologies as a service-based offering is less about testing the tools and more about exploiting the potential.

As far as an enterprise is concerned, the key concept is *service*. However, whilst Chap. 1 explained that cloud computing was all about computing utility delivered as a service, if an enterprise sees the cloud as yet another service to consume, then the business benefits will be limited. In fact, for many cases the purported savings will not be achieved. *Virtualisation* of your on-premise servers will only deliver tangible efficiency savings if (a) you have enough redundant capacity to aggregate into a useful resource and (b) you have identified sufficient numbers of paying customers to consume your service. On top of this, it's probable that IaaS/PaaS is not core to your business, so you will need to develop experience in this new market, against bigger players like Google and Microsoft (best of luck!).

So what does this mean for enterprises who want to fully exploit the cloud? Well, to reiterate the key concept is still *service*. When we talk about cloud computing, there is an implicit assumption that we are referring to the technologies that support a utilitarian model of IT delivery. However, the focus upon service in the context of Enterprise Cloud Computing is more about what business value can be derived from the innovation potential of the cloud. Therefore, in this chapter we shall start by discussing the concept of *cloud services*.

9.2   Cloud Services

To date, most conversations about cloud computing relate to technical concepts: What the technology is, how it can be specified, when it is useful, how it can be integrated. But as we have seen so far, the notion of cloud as a utility suggests that we should be talking about the business drivers for competitive advantage. As such, cloud computing implies a technological vocabulary. In contrast with this, cloud services frame the conversation around the *use of technology* for business advantage. Enterprises that want to adopt cloud computing need to be able to represent and coordinate their own functionality as a collection of services, after which a move to the cloud is simplified. We refer to such enterprises as *Service-Oriented Enterprises* (SOE).

9.3 Service-Oriented Enterprise

An SOE exposes its internal business processes as services to other enterprises. To do this, an SOE must have a definitive understanding of the business functionality it offers and can describe this functionality as value-driven services. An SOE also understands that services are rarely static and that new opportunities for value creation are occurring all of the time. This understanding manifests itself in a business architecture that makes specific demands of an IT architecture, such that the services are assembled from reusable components, to suit the current need. As new requirements emerge, new services are configured and deployed from the reusable building blocks of business functionality.

The exposure of these services deepens the relationship between collaborating enterprises, whilst also promoting agility. Rapid shifts in market demand can be accommodated easier, with the associated benefits being shared between collaborating enterprises. So far this description is of an organisational entity that is acutely aware of the business drivers, the nature of these drivers and the financial impact of engaging with the drivers (or not). The response to this has to be an IT architecture that can deliver 'rapid agility' and 'collaboration capabilities' through a service-enabled infrastructure. Cloud architectures provide the elasticity and utility that underpins the requirements of a service-based approach.

You might now be wondering what is the actual difference that cloud architecture brings. After all, the IT industry has spent the past 10 years trying to adopt *Service-Oriented Architecture* (SOA), and it sounds as if this is what an SOE needs. The difference is explained again by the vocabulary that is adopted. SOA has transformed the re-engineering of back-office systems, enabling faster and more flexible opportunities to integrate increased numbers of disparate IT systems, often by centralising and sharing services. Thus, it is essentially a technology-driven transformation.

Cloud services, on the other hand, are about deriving value from customer-facing *front-office* interactions. The external facing interactions create an immediate need for response both in terms of existing service delivery as well as new service composition to enable differentiation in the marketplace. This is a business-driven transformation that mandates rapid agility and collaboration, thus suggesting the adoption of the cloud. This is not to say that SOA is inappropriate for the design of cloud services. But the drivers that define the decomposition of business functionality into services fundamentally alter the way in which SOA is utilised to embrace the cloud.

9.3.1 Realising the Service-Oriented Enterprise

As new business markets emerge, the legacy silos that were created to deliver value through efficiency are starting to limit future growth. Systems are added to and held together with bespoke program code that requires specialist maintenance. Large systems such as *Enterprise Resource Planning* (ERP) and *Customer Relationship Management* (CRM) tend to be tightly coupled to the functionality that an organisation offers. Indeed, in many cases an enterprise has changed its way of doing business to suit the IT system, which is rapidly becoming unacceptable for customers who just want excellent service. As a result, an overhead is generated purely by the operation and customisation of legacy systems that ultimately limit the free cash that can be invested towards innovative activities.

The emergence of the World Wide Web, together with its associated standards for interoperability, is driving the creation of systems that can now aspire to be service oriented. Web services are an example of a technology standard that facilitates a more flexible IT architecture, by using open standards for inter-service communication. Of course, as a technology standard, web services don't help an enterprise specify its services, but they are a fundamental part of the solution.

We should now observe that some characteristics of an SOE are starting to emerge. First of all, an SOE can change the internal services that it offers externally, quickly, in response to customer demand. Secondly, an SOE is not constrained by its back-office IT architecture, though it might incorporate useful legacy functions as required by the needs of the business. Finally, it uses open communication standards to facilitate interoperability between all services, whether they are internal or external to the enterprise.

The reality is that most enterprises have these characteristics as goals rather than as a description of the current state. Changes to IT systems invariably are driven by an impetus to increase efficiency and reduce costs by rationalising technical functionality. This isn't necessarily a bad goal to pursue, but it is the approach that is taken that may impede future potential.

For instance, the IT Director may see cloud as a means of reducing IT staffing costs. Simply outsource the internal repositories to data centre. At a stroke, the management of the systems is delegated to a supplier and operational costs are reduced. However, aside from scalability of the existing infrastructure, what contribution has this made to the future development of innovative systems?

The legacy systems have not been specified as services, so any new customer requirements will require re-engineering. This, of course, also maintains a requirement to maintain any bespoke program code that exists. So, the cloud characteristic of rapid agility is only satisfied in part, and it relates to the back-office capabilities, not the front-office, customer-facing part of the system. As far as collaboration is concerned, this has not been achieved. The technological infrastructure has become more optimised, but the business stays the same.

Therefore, the adoption of Enterprise Cloud Computing, through cloud services, requires not only a technical shift but also a cultural shift. It is all about considering the needs of the business and being in a fit and agile state that is ready to exploit new opportunities as and when they arrive. This new mindset assumes continuous change and that the enterprise needs to take a process-centric view of its operations. The traditional, project-based approach to IT systems change is just too restrictive for today's marketplace. Project management is too focused upon delivering static objectives, which, due to the size of most IT projects, results in the objectives having changed over time. What is required is an approach that embraces emergent outcomes, by engineering incremental changes into the operations of the enterprise.

9.4   Enterprise Architecture

The collaboration potential offered by cloud services means that it is now feasible to develop deep relationships with both customers and other businesses. Such collaboration opens up channels of communication that should lead to more optimised service delivery, through constant review and enhancement. Processes will be tailored to specific need, yet delivered through carefully orchestrated internal services. To manage this requires an approach that has process change at its core, such that the continuous change is managed, supervised and exploited as required. *Enterprise Architecture* (EA) is a means by which the traditional technological hurdles are removed and replaced with open standards for enterprise interoperability. EA uses continuous improvement to build-in agility and responsiveness into an IT architecture, whilst retaining the focus of serving the needs of the business.

When we think of architecture, we typically consider buildings. A simplistic view of architecture is that it is the practice of arranging entities and the relationships between those entities. An architect represents ideas through drawings, plans and models. The same can be said of an enterprise's IT infrastructure. It comprises many different entities, often with complex arrangements and relationships between those entities. The representation of that architecture may exist, or it may not. The collection of entities may have evolved over a period of time, in response to technical demands or in response to a business need that has been identified. Here is the crux of the topic; the representation of the IT entities and their connections needs to be aligned with the business needs of the enterprise. Thus, EA is more than a description of an enterprise's IT architecture; it is a process of change that includes a description of how the system will evolve to meet the needs of a future state. In EA language, the future is described as the 'to be' state. Unfortunately, for many enterprises, the 'as is' state is characterised by the following:

- Information about customers or process performance is difficult to access, making management decision-making difficult.
- Knowledge workers must interrogate a number of different systems to enable them to make inferences on a daily basis.
- Processes are duplicated and not optimised for efficiency.
- It is impossible to quantify the value that the IT systems provide.
- Processes are not agile and customisation is a lengthy and expensive process.
- Answers to queries vary depending upon which part of the enterprise is questioned.

EA thinking promotes the enterprise as a holistic entity, whose single purpose is to derive value from offering services to customers. There is nothing new in this of course, but it is the way that this is devolved as an 'outside-in' approach that sets EA apart from more traditional methods of transforming IT. As such, EA is as much a product as it is a process. The artefacts created during the process of documenting the existing (as is) IT architecture, as well as the strategic goals that the 'to be' state will successfully achieve, constitute the *product*. The *process* is the means by which the architecture is transformed by a combination of strategic, management, operational and technical decisions, usually under the guidance of an EA framework.

9.4.1   Enterprise Architecture Frameworks

Since enterprises are typically complex, the move towards a more business-driven architecture is often very challenging. Whilst the abstract view of an enterprise can improve strategic focus, the underlying detail and complexity has to be dealt with if the agile, collaborative organisation is to be realised. In recognition of this, a number of frameworks have been developed that aim to assist enterprise architects develop and maintain a more agile 'to be' state. The most prevalent frameworks referred to are:

- *Zachman Framework*. John Zachman pioneered the thinking that technology needs to be aligned with business, and thus a process for developing this coupling was required. This influential work was adopted by the United States of America's Department of Defense and was implemented as the Technical Architecture for Information Management (TAFIM).
- *Federal Enterprise Architecture Framework (FEA)*. The United States Federal Government developed their own interpretation of EA, again using Zachman's work as the inspiration.
- *The Open Group Architecture Framework (TOGAF®)*. This came about after the TAFIM framework was given to The Open Group (http://www3.open-group.org/).
- *The Oracle Enterprise Architecture Framework*. Oracle developed their own EA framework from a hybrid of TOGAF, FEA and others.
- *SAP Enterprise Architecture Framework (SAP EAF)*. SAP used TOGAF as the basis of a framework that is contextualised within an SAP environment.

In practice, the predominance of Oracle and SAP systems worldwide, together with the fact that most large systems need to interface to many small systems, means that TOGAF tends to be the reference approach for EA.

9.4.2   Developing an Enterprise Architecture with TOGAF

The fundamental thrust of TOGAF is that it should be a generic, open framework for architecture development. Whilst other EA frameworks specify architectural deliverables that should be produced, TOGAF places more emphasis upon a method by which deliverables will be produced. This allows TOGAF to be used with any number of specific deliverables that are a requirement for other EA frameworks, thus widening its applicability to all EA scenarios. TOGAF comprises three key components: (1) the Architecture Development Method (ADM), (2) the Enterprise Continuum, and (3) the Resource Base. Of these, the ADM is the fundamental

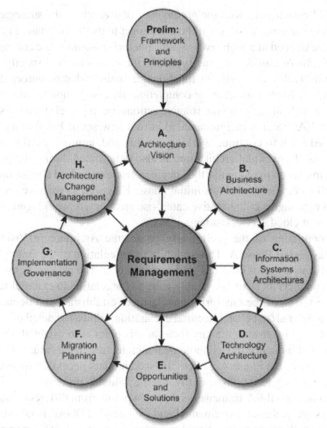

Fig. 9.1 TOGAF architecture development method (ADM) cycle © The Open Group

description of how the framework is utilised. As an enterprise engages with the ADM, architectural artefacts are generated and stored within the Enterprise Continuum. In the meantime, reference documentation and templates are drawn from the Resource Base as the ADM is followed.

9.4.3 The Architectural Development Method (ADM)

An enterprise architect will spend most of their time navigating each of the stages of the ADM. The method is cyclical, and it is anticipated that not only will the whole cycle be iterated, but individual stages will need to be repeated as necessary. Iteration is a deliberate intention of the ADM; stages are not always completed at their first attempt, and repetition and refinement encourages reflection and evaluation of work done. Figure 9.1 illustrates the ADM cycle in its entirety.

The ADM commences with the *preliminary phase*, where the strategic aims are used to define the approach that will be used to get to the 'to be' state. Fundamental principles are defined at a high level, as any enterprise would at the commencement of a programme of transformation. Typically, the enterprise will specify the scope of the activity (entire enterprise or functional domain), what resources it wants to dedicate and the likely timescale for completion. By completion we are referring to the point at which all of the transformative actions are in place, since the successful adoption of EA requires maintenance akin to a new set of behaviours that must be embedded for it to continue working. To this end, control and the subsequent governance of the eventual architecture is also determined during the preliminary phase. It is important to recognise that an enterprise may indeed choose not to adopt a cloud architecture as part of this initial phase. However, as we have seen so far, a desire for a more agile, collaborative enterprise architecture would tend to advocate the adoption of cloud services at least.

Upon completion of the preliminary phase, the Architecture Vision is then developed as part of Phase A. This vision is an articulation of the strategic aims of the enterprise in terms of business goals and mission. The principles by which the enterprise conducts its business, strategic drivers in relation to external factors and the ultimate vision of the enterprise are clarified, established and documented by way of an 'as is' and 'to be' architectural declaration. Whilst the detail of the existing architecture may be absent, the key focus at this point is to establish the business drivers that will influence the technological architecture in the future. There is also the added benefit that Phase A gathers the stakeholders necessary to discuss business and technology as a holistic entity, itself a valuable process.

It is common to all EA frameworks that viewpoints from different collections of stakeholders are gathered, documented and evaluated. TOGAF is no different and considers the following organisational groupings:

- *Business architecture.* What is the strategy? How will the business be governed? What are the business processes required to deliver the strategy?
- *Data architecture.* What are the logical and physical data structures? How is data managed through the enterprise?
- *Applications architecture.* What specific application architectures are already in place? How are applications related to key business processes?
- *Technology architecture.* What software and hardware standards are utilised? What is the network topology/organisation/management? Which middleware technologies are in use?

After Phase A is deemed complete, Phase B is concerned with the *business architecture.* Phase C considers both the *data architecture* and the *applications architecture.* Finally, Phase D considers the *technology architecture.* Each phase has a set of guideline artefacts to produce, ensuring that sufficient documentation is generated upon which informed decisions can be made. The *opportunities and solutions* stage (Phase E) is used to define the activities required for implementation, such as projects in different domains. This work is detailed enough to specify what the actual activities are. Subsequently, Phase F (*migration planning*) is then used to schedule the implementation projects into a practical order, recognising the availability of resources and placing the implementation into the context of normal business operations. Phase G (*Implementation Governance*) is concerned with the overall management of all of the implementation activity. Phase H, the final stage in the ADM cycle deals with the processes by which any ensuing change will be managed. Central to all of the phases is that of *requirements management*, which during a traditional transformation project is likely to change as the new architecture matures. However, if we think about the opportunities afforded by cloud services, we can see that the ability to change and respond to requirements is a desirable trait of an SOE, so we should expect the requirements to remain dynamic and central to all of our architectural activities.

The Enterprise Continuum is a collection of architectural artefacts that have been produced as a result of engaging with the ADM, as well as artefacts from outside of the enterprise. The actual artefacts are varied, but they typically include relevant documents from the enterprise, data models, specifications, strategic documents, etc. This is augmented with external artefacts such as other architecture specifications, design patterns and examples of best practice from other enterprises. Together, these artefacts form a rich repository of information, experience and inspiration that can be reused as applicable within an emerging architectural specification. Experienced enterprise architects can also use the Enterprise Continuum as an indicator of architectural maturity; how far has the transformation progressed from the initial iterations of the ADM?

All of the activities of the ADM are supported by the *Resource Base*, which sets out the guiding principles of enterprise architecture through documented standards, methods, processes and case studies. Additionally there is guidance on the staff skills required to contribute towards an EA transformation.

The adoption of EA should be seen as a key enabler of business value realisation. In terms of Enterprise Cloud Computing, it is necessary to embrace the concept of cloud services and facilitate an approach whereby the enterprise scrutinises its operations from the outside-in. An SOE is achieved by understanding that agility and collaboration must be designed into the fabric of an enterprise, by engaging in architectural principles that will enable the enterprise to adapt and exploit emerging business opportunities. So if we have a flexible architecture in mind, how do we realise it with the cloud?

9.5 Building on Top of SaaS

Elsewhere in this book we have discussed the three service models of cloud computing: infrastructure as a service (IaaS), platform as a service (PaaS) and software as a service (SaaS). We also briefly introduced a fourth service model in Chap. 1 (illustration repeated in Fig. 9.2): business process as a service (BPaaS). To understand why BPaaS might be important, we should first consider how an SOE enables a brighter business future. To quickly recap, an SOE:

- Exposes its internal services to an external marketplace.
- Can change its services rapidly to help optimise the business operations.

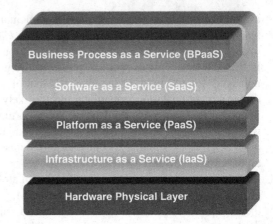

Fig. 9.2 The Cloud stack
extended by business process
as a service (BPaaS)

- Uses open standards for communication between its internal and external services.
- Facilitates enhanced collaboration with customer and business partners.
- Uses the concept of EA to embed a culture of continuous change and to deliver competitive advantage now and in the future.

We have discovered so far that these characteristics are best achieved by the adoption of service orientation. The declaration of business functionality from an external perspective makes our services more adaptable to the emerging needs of customers and avoids the shackles that an internal service-based perspective might present.

As we architect a new vision of business that is facilitated by technology, it becomes apparent that IaaS, PaaS and even SaaS cannot offer what an enterprise truly seeks. SaaS is effectively pre-packaged applications that are made available over the Internet, offered on a multi-tenancy, pay-per-use delivery model. The application might be an ERP or CRM 'solution' that negates the need for an enterprise to own and manage significant on-premise resources. But these solutions are still limited by silo, application-based thinking, whereas the SOE, as we describe it, needs the flexibility to be able to reconfigure and extend itself as new business opportunities emerge. Thus, we have the need for a fourth layer that enables end-to-end business processes to be created and managed.

BPaaS is a more horizontal approach that is concerned with process fulfilment through service orchestration. Considering that the typical value chain can contain upwards of ten different suppliers, competitive advantage is more likely to be gained by providing a mechanism that supports deeper collaboration between the different suppliers, rather than attempting to package together a one-size-fits-all solution. One advantageous aspect of this approach is that it directly facilitates the *emergence* of processes, as each contributor optimises their own contribution, and is therefore a key enabler for those enterprises who view the business opportunity as an architectural challenge rather than a self-contained project.

It follows that BPaaS is a logical extension of a service-oriented architecture that, in turn, is delivered by a service-oriented infrastructure. It is also logical to deduce that a service-oriented infrastructure is to all intents and purposes a cloud-oriented infrastructure. Therefore, to maximise the potential of the cloud requires an organisation to transform itself into an SOE.

9.6 Managing a Process-Centric Architecture

An enterprise that recognises the need to declare and expose its functionality as services has made the conscious decision to focus on the front office of the business. The customer wants service and interacts with process. Business people understand what the processes should deliver and how this might be achieved, but pressure exerted from decades of traditional, centralised IT systems often means that both customers and front-office personnel are frustrated. This is often compounded by processes which are obscure or hidden; information regarding process performance may be absent or difficult to obtain, reinforcing the divide between business and IT functions.

Enterprise Application Integration (EAI) has been an attempt to 'glue' disparate systems together, often resulting in message routing/brokering systems that serve as an interface between heterogeneous applications. These, by nature, tend to be very technical solutions as the myriad differences in message-passing protocols are mapped against differing database schema. This all results in considerable effort expended to connect the systems together and a reluctance to revisit the customisation if a process already works. In short, enhancement is too difficult and expensive to achieve. On top of this, the solution is too technical for business people to engage with, or even understand, so the process if left alone or new, informal systems to circumvent the problem are created.

Whilst there have been attempts to bridge the business/IT gap, the technology and how it is packaged has genuinely created challenges so great that the divide has been embedded into the fabric of enterprises. The advent of web services has enabled workflow systems to break free from proprietary standards, thus enabling disparate systems to be connected together with a common language for invocation. What has been lacking, however, is a generalised platform that is abstracted away from the detail, but which allows interoperation through open standards.

9.6.1 Business Operations Platform

Orchestration is a key concept for the management of business processes. An enterprise that has clearly defined (cloud) services needs to have an architectural layer that allows business people to maintain, modify and create new business processes from the services that exist. Indeed, an SOE that maintains relationships with other external SOEs can also make use of their services to complete a value chain. The orchestration layer thus decouples business process management from the underlying technical, transaction level of the IT systems. A *Business Operations Platform* (BOP) serves not only as an orchestration layer to represent system complexity as business processes, but also as a performance monitoring dashboard for the enterprise. Process performance can be assessed and evaluated, and quickly reconfigured for the purposes of optimisation, from the perspective of the customer. This alone differentiates BOP as part of a BPaaS solution from SaaS, since the SaaS users can only offer the services that the SaaS application provides. SaaS offers little scope for differentiation in the marketplace, whereas BOP offers the ultimate scope to exploit new trends.

So we can see that a BOP improves the agility of an enterprise, but what about collaboration? One significant advantage of a BOP is the way in which an enterprise can collaborate with its partners or customers to tailor and optimise a business process. Since the BOP facilitates process enhancement, an enterprise can actively seek out ways in which the process can offer a customer or supplier a better service. The changes can then be made easily (by business people, not a change request submitted to the IT department) and the benefits realised much quicker. Whilst this in itself would offer substantial advantages for many enterprises, there is also the ability to exploit this in a more entrepreneurial way.

Throughout this book there are examples of how the elasticity of the cloud can facilitate the prototyping of innovative business ideas. However, the examples usually relate to existing applications that may require extra resource if they become popular. A new e-commerce website is one such venture. If an enterprise has adopted a cloud services architecture that is orchestrated by a BOP, then there is now the capability to rapidly assemble business processes for a particular purpose or event. In fact there may be something occurring in the near future that will create new opportunities to conduct business (such as the Olympic Games being hosted in a country) that could be better exploited with bespoke business processes. After the event closes the processes may never be used again, but the speed with which they can be configured means that for a minimal investment (time), new business can be generated. These developments have the capabilities to turn business entities into different beasts; services are offered and consumed that may not directly relate to the original purpose of the business. Who would have thought that Amazon, the online book seller, would eventually be offering a cloud-based e-commerce platform as part of its business model?

9.6.2 Even More Agility

Since a cloud architecture can provide the illusion of 'unlimited' resource, and an SOE can orchestrate its services to form business processes that are relevant to customer value chains, then the natural extension to this is to provide automation. Back in Chap. 1, we saw that one of the technologies that has helped make the cloud delivery model work is that of autonomic computing. Along with virtualisation, this is one of the critical mechanisms behind dynamic provisioning that enables the cloud to appear homogeneous and limitless, from an infrastructure that comprises many discrete servers. If a cloud provider sees that demand is increasing, the autonomic control software manages the allocation of extra computing resource to suit the new demand.

Similarly an SOE with a BOP has already identified the core services that are to be offered, and the BOP already has mappings from internal and external (partner) services onto end-to-end business processes. Automation can now assist in two ways.

First, new instances of established processes can be dynamically provisioned for use with new customers. Secondly, and perhaps more innovatively, existing processes can be modified at run-time. This means that an end-to-end business process that has started can have services replaced and augmented during the execution of the process. This is made possible by using the data gathered by the BOP to act as an environmental sensor – what is happening in the marketplace – which then optimises the process accordingly. This is the true realisation of orchestration, without human intervention.

Autonomic orchestration has particular value when processes emerge in a market, and therefore the preliminary use cases and alternate use cases have not been ascertained yet. From a systems perspective, this opens up the possibility of goal-driven services, where business people delegate their goals for cloud services to achieve.

As we introduce flexibility into our systems, enterprises will be required to become more comfortable with emergent outcomes and system complexity. Such environments need businesses that can adapt in rapid, rational ways, and the two fundamental aspects of Enterprise Cloud Computing – rapid agility and collaboration – will undoubtedly change the way that business is conducted.

9.7 Summary

Business is becoming more about faster change and adaptability. The cloud can assist this transformation by building responsiveness into the IT architecture of a business, through engagement with *Enterprise Architecture*. Rapid service construction for cloud-based applications can only be effectively realised if there is a service-based approach to the design of business processes. The business realisation of services is through the understanding and implementation of *processes*; for this to harness the elasticity and scalability characteristics of the cloud, it requires processes to be described and mapped to services that can be adapted at run-time. Thus, a *Service-Oriented Enterprise* is best placed to exploit fully the benefits of the cloud. Business owners will need to represent their business operations in such a way that the dynamic capabilities of the cloud can be translated into services that are elastic and scalable. If we move our existing business applications to the cloud without understanding the potential of a service-oriented enterprise, then we can only achieve cost reductions in relation to infrastructure management at best. The cloud is already a collection of services that are ready for exploitation, and through business process *orchestration*, enterprises can use this to develop and offer more modular, flexible ways of service fulfilment.

9.8 Review Questions

The answers to these questions can be found in the text of this chapter.
1. Describe the key characteristics of a service-oriented enterprise by way of example cloud services.
2. Briefly discuss the impact of SOA upon enterprise architecture and explain what is meant by the 'outside-in' approach.

3. Compare the concepts of Service-Oriented Enterprise with Service-Oriented Architecture.
4. Describe BPaaS and illustrate with an example how different cloud service models are utilised.

9.9   Extended Study Activities

These activities require you to research beyond the contents of this book and can be approached individually for the purposes of self-study or used as the basis of group work:

1. You have been asked to lead an EA project using TOGAF. What strategic information and documentation would you seek as part of the preliminary phase? Prepare a checklist of items to consider.
2. You are investigating an end-to-end value chain that consists of three separate enterprises. Prepare a case for the adoption of cloud services and identify any risks that will affect their successful implementation. For each risk identified, describe a mitigating action that may prevent the risk from adversely affecting the project.

References

Mulholland, J.A., Pyke, J., Fingar, P.: Enterprise Cloud Computing: A Strategy Guide for Business and Technology Leaders. Meghan-Kiffer Press (2010). ISBN 0929652290
Sapir, J.: Power in the Cloud: Building Information Systems at the Edge of Chaos. Meghan-Kiffer Press (2009). ISBN 0929652312

Cloud Security and Governance

10

What the reader will learn:

- The nature of security risks surrounding public cloud services
- Approaches to mitigate against security risks
- That data in the cloud can be secure
- Why IT governance is important for cloud computing

10.1 Introduction

Information Technology is so pervasive now that it is difficult to imagine doing business without it. Organisations record their transactions in databases and save their documents in networked file storage. Some of that information is crucial for competitive advantage, so clearly the security of that information is important. Every day, organisations expend more funds to secure their IT operations, whether it be physical security (swipe card access to underground server bunkers), technological security (encryption) or process security (policies). With all this investment in place, why would any organisation even consider giving away the responsibility of managing their data, when you don't know where it will reside, and you can only access it over an Internet connection?

This chapter attempts to explain what the key concerns of an organisation should be and identifies the typical questions that an organisation should ask of a cloud provider. The discussion is placed in the context of a public cloud infrastructure, which is deemed to be the most stringent test of any security strategy for an organisation.

The prospect of introducing cloud-provisioned resources can strike fear into the management of IT departments. First of all, it can seem insecure. Second of all, it might bring to the surface existing vulnerabilities that need tackling before anything is deployed to the cloud. In fact, cloud security should be approached in a similar way to cloud migration in general; ensure that you have prepared the ground properly with your existing infrastructure. As we can see in Chap. 9 (Enterprise Cloud

R. Hill et al., *Guide to Cloud Computing: Principles and Practice*, Computer
Communications and Networks, DOI 10.1007/978-1-4471-4603-2_10,
© Springer-Verlag London 2013

Computing), the business value of cloud computing cannot be realised unless a service-oriented view to systems development is adopted. Similarly, a poorly secured infrastructure will become a remote set of vulnerabilities if it is moved to the cloud. Whilst cloud services bring new security issues to consider, it is essential to have an effective strategy in place beforehand.

Since cloud computing is about services, there is a temptation to delegate excessive responsibility to the cloud providers. Each cloud provider will have their own practices, which may or may not operate harmoniously with an enterprise's existing operations. If an enterprise finds itself in a situation where the strategy it uses is ineffective, there may be serious repercussions if some legislation is breached. Just because the systems management has been devolved to a cloud service provider does not necessarily mean that the responsibility has been devolved along with it. Again, referring to the concept of Enterprise Cloud Computing (Chap. 9), we observe that the key driver must be the business case. If the business case relies upon secure data, then cloud computing is a means of outsourcing the technology, not the business responsibility. It is incumbent upon the enterprise to ensure that the cloud provider has the correct policies, procedures and practices in place. Thus, strategy for the adoption of cloud services must have explicit links with an over-arching security strategy for the enterprise. Indeed for the Service Oriented Enterprise, such a strategy would be a component part of the Enterprise Architecture.

10.2   Security Risks

Not all cloud providers are the same, so it is important to understand the risks of inadequate security so that an enterprise can make an informed judgement about what, if any, information should be trusted to the cloud.

Since the actual risks to a system are varied, an enterprise typically takes a generalised approach to security and then manages exceptions separately, for instance, identity management; it is usual for an employee to require a user identity for access to a system when on the organisation's premises. But this access has a different set of potential vulnerabilities if the employee is working at home or in the field. These specific situations might not apply to the cloud provider, who will by default create security strategies that are relevant for that type of business. The individual security mechanisms that a number of applications use may not transfer easily to a cloud environment, and therefore, a detailed understanding of the approach taken towards security is required if further, unintended vulnerabilities are not to be introduced. This situation is not new; organisations have been outsourcing data storage and telephone call centres for some time now. What is different about cloud, however, is the depth of the infrastructure that is being entrusted into the cloud. Both data storage and customer care management are discrete, vertical functions that have been devolved to third parties. The devolvement of infrastructure/applications/services is a horizontal function that contains the heart of the organisation's operations.

Such is the potential complexity of the situation that enterprises adopt a risk-based approach to security. This is where controls are prioritised towards areas where security risks are the most damaging. One part of a risk-based approach is to ensure that service-level agreements (SLA) are in place. However, SLAs are often used to protect the supplier, not the customer, again underlining the importance of understanding the security detail so that the requirements are catered for properly. So, even though you may be impressed with the physical security during the sales tour of the cloud provider's premises, it is still your responsibility to ensure that all of the other aspects of security are assured as well.

Access control is an example of perimeter security. Without an account and a password, you cannot penetrate the perimeter of the network. This assumes though, that those who have an account are honest and trustworthy. Unfortunately, most breaches in security are the result of employees who have legitimate access, and they are rarely detected. These internal threats don't go away if you move to the cloud, unless the cloud provider offers a more secure service that you can utilise, that adds protection over and above what you are currently using.

When dealing with security, it helps to be paranoid. Migrating systems to the cloud might increase the headcount of people who have access to your data, so your security strategy must have a provision to deal with threats from the inside. Whilst virtualisation is seen as an example of a specific technology that has enabled the cloud delivery model to become workable, it also complicates the demands placed upon a security strategy as servers, storage and even networks are now executing in virtual environments. Rather than the traditional risk of an employee divulging a password or snooping around a system, an employee of a cloud provider might only have to provide access to the virtualisation layer for havoc to be wreaked. In fact, if we consider the elasticity function of a cloud resource, any hacker would have plenty of compute resource to use for nefarious purposes if granted some access to a cloud.

The provision of IT security is a challenge, and the effort required to do it can make the migration to cloud appear an attractive one if it reduces the hassle. However, the enterprise is placing trust in its provider and needs to assure itself that the provider's capabilities are at least as good as the current architecture. Another factor is that today's IT systems are complex and becoming even more intricate and bespoke. The traditional model of security is to define a hard security perimeter (usually around the data centre) and monitor all inbound and outbound traffic. The problem with multi-tenant clouds is that all sorts of traffic will be present at the access point, and in fact another enterprise's traffic might be deemed as hostile, even though the public cloud architecture is designed to have multiple sets of data coexisting in one virtual appliance. This arrangement means that it is meaningless to have systems in place that can both monitor and proactively protect against potential breaches. The system has to be secure at the point of access.

The reality is that breaches happen, and then enterprises need to quickly plug the hole, trying to understand what went wrong afterwards. In the case of serious breaches, the default behaviour might be to shut a system down completely, which is massively disruptive for a business. Finally, when an enterprise is choosing a potential cloud provider, it may find it difficult to assess a candidate supplier, since they don't release details of their internal services for the purposes of maintaining security.

10.3 Some Awkward Questions

The main purpose of any interaction with a potential cloud provider is to establish whether their security strategy is harmonious with a particular enterprise. This becomes more difficult as an enterprise moves up the cloud computing stack. For instance, if an enterprise is seeking IaaS, then all of the OS security upwards is the responsibility of the enterprise, not the cloud provider. If PaaS is required, then there is some responsibility for the provider to ensure that the OS and platform layers are secure, but again, role-based permissions that are part of the application layer are ultimately the responsibility of the consuming enterprise. This becomes more complex if access control is associated with OS-level security. For SaaS, the provider maintains the access to the application, but access within the application may be managed by the customer.

Again, this becomes ever more complicated as external services are consumed, thus reinforcing the need to understand security in the context of an SOE, before a cloud migration takes place. A solid implementation of security in a service-based environment is much easier to transfer to the cloud, irrespective of the level in the stack that is required. The key concept here is to establish where the boundary of trust exists between the consumer and the provider. This needs establishing up front to prevent costly confusion in the future. Table 10.1 illustrates some pertinent issues to raise with a potential cloud provider.

Chapter 2 introduced the model proposed by the Jericho security forum of the Open Group (Fig. 2.2), which succinctly illustrates the concept of de-perimeterisation. Modern SOEs require secure architectures that protect even when internal services are exposed to third parties. This creates a significant challenge for enterprise architects and application developers who cannot rely on a fixed, hardened security perimeter. Every way into an application or system service has to be individually protected.

10.4 Good Practice for Secure Systems

As described above, a move to a cloud provider means that an enterprise will have to establish a level of trust with the provider. The process of building trust involves open communication and sufficient understanding on the part of the enterprise, to ask the pertinent questions. We shall now consider six key functional areas of security, in order to derive a checklist of security fundamentals that must be present before migrating to a public cloud (ENISA 2010; Intel 2011):

- Identity management
- Network security

Table 10.1 Security risk areas to consider when selecting a potential public cloud provider

Issue	Questions for potential public cloud providers
Architecture	Is the provider's security architecture available for scrutiny? What is the architecture for access management?
Risk assessment	Do you utilise an independent authority to assess and monitor security risks?
Legislation, compliance and governance	What controls do you have in place to ensure that domain specific legislation is complied with?
Information location	Where will the information reside?
Segregation	Will the applications/tools be shared with other tenants? Which application/tools will be shared?
Service level	What service level is to be guaranteed and what measures are in place for access to data during downtime? What is the scope of any penalties for downtime/loss of access?
Portability	What standards are employed to guarantee data/application/tools/process portability?
Physical security	To what standard is physical security provided?
Management tools	How are software updates and patches managed to minimise service disruption? What monitoring tools are provided?
Perimeter security	What controls are in place for firewalls and the management of Virtual Private Network (VPN) access?
Encryption	What standards for encryption are in place? How are public keys managed? How is single sign-on (SSO) implemented?

- Data security
- Instance security
- Application architecture
- Patch management

10.4.1 Identity Management

The first area is that of identity management. The nature of cloud services means that identity management is paramount if end users can securely access the services that they need to do their jobs. Since we anticipate a user to be interacting with a business process that is composed of one or more cloud services (for more detail on business processes and services, see Chap. 9, Enterprise Cloud Computing), we wouldn't expect the user to have to manage separate access details for each separate service that was invoked. In fact, in a web browser environment (the default interface for cloud services), this would be particularly dangerous as users would simply let their passwords be saved for convenience. So, along comes another person, who does not have access to the payroll reports, and they use a computer where the passwords have been saved in the web browser. Chaos ensues! Single sign-on (SSO) is one example of a system where user identities are managed across a number of separate systems. The user signs in with their account, and they are automatically authorised to access business processes that they have been granted permission for. Behind the scenes this needs a role-based permission system so that access rights can be quickly assembled, maintained and revoked, for individuals and en masse. An additional benefit is that all users of the services benefit from the simplification of SSO, which in an SOE setting means the suppliers as well.

The IT department also finds that SSO assists the management of user profiles in that, firstly, they won't have to manage individual accounts on a per-service basis (a lot of work) and, secondly, much of the account maintenance can be automated. For example, a default set of identities can be created for a number of job functions, which can be automatically provisioned for new users. These may either be suitable already or can be augmented with other capabilities quickly. This of course, reinforces the need to have a comprehensive understanding of a service-based architecture, in relation to the business that is being conducted. Once an identity management mechanism is in place, account migration to the cloud is simplified.

10.4.2 Network Security

Network security is of course an important concern for any corporate, distributed system. The one issue that a move to a cloud brings is the fact that an enterprise's application network traffic is transported along with every other application's network traffic. This means that packets that are exchanged between secure access points are mingling with packets that are exchanged between less secure applications. Whilst cloud providers appear to segregate network traffic by utilising virtual local area networks (VLAN), the separation is virtual (as the name implies), and therefore, at packet level, the traffic is still mixed and shares the same cable. So, the sensitive accounts data for payroll is present on the network, along with the (relatively) less sensitive sales figures for the last quarter.

This data can't be accessed without the correct permissions, but it does mean that an employee with network administration rights could, with a bit of work, have sight of the confidential information, even though they would not have any operational need to do so. The traditional model of security in this case has relied on trust, but in the context of a cloud environment (where the network administrator is not directly on your payroll), there is a need to actively control exactly who has access to what.

Since cloud adoption means that an enterprise has devolved all responsibility for the infrastructure, it is not possible to build a private, physical network, nor is it good practice to trust the honesty of a VLAN administrator. The solution in this case is to provide end-to-end encryption of data packets, between authorised applications. The fear of packets coexisting with other packets has much greater ramifications when the owner of the other packets might be a competitor. This is bound to occur at some point if access to the cloud services is made over publicly shared Internet connections (which they are). It is possible to acquire a private leased line to a cloud provider, but this creates an architecture that is more like a traditional data centre.

At some point an enterprise is going to need access to a service that is outside of this infrastructure. The more comprehensive alternative is to create a Virtual Private Network (VPN) connection to the cloud provider. This can be terminated upon entry to the cloud provider, or for maximum security it can be terminated at the application.

Of course it is rare to get something for nothing. Data encryption is costly in terms of processing overhead and directly increases network latency, reducing throughput performance. It is therefore prudent to consider what data needs encrypting, and what the risks would be if it ever got released publicly. You would expect an enterprise's salary information to be kept private, but a lot of the standard transactional reporting data might be safe enough in a VLAN scenario. It follows that a security risk assessment should be an integral part of the planning for a security strategy.

10.4.3 Data Security

There is no question that data is the key asset of an organisation. Data Security is therefore a fundamental component of the security strategy for a cloud migration. If data is lost, or inaccessible, then the effect can disarm an enterprise. There are many instances where an enterprise suffers a major infrastructure failure and the data is securely backed up somewhere, but the systems cannot be reconstructed quickly enough afterwards, causing revenue losses. One of the apparent comforts of owning your hardware is that you feel in control when disaster strikes. If you delegate this control to a cloud provider, what measures should be taken?

In terms of responsibility, the cloud provider is wholly accountable for the provision and maintenance of hardware. Since a consumer of cloud services no longer has the responsibility for the infrastructure, they need to find a way of dealing with the overall responsibilities associated with managing data security, such as protecting against data theft or malicious change and compliance with legislative measures for the transport, storage and expunging of data.

In terms of data transport, this can be dealt with by utilising VPN mechanisms as described earlier. In terms of data storage, a move to the cloud means that by default external parties now have access to the infrastructure that the data resides on, and by implication, also have access to the data itself. If an enterprise assumes a paranoid stance, then the only option is to encrypt the data and concentrate upon developing a secure mechanism for encryption key management, stored in a place where they cannot be accessed by external parties. The administrators of the cloud provider can of course still see data; it's just that they can't make sense of it.

Whilst the discussion has separated network security from data security, the reality is that they should be considered together when planning the security strategy. A risk assessment will determine which parts of the system must be encrypted, and if transport encryption is required, then the data must be sensitive enough to protect, so storage encryption will be required also. The extent of this security will be determined by what the likely risk of data leakage being, as a trade-off against reduced network performance.

Another major shift in security thinking for cloud deployments is created by the dynamic environment of virtualisation. Traditional approaches to IT security assume a static infrastructure that expands in a planned, orderly way. If more storage is required, it is designed, incorporated into the overall security strategy and then implemented. Security policies are amended if need be, and new procedures commissioned accordingly. Usually the data store is deep within a hardened security perimeter. In terms of off-premise data centres, this is certainly the case.

10.4.4 Instance Security

However, the agile, collaborative environment of the cloud, which exposes internal services for external consumption, which dynamically provisions extra compute and storage resources on demand, is a more challenging beast to tame. An enterprise must now be more concerned with instance security. The secure data store is now a virtual entity, composed of a number of secure repositories that are associated with individual service instances. Whereas the scope of a traditional security model was that of the system to be secured, the scope is now limited to a particular instance, but also is multiplied by the number of instances that are executing at any one time. It follows that centralised management of security is more complex, and more of the security controls require delegating to the individual services themselves. Instance security is provided in the following ways:

1. *Instance-level firewall.* Typically, the cloud provider will provide a firewall for each VLAN that is present. This firewall serves to virtually separate the traffic between user's respective VLANs. Bearing in mind the caveat mentioned earlier that the physical separation of traffic is not implemented with VLANs, it is necessary to ensure that each instance has a firewall to marshall only authorised traffic into the associated virtual machine. As this relates to application security, it is clearly not the responsibility of the cloud provider and therefore may require extra in-house expertise developing on the part of the consuming enterprise. Individual instance firewalls are controlled on a fine-grained basis, and it is likely that different instances will present different requirements. However, this is the maintenance cost of ensuring that only the appropriate data is passed onto each instance.

2. *Daemons/background services.* Anyone who has set up an externally exposed server and then 'hardened' the build will be aware of background services that can be exploited by those with malicious intent. Each instance must be assessed to understand what operating system services are required to complete the job and ensure that nothing else is enabled.

3. *Penetration testing.* There are two parts to this activity. First, an audit mechanism should identify if the existing security measures have been properly implemented. The outcome of this might be a list of items that need attention to ensure that the overall security strategy is maintained. Secondly, a series of invasive tests simulate the effects of the instances in response to external attack. These tests place the system under load, which may expose hitherto undetected vulnerabilities. In practice such auditing and testing is at the fringe of the

relationship between an enterprise and a cloud provider, since the provision of shared services to a number of enterprises potentially puts all of them at risk if one particular enterprise starts doing penetration tests. Cloud providers have responded in two ways. The first is to have vulnerability testing as a cloud service (SaaS), which can perform some of the work required. The second approach is to develop in-house penetration capabilities at the cloud provider, who will conduct tests and present a list of recommendations for the enterprise to consider.

4. *Intrusion detection/prevention.* Intrusion Detection Systems (IDS) monitor network traffic and report anomalies in relation to pre-determined security policies. The logs generated can then be used to identify areas that may need hardening, or they may be used as part of a forensic investigation after a breach has occurred. An Intrusion Prevention System (IPS) takes any anomalous behaviour and proactively alters a firewall to prevent a recurrence of the behaviour by stopping the traffic from accessing the instance. For cloud environments, host-based variants of IDS/IPS are required (HIDS/HIPS) for each application instance that consumes external traffic. Again, the extent to which this security measure is deployed will be dependent upon the risk profile produced by the initial assessment.

5. *Application auditing.* There are still cases where unwanted intruders can circumvent network security and gain access to applications. Automated application auditing monitors the applications that are installed and raises an alarm when files are changed. This is often referred to as file change monitoring and can be applied to any application or system files where changes would not normally be expected.

6. *Antivirus.* One approach to prevent viruses or malware being installed is to robustly prevent users from installing applications themselves. However, this does not stop emails being opened, nor in the case of the cloud-based SOE, does it mean that the business partners of an enterprise enforce such policies. In the same way that other vulnerabilities at instance level need to be protected, the same applies to the prevention of malicious programs being allowed to penetrate and infect the service. Each instance should ideally be checked with the latest signature file every time that it is executed to maintain maximum protection. This does create a significant overhead for services that are in frequent use, and therefore, a cloud-based antivirus/malware service may be more appropriate. Such a service ensures that the latest signature files are present, without using the execution of a service to trigger an external check.

In summary, the concept of instance security for cloud services does not so much rely upon new technology, but more a rethink in terms of how existing solutions are deployed.

10.4.5   Application Architecture

A common approach to application architecture is that of separating the architecture into tiers, whereby communication access between tiers is tightly controlled. This serves to constrain any problems in one tier without adversely affecting the other. For instance, a web application tier might be kept separate from the back-office system tier. In between the tiers would be a firewall that restricts the network traffic between the two tiers.

As mentioned earlier in the chapter, the multi-tenant environment of a public cloud prevents physical network infrastructure from being inserted. At best an enterprise could create VLANs, albeit that the network traffic is still physically intermingled.

One approach is to seek out a cloud provider who is willing to allow the user to define subnets as part of the rented infrastructure. This would permit an enterprise to replicate some of its more traditional architecture within a virtualised environment and achieve its desired network topology. Another approach would be to persist with instance-level management and implement tier separation at the instance firewalls. This increases complexity somewhat, but it could be argued that it fits more cohesively with the 'instance approach' to managing security in a robust way by treating each appliance as a discrete service provider.

An alternative option is to adopt the services of a cloud provider to help in the management of security. Some cloud providers are now offering security layers which mimic instance-level firewalls. Such layers are convenient to use, though they have the potential to increase vendor lock-in until more open security standards are developed.

10.4.6 Patch Management

Patch management refers to the constant checking and maintenance of software during its use. As bugs and vulnerabilities are discovered, the corrections may result in software patches that need to be applied. The resourcing and management of software patching is perhaps one of the motivators for considering cloud adoption, since anything relating to the services that are provided will be managed by the cloud provider. SaaS is the best example of fully delegating the responsibility to the provider; for IaaS it only applies to the infrastructure itself, not the systems or services that run on them.

However, one aspect that enterprises should consider is the way in which a cloud provider manages the installation of patches, particularly those cloud providers who originate from a history of being a data centre. Traditionally, images of the system would be created by the data centre, which was a snapshot of a particular instance. This could then be deployed rapidly, without having to build an installation from scratch every time. In the era of rapid provisioning, this means that new images have to be created each time a patch is installed, resulting in lots of images being created. As the cloud computing industry matures, more and more cloud providers will reject this practice and utilise automation to dynamically build instances on top of very basic images. This ensures that the latest software updates are incorporated into the instance but also permits extra instances to be dynamically provisioned to enable service elasticity. Thus, software patches can be kept in one repository (and therefore managed) and be called upon only when they are required.

This is an important issue to consider for an enterprise. The IT department does not want to be investing significant resources into protecting instances, only to find that the instance is built upon an image with a known vulnerability.

10.5 Assessing a Cloud Provider

A report by the European Network and Information Security Agency (ENISA 2009, 'Benefits, Risks and Recommendations for Information Security') suggests the following security risks as being priorities for cloud-specific architectures:

- *Loss of governance*. Governance is complicated by the fact that some responsibilities are delegated to the cloud provider, but the lines of responsibility do not fall across traditional boundaries. These boundaries are less well established and may need to be debated with the cloud provider in terms of what responsibility they will wholly adopt and what responsibility needs to be shared. The traditional approach is to draw up service-level agreements (SLA), though these, without sufficient scrutiny, may leave security gaps.
- *Lock-in*. At the time of writing, there is a lack of consensus with regard to tools, procedures or standard data formats to enable data, application and service portability. Cloud consumers who wish to migrate to other cloud platforms in the future may find the costs too prohibitive, therefore increasing the dependency between a cloud provider and consumer.
- *Isolation failure*. The pooling of computing resources amongst multiple tenants is a classic cloud environment. It is therefore necessary to have mechanisms in place to isolate any failures to the minimum number of instances possible. This can also be the source of a security vulnerability exploit ('guest hopping' attacks), although it is more challenging to successfully attack a hypervisor (where the resource is isolated from the infrastructure) rather than a traditional operating system architecture.
- *Compliance risks*. Enterprises that have invested heavily in the attainment of industry standard or regulatory certification may risk non-compliance if the cloud provider cannot evidence their compliance or if the cloud provider does not permit audit of its own facilities. In practice, this means that certain certifications cannot be achieved or maintained when using public clouds.
- *Management interface compromise*. The web-based customer management interfaces that cloud providers supply are also an extra risk with regard to extra opportunities to compromise a cloud system.
- *Data protection*. An enterprise may not be able to verify how a cloud provider handles its data and therefore cannot establish whether the practices employed are lawful. In the case of federated clouds, where different clouds are linked by a trusted network, this challenge is more complicated. Some cloud providers have achieved certified status with regard to data handling.
- *Insecure or incomplete data deletion*. The request to delete a cloud may not result in the data being completely expunged, and there may be instances when immediate wiping is not desirable. For instance, the disk to be deleted may

contain data from another cloud service consumer. Since the multi-tenant model assumes that hardware will be pooled and shared, the risk of data remaining undeleted is much higher than if the enterprise had ownership of its own hardware.

- *Malicious insider*. The potential damage caused by a malicious insider is much greater when using a cloud provider, purely because of the administrative access that is granted to be able to manage the infrastructure.

Whilst it is desirable to transfer risk to the cloud provider, it is not always practical to do this. Responsibility can be outsourced, but accountability cannot. Bearing in mind that most enterprises do not have the capability to perform large-scale assessments of cloud provider security, there is a tendency to rely upon legal agreements in order that should a breach become evident, the blame (and any compensation) can be clearly directed at the offending party. Such legal agreements make reference to standards or certified evidence that a cloud provider can demonstrate compliance. We shall now consider certification that is applicable to the provision of cloud computing.

10.6   The Need for Certification

It is evident that to stand any chance of successfully evaluating a cloud offering requires considerable expertise. Arguably, the expertise can only be acquired by undertaking the provision of cloud services itself. The nature of IT is that it is a domain that is constantly faced with newly emerging technologies, approaches and models, and therefore it is not atypical to be faced with the business case driving a fundamental change, without fully comprehending the impact that this change is likely to make.

The normal response from the IT industry is to create a body of industrial partners, many of whom will have a vested interest in the products that are on offer (it's usually a technology for sale). Industrial parties are joined by representatives from government or trade bodies and sometimes from regulatory agencies. Once formed, the body works towards a standard that can be used to harmonise the approaches taken towards the adoption of the new technology, including the specification of new products that adhere to the standard. The implementation of a standard makes the process of evaluation, and ultimately comparison with other technologies much more straightforward, and also enables comparisons to be made more effectively with technologies that are clearly different to the standard.

Unfortunately, the standard itself does not mean that an end user is proficient enough to evaluate against it correctly, and there is always the risk of bias affecting any qualitative judgements that have favourable market consequences for the enterprise concerned. This is normally addressed by the use of an impartial third party, who can conduct the evaluation without any vested interest and, through the process of auditing, can certify that a given standard or standards have been complied with. This process is more rigorous in terms of quality assurance and more expedient in that end users are not repeatedly conducting evaluations, an activity that they are not practiced at.

Table 10.2 Some common IT certification standards that are relevant to cloud computing provision

Standard	Remit
Control Objectives for Information and Related Technology (COBIT)	A set of process declarations that describe how IT should be managed by an organisation
National Institute of Standards and Testing (NIST) SP 800-53	The quality assurance of secure information provision to US government agencies, being audited against the Federal Information Security Management Act (FIMSA)
Federal Risk and Authorisation Management Program (FedRAMP)	Quality assurance is achieved by collectively achieving multiple certifications that are compliant with FIMSA. This is intended for large IT infrastructures where compliance can be a largely repetitive process
ISO/IEC 27001:2005—Information Technology, security techniques, information security management systems—requirements	Security controls to assure the quality of information service provision
Statement on Standards for Attestation Engagements (SSAE) No. 16, Reporting on Controls at a Service Organisation	This standard supersedes the Statement on Auditing Standards (SAS) No. 70, Service Organisations. SSAE 16 describes controls for organisations that provide services to users, including an assessment of the reliability and consistency of process execution
Generally Accepted Privacy Principles (GAPP)	This standard is primarily concerned with information privacy policies and practices

The certification process consists of an approved auditor inspecting the system or infrastructure to be scrutinised, and then making an assessment against a set of formal criteria. Satisfaction must be achieved in the criteria assessed in order to be awarded a certificate of compliance. Having such a scheme in place is invaluable when faced with the prospect of selecting a provider of services; a simple filter is whether the candidate service provider has the relevant certification. From then on, there is the assurance that the standards for that particular domain have been certified.

Table 10.2 summarises some of the more prevalent standards that are applicable to cloud computing. The multiplicity of standards does imply overlap, and this can create complications for organisations engaged in a variety of industrial domains (public cloud providers for instance). Having said this, should an enterprise who already has certified compliance with a standard decide to select a cloud provider, the details of the compliance will make comparison with the cloud provider's offering more straightforward.

The Cloud Security Alliance (CSA) is a not-for-profit organisation that provides recommendations for the planning and implementation of security in cloud systems. Its mission is:

To promote the use of best practices for providing security assurance within Cloud Computing, and provide education on the uses of Cloud Computing to help secure all other forms of computing.

https://cloudsecurityalliance.org/

It comprises technology vendors, users, security experts and service providers, who collaborate to establish industrial standards for the execution of secure cloud environments. The CSA has an international remit and organises conferences and local meetings to exchange ideas with regard to cloud security.

This focus upon security has led to the publication of research into cloud computing, including user's experiences of compliance with the myriad standards.

So far, we have seen a number of factors that need to be considered when thinking about a move to a cloud infrastructure. The number of potential issues arising from neglecting any aspect of cloud security is large, and the implications can be catastrophic. Whilst some of the items are mostly applicable during the preparation for a switch over to cloud, many of the pertinent activities remain afterwards and require careful management. It is the overall management of the business assets that should provide the focus for how security (amongst other things) should be considered, and this management is generally referred to as *governance*.

10.7   Governance and the Cloud

Governance is oft-talked about in the context of *corporate governance*, the rules, practices, customs, policies and processes, which define and steer how an organisation conducts its daily business. Typically, the act of governance results in two key functions (de Leusse et al. 2009):

1. Providing defined chains of authority, responsibility and communication to empower the appropriate staff to take decisions
2. Defining mechanisms for policy and control, together with the associated measurements, to facilitate roles for staff to undertake

As you would expect, corporate governance is all encompassing when it comes to the operations, strategy and future trajectory of an organisation. It has tended to have been regarded as applicable to more traditional demarcations within business, such as the accounting, sales, human resource management or production functions, to name a few. However, as we have seen in this book and in Chap. 9 specifically (Enterprise Cloud Computing), the opportunities created by consuming IT as a utility have the potential to completely transform how business is conducted.

As such, there is emerging recognition that the impact of IT on a business is crucial to its survival, and as more and more legislative and policy controls now assume the use of IT, the need to govern the IT *function* is now paramount. As we have found elsewhere in this book, cloud computing presents a convergence of the IT and business functions, and thus, the governance of IT is a logical next step for organisations who choose to embrace the cloud.

10.8   Governance in Practice

The practice of IT governance needs to understand the different ways in which IT services are delivered and maintained in the presence of a cloud infrastructure. For instance, for each of the issues identified in Table 10.1, the governance body needs to understand the implications of noncompliance with regulatory, ethical, business and political constraints, as well as be suitably prepared for unforeseen circumstances in the future. The management of this activity requires delegation to a body that can oversee and marshall the holistic perspective, whilst also having the authority to intervene when required. However, it is unlikely that the governing body can understand the totality of detail that increasingly complex technology involves, so there are needs to be a number of items to consider as follows:

- Whilst IT governance is concerned with the technical capabilities and requirements of technology, the adoption of cloud services, together with the associated delegation of authority (but not responsibility) to external partners, reinforces the need to understand the issues that affect the business. Governing IT that includes clouds means that an intimate understanding of the responsibility boundaries is as important as whether there is sufficient bandwidth at each point of access.
- A governance perspective usefully tends to bring to the fore the potential myriad of services that may already exist. This list of services is likely to increase in the future, so it is important to empower the governing board to be able to rationalise and standardise where practicable. This in itself demands a blend of technical and business expertise that the governing board can call upon to inform its operations.
- The pace of change is rapid, and cloud adoption will only accelerate this change. Meaningful data is required to inform the decisions taken, and therefore it is necessary to not only understand what metrics need to be monitored and reported, but the mechanisms that do this must be automated.

IT governance should be seen as an opportunity to manage the emerging organisation that aspires to align its IT and business needs to generate value. It is likely that this will require a risk-based approach to management, which of course is hugely dependent on the quality of information used to assess and monitor risk. Standards such as COBIT assist the creation of benchmarks upon which monitoring can take place, but the resulting actions that are derived from this approach should not be underestimated. How many in-house applications are subject to security auditing for instance? What are the implications of executing tested, but not audited code on public clouds?

The ability to govern effectively means that an organisation must ensure that it can attribute cause to effect, be flexible in its operations and have the capability to accurately monitor its activities.

10.9   Summary

Clearly cloud computing can be an exciting and also potentially hazardous field to enter. Fortunately the topic of computer security is quite well established, and therefore there exists a plethora of approaches to managing the design and planning of secure systems. In short, these approaches are useful when considering the adoption of cloud services, and thus an organisation that already understands computer security will find the move to cloud can be accommodated by augmenting their existing practices. Similarly, an organisation that has already established the function of IT governance will be better prepared for the inclusion of emerging delivery models.

However, the abstraction of technicality and simplification of acquisition of cloud resources also means that organisations without experience of managing computer security, or who have not previously foreseen the need to establish IT governance, may unwittingly find themselves unduly exposed to new threats. The way forward is to adopt a risk-based approach to cloud security; at the very least, an organisation will have a more accurate and in-depth understanding of its existing practices, and it will be aware of the possibilities that cloud infrastructure brings to make the business less susceptible to security risks. Cloud computing brings what was traditionally *enterprise-class capability* to organisations that have not managed *enterprise-class operations* before. Therefore, organisations should clearly identify the business risks that are directly influenced by IT decisions and use these to develop the future *business technology* strategy.

10.10   Review Questions

The answers to these questions can be found in the text of this chapter.
1. Create a list of questions that an organisation should consider asking prospective cloud providers. For each question, define the evidence that you would expect to see that would convince you that the provider will practice due diligence.
2. Explain how 'data security' will impact upon the specification of a cloud offering and contrast it with the requirements of 'network security'.
3. Compare and contrast *IT governance* with *corporate governance*. Illustrate your answer with an example.

10.11   Extended Study Activities

These activities require you to research beyond the contents of this book and can be approached individually for the purposes of self-study or used as the basis of group work:
1. Your organisation has decided to migrate its core IT provision to the cloud. You have been nominated to assemble an IT governance board. What essential skills and experience will you require, and what will be the scope of the board's responsibilities?
2. A medium-sized enterprise of 180 staff, of which 40 are employed in the IT department, has decided to explore the use of cloud computing for software testing and quality assurance. Two directors of the company are concerned that the use of clouds will introduce intolerable security risks. Prepare two cases: The

first case should advocate the move to clouds. The second should oppose the move to utilise clouds. If there are sufficient numbers in the class, then this topic can be debated.

References

de Leusse, P., Dimitrakos, T., Brossard, D.: A Governance Model for SOA, ICWS 2009. IEEE International Conference on Web Services, pp. 1020–1027, 6–10 July 2009 (2009)

ENISA: Cloud Computing: Benefits, Risks and Recommendations for Information Security. European Network and Information Security Agency. http://www.enisa.europa.eu/activities/risk (2009). Accessed Mar 2012

ENISA: Cloud Computing Information Assurance Framework. European Network and Information Security Agency. http://www.enisa.europa.eu/activities/risk-management/files/deliverables/cloud-computing-information-assurance-framework/at_download/fullReport (2010). Accessed Mar 2012

Intel: Planning Guide, Cloud Security. http://www.intel.com/content/dam/www/public/us/en/documents/guides/cloud-computing-security (2011). Accessed Mar 2012

Opengroup: Cloud Cube Model: Selecting Cloud Formations for Secure Collaboration., Jericho Forum. https://collaboration.opengroup.org/jericho/index.htm (2010). Accessed Mar 2012

Developing a Cloud Roadmap 11

What the reader will learn:

- Appreciate the need for having a strategic approach to cloud computing
- Understand the strategic planning process for cloud
- Understand the need for business and cloud alignment
- Appraise the appropriateness of tools and techniques for strategic planning for cloud
- Plan and develop a strategic cloud roadmap

11.1 Cloud Strategy

The pace of change and innovation in Information Technology and its increasing contribution to business transformation has been a major source of spending in organisations. At the same time, companies of all sizes have increasingly been affected by unpredictable and uncertain changing business environments in recent years. Whilst externally current business landscape is driven by new hurdles and opportunities such as challenging economy, emerging technologies, increasing commoditisation of technology, shorter information life cycle, increased transparency along the supply chains, changing customer demands and preferences, evolving issues around transparency, privacy, security, as well as associated regulations, compliance and standards, internally organisations are challenged by tighter budgets and emphasis on managing investments effectively, reducing costs, managing the evolving complexity of markets, managing new relationships including developing new business models to differentiate and stay competitive, harnessing the technology capabilities for efficient and effective business delivery, process and operational efficiency, strategically aligning IT resources to business needs for optimised business benefit realisation, managing risk and many more.

Addressing the above concerns and maintaining growth and delivering business value has more than ever driven organisations to focus on their core competencies by carefully designing and leveraging the unique and differentiated processes,

R. Hill et al., *Guide to Cloud Computing: Principles and Practice*, Computer Communications and Networks, DOI 10.1007/978-1-4471-4603-2_11, © Springer-Verlag London 2013

architectures, skills and competencies and relationships across their business ecosystems. IT as a valuable strategic asset has also been the centre of attention due to its significant business impact and also the investment requirements and the need to lower operations cost, deriving business benefits, improved productivity and performance, streamlined processes and services, just to name a few.

Cloud computing is an important development in the landscape of computing options. Although cloud technologies have been around for some time, it has only been until very recently that the cloud as a business model has gathered momentum. Cloud is viewed as a business–IT innovation that is expected to accelerate the pace of some of the changes mentioned above as well as an opportunity to foster new business models and innovative solutions. Cloud technologies have come a long way and are maturing fast along the evolving business models, and companies need to look beyond the hype to fully exploit these emerging opportunities.

Any wave of industry hype gets fevered and loud, and many organisations try to create a new strategy for the new industry favourite. In case of cloud too, most of the conversations revolve around placing the strategy focus on the technology often at the expense of real business benefits. The cloud hype proposes that cloud adoption is a sure path to business benefits, often not articulating in balance the cloud option against the trade-offs and interdependencies.

What shouldn't change with cloud as an emerging technology is the need for a business-focused strategy that takes account of cloud, its capabilities and fit within the organisations business and technology portfolio. IT decision-makers need to determine where and how cloud could offer business value for their organisations by establishing a strong foundation for a long-term evolution towards cloud and other emerging options as they mature over time.

Just like any (information) technology solution, cloud computing offers tools and techniques that may or may not fit business needs. It is hence imperative to consider the impact of cloud adoption on short, medium and long-term business strategy and operational delivery.

This chapter will examine the strategic context of cloud and some key ingredients of strategic planning to realise cloud business benefits.

11.2 Planning for the Cloud

What is strategic value of cloud? Strategic value of cloud is demonstrated when it plays a key role in an organisation's achievement of overall business strategy. As an ingredient of the IT portfolio, cloud strategy needs to be focused on business outcomes and play significant role in optimising and improving core value chain processes and drive innovation that enables new technology-enabled product and service revenue streams. The results can be translated into and measured by improved customer satisfaction and market share.

It is important to consider cloud in its totality in relation to as-is and the to-be context of the business. This means that companies should see cloud as a mix of many options in terms of business models, deployment models and technology architecture. Business benefits will often be achieved as a result of careful and smart integration and configuration of various cloud options.

As organisations take the strategic information era further into the innovation era, they need to be able to develop a fitting strategic view of the nexus between their Information Technology and business performance and in the way it impacts their competitive position. Cloud computing reduced barriers to entry, accelerates innovation cycles, as well as time to value and markets, and commoditises the once unique technical capabilities companies invested in to design and develop. The dynamics are creating a new paradigm: commoditise to differentiate. Organisations of all sizes now have incredible opportunity to review their current business processes and technology portfolios and identify scope for simplification and new efficiencies and focus on their core business where they can develop differentiating capacities. This exercise requires smart planning not only of technological order but rather a very important business activity. Organisations need to appreciate the relationship between technology in general and cloud fit, more specifically, to their business and develop a holistic view of impacts of various business models and scenarios in the context of their industry and their business. It is important to realise the need to look beyond the boundaries of their organisations and consider the value chains and complex ecosystems that make up the future successful cloud implementations. Although it is stated that switching cost from one cloud provider to another is significantly lower than the equivalent traditional IT, the industry is still taking shape and the risks need to be fully accounted for as well. The outcome would be developing integrative business–IT strategies that leverage cloud for business benefits realisation.

Therefore, the underpinning premises of the planning for cloud include:
- Going into the cloud requires strategic planning that leverages the business effectiveness.
- A strategic planning framework can help ensure that cloud investments are aligned with and support the strategic business objectives.
- Cloud can contribute to developing a sustainable competitive advantage.
- Cloud and other emerging technologies should be recognised as strategic opportunities.
- Cloud and other emerging technologies need to be managed in a wider context of a sustainable IT portfolio.
- Business and enterprise architectures should be made cloud compliant to link the multiple strategic business and technology priorities and operational delivery.
- Internal and external business environments will have bearing on the cloud options and provision configuration.
- Cloud implementation will imply business and organisational change and can in turn drive or support it.
- Perhaps most importantly, it is imperative to strike a balance between information and technology and business and IT.

IT-led-competitive advantage has been the concern of many insightful debates over the years. Some perspectives challenge the gains of being a first mover in relation to emerging technologies including cloud which may or may not have been at the early stages of their maturity. However, there is compelling argument that an effective implementation and management of innovative technology resources aligned with business has been a prime critical success factor for many organisations.

The following issues are all relevant to the discussions and some have been assessed in previous sections:

- The importance of business–IT alignment
- The differing business priorities and requirements at different organisational levels
- The importance of data, information and related processing systems as strategic assets to the business and how they address the business priorities
- Technological advancement and innovation which will/may change the way organisations are structured
- The importance of (operational) partnerships with technology suppliers and business customers which span organisation boundaries beyond service level agreements (SLA)
- Importance of a holistic reference model/framework that focuses on business realisation and innovation

  Hence, a cloud computing strategy needs to aim to:
- Articulate the value, benefits, risks and trade-offs of cloud computing
- Provide a decision framework to evaluate the cloud opportunity in relation to strategic business and technology direction
- Support with development of an appropriate target architecture
- Support with adopting an appropriate cloud choice and infrastructure to deliver
- Provide a roadmap and methodology for successful implementation
- Identify activities, roles and responsibilities for catalysing cloud adoption
- Identify measures, targets, initiatives that support monitoring, optimisation and continuous improvement

11.3   Some Useful Concepts and Techniques

Developing a cloud strategy is not an easy and can be a complex task even more so if these strategies need to support business strategies.

How these strategies are formulated and managed will depend on the organisational structure, culture and organisational pressures both external and internal. The environment may be stable and allow for structured planning to take place, or the organisation may be operating in a volatile changing environment where there is a requirement to respond to immediate issues and develop emergent strategies fast.

There are a range of traditional tools and techniques that can assist in the planning process to develop a cloud roadmap. Indeed, a general understanding of the following planning tools and techniques will be useful in order to be proactive in any IT planning process (Robson 2002; Ward and Peppard 2002):

- SWOT analysis
- Critical success factors analysis

- Stakeholder analysis
- PESTEL analysis
- Value chain analysis
- Value management
- Business competitive environment analysis (Porter's 5 forces model)
- Strategic thrust analysis
- Product portfolio analysis (Boston Matrix)
- IT portfolio management
- Business process modelling and analysis
- Enterprise architecture
- Governance and risk analysis
- Capability maturity model/analysis
- Investment appraisal and benefits analysis

There are many frameworks to choose from and in practice organisations adapt frameworks to identify the strategic drivers (alignment or business impact) and use the most suitable tools and techniques to carry out the necessary strategic investigations.

The frameworks should be aligned with the drivers for change, that is, is the organisation seeking to assess whether cloud can have a positive impact on the quest to gain sustainable competitive advantage by changing strategic direction? Is the organisation seeking to align the cloud provision with the strategic business objectives? Is the organisation seeking to differentiate by achieving streamlined efficiencies across information processing systems?

11.4 Developing a Cloud Strategy

Strategic planning for cloud is the effective and sustainable management of cloud provision and its optimal technology and business impact. It also includes the inter- and intra-organisational elements such as change management, process management, governance, managing policies and service level agreements.

Broadly speaking, there are three areas that should be considered in any such strategic planning exercise (Ward and Peppard 2002):

- Managing the long term and optimal impact of cloud provision in the context of organisation including management of the cloud service and the inter- and intra-relationships with the stakeholders including the user community, service providers and other stakeholders, policies and process management: this level of strategy is predominantly concerned with management controls for cloud and broader IT systems, management roles and responsibilities, cloud performance measurement, optimisation and continuous improvement.
- Managing the long term and optimal impact of cloud in the broader context of the information systems strategy: this level of strategy will be primarily concerned with aligning cloud investment with business requirements and seeking strategic advantage from cloud provision. The typical approach is to formulate these strategies following formal organisation's strategic planning frameworks to

align with the organisation's business strategy. The resulting action plan should consist of a mix of short-term and medium-term application requirements following a thorough review of current technology and systems use and emerging technology issues.

- Managing the long-run and optimal impact of cloud in the broader context of underlying IT infrastructure and application portfolio: the cloud strategy will be primarily concerned with the technical policies relating to cloud architecture (and its fit within the broader IT architectures), including risks and service level agreements (SLAs). It seeks to provide a framework within which the cloud provision can deliver services required by the users. It is heavily influenced by the CIO and IT specialists and is likely to be a single corporate strategy. Separate federated cloud strategies may be required if there are very different needs in particular business units.

In practice, all three of these are interlinked and need to be managed accordingly to ensure a coherent and strategic cloud provision.

The planning process seeks to answer some basic strategic questions of:

- What is the current state of the business in terms of the management and utilisation of current business and supporting information systems and technologies (as-is analysis)
- What is the desired state of the organisation in terms of the management and utilisation of business assets and IT resources (to-be analysis)
- How can the organisation close any strategic gaps identified in its management and utilisation of cloud as an IT resource (transition plan)
- How can the resulting information systems plans be implemented successfully (realisation plan)
- How to review progress through effective business metrics and control structures and procedures (fine-tuning, optimisation and continuous improvement)

11.5 Benefits of Developing Strategies for Cloud

It is important to revisit the organisation's overall business and information management strategies to ensure that the cloud provision is in line with the direction of development. For most SMEs and certainly larger enterprises, cloud could present them with an opportunity to adopt and enhance such strategies. Strategic planning aligned with business objectives will imply that cost-effectiveness is measured over the longer term and that there is significant element stability in the infrastructure framework of the organisation and its operations. It will allow for continuing incremental fine-tuning and optimisation of the systems, products and operations, building on a sure base and a solid systems infrastructure and adaptable architectures.

Some of the key drivers for developing strategies for cloud include:

- Business-aware deployments
- Developing flexible and innovation-aware business
- Risk-aware business and technology models

- Strategic development of applications portfolio
- Improved software and management/resource allocation
- Ability to scale IT resources
- Reduced operational and maintenance costs
- Improved decision-making
- Improved coordination across business and technology units
- Sound management practice

11.6   Issues Around Implementing Strategies

What is clearly evident is that the whole process of strategy development relies on different groups of stakeholders in the organisation working together to assess business and process requirements and the information needs, and the steps towards developing implementable strategy.

The caveat to this is that there are wide ranging issues that need to be mitigated to ensure that implementation of the cloud strategy can be successful. The issues encompass various areas including internal competencies and experience of the strategy development as well as cloud delivery teams, organisational change management, project management, technical solution management, data governance, just to name a few. It is therefore imperative that the cloud business case and roadmap consider a holistic view that cuts across people, systems, architectures and business processes for successful implementation and optimising business benefits (Ward & Peppard 2002).

11.7   Stages in the Planning Process: Cloud Roadmap

The cloud roadmap should ensure close alignment of the target architecture goals, measures and initiatives with the strategic business objectives that address the operational requirements of the business.

As mentioned above, it includes five key elements which we expand upon below.
- As-is (baseline/current state) analysis
- To-be (future/target state) analysis
- Transition plan
- Realisation plan

11.8   As-Is Analysis

The main deliverable of the as-is analysis is establishing business direction and needs stemming from its strategy and business architecture and the collection of demands from the current business operations in its internal and external context.

The assessment of the current broader information systems and supporting technology landscape indicates the existing capabilities and resources in support of the current business strategy. There will almost certainly be gaps between the current resources and competencies and those needed to satisfy the cloud-enabled information system.

11.8.1 Analysing the Business Context and Technology Requirements and Opportunities

This stage of analysis considers the macro-context of the business. It is important to indentify the trends that can affect the business positively or negatively. This has strategic significance and cloud affects the choice of cloud model an organisation opts for or the pace of change required and potential risks that might affect the implementation plans.

To help analyse the environmental context of the business, PESTEL framework could be a useful tool.

- Political influences and issues—Partnerships, vendors, ecosystems, etc.
- Economic influences and issues—Changes in customer activities, competitor activity, cost efficiencies as a result of flexible payment options, etc.
- Social influences and issues—Demographics, social technology trends, behaviours and expectations, etc.
- Technical influences and issues—IT innovations changing industry generally, governance, security, service-orientation, service quality, service customisation and extension, etc.
- Ethical and environmental considerations—Privacy, environmental impact of operations (reducing carbon footprint), etc.
- Legal issues—Governance, SLAs, service reliability and availability, etc.

It is also important to consider the level at which the framework is applied. It may be helpful to narrow down to a particular part of the business and analyse the impact of cloud at that level as it will provide an opportunity to focus on more relevant and specific influences and issues. Similarly it is useful to consider the local as well as global context of the business in the cloud.

Some of the other concepts, tools and techniques that help with internal and external analysis include:

- Brain storming sessions involving both business and IT users, influencers, specialists and decision-makers to identify and evaluate the potential cloud opportunities
- Porter's five forces analysis to identify possible supply chain linkages with customers and suppliers, and other actors such as service providers or service brokers should also assist in evaluating stakeholder activity and their interests in the cloud ecosystem
- Value chain analysis to identify if cloud could improve efficiency or effectiveness or provide competitive advantage through linkages within the internal and external value chains

11.8.2 Analysing the As-Is Business Architecture

Analysing the cloud in isolation of the business architecture and narrowly focusing the roadmap on the technical implementation of cloud is unlikely to deliver a holistic picture of existing concerns nor will it realistically address the potential business benefits and the wider impact that it has on the entire organisation.

This stage of analysis requires critical evaluation of the business environment, business and technology drivers, business processes and organisational change programmes. In essence, it is an audit of the organisation's current context, direction and capabilities. This exercise is similar to an enterprise architecture development, and its purpose is to establish the business case for cloud by modelling a clear understanding of the vision and existing level of business and technical maturity to determine what factors need to be introduced or improved in successful path towards the cloud implementation.

You may identify appropriate tools and techniques to capture, model and analyse the business. Depending on the degree of sophistication, these may comprise simple documents or spreadsheets, or more sophisticated modelling tools and techniques, business process models, use-case models, etc. Some example useful concepts and tools that can contribute to this stage of analysis are:

- Use-case modelling and analysis
- Business process modelling and analysis
- Value chain analysis
- Stakeholder analysis
- Information intensity grid
- Porter's models
- PESTLE analysis

11.8.3 Analysing the Current IS and IT Provisions

Parallel to the business context and strategy context analysis, it is imperative to determine the existing technology maturity of the business. At this stage, we want to establish how information systems (IS) contribute to the business and what underlying IT infrastructure and architectures support the IS provision. The key activities involve compilation of the current systems portfolio followed by critical evaluation of effectiveness and efficiencies and any issues or shortcomings that can be addressed. In this context, we need to critically evaluate the nexus between IT and business, that is, IT contribution to business and the extent to which business is able to leverage the existing IT capabilities to achieve strategic objectives and goals. Establishing the strengths and weaknesses of the current provision and identifying potential opportunities and risks will also be an important deliverable at this stage.

Some of the useful concepts, tools and techniques that can help with this analysis would be:

- McFarlan's IT portfolio grid analysis: that is, strategic, high potential, key operational, support systems

- SWOT analysis for each system
- Evaluate each system utilising the business value versus technical quality assessments

11.9   To-Be Analysis

The key task here is to develop appropriate target/desired cloud solutions. This encompasses both business and technical aspects of cloud deployment. The core focus is to identify, define and configure cloud-enabled information system architecture and application portfolio that support the business architecture. At this stage, we also consider what aspects of business operation and what business processes in what part of the business will be affected and how. A detailed definition of target business and technology infrastructure, application and data architectures in relation to a suitable cloud deployment model will be a key deliverable.

The scope and level of granularity and rigour of decomposition in this exercise will depend on the relevance of the technical elements to attaining the target cloud model, maturity of existing infrastructure, existing architecture models and descriptions, and the extent it can sufficiently enable identification of gaps and the scope of candidate/target cloud provision.

Some of the key considerations at this stage will span data (service), application and technology. The Chaps. 3, 5, 6 and 7 have particular relevance here.

11.9.1   Data for the Cloud

Undertaking transformation towards cloud requires careful understanding and addressing information lifecycle management and governance issues. Some of these issues relate to risk and security concerns that will constrain the choice of platforms, cloud deployment architecture, service level agreements, etc. Some of the finer grain considerations in data management for cloud include access and identification, authentication, confidentiality, availability, privacy, ownership and distribution, retention and auditability. A structured and comprehensive approach to Information Lifecycle Management (ILM) and data management will not only address data security concerns but will also leverage data effectiveness for competitive advantages.

The purpose of the to-be architecture for data for cloud is to define the data entities relevant to the enterprise that will be processed by the service and cloud-enabled applications.

Cloud implication for data spans across the following domains:

- Data architecture
- Data management (processes)
- Data migration
- Data integration
- Data governance

Data architecture is expected to map a clear model of which application components in the new landscape that includes cloud services will serve as the reference system for enterprise master data. Moving to the cloud may critically require data transformation and migration; hence, one concern will be adopting suitable standards and processes that may affect all data entities and processing services and applications whether existing or in the target applications and architecture.

Previous chapters on data in the cloud cover many aspects of the data considerations towards development, implementation or consumption of cloud provision.

11.9.2 Cloud Application

Similarly in the case of target cloud technologies and applications, the objective is to define the relevant types of applications and enabling technologies necessary to process the data and information effectively and efficiently to support the business. In this sense, we need to logically group applications in terms of capabilities that manage the data objects defined earlier in the data architecture to support the business functions in the business architecture. Although generally these application building blocks are stable and remain relatively unchanged over time, we are seeking fresh opportunities to improve, simplify, augment or replace components for the target cloud-enabled systems landscape. The business architecture and the application portfolio analysis in the as-is assessment will inform the list of affected or required logical and physical components in the application stack. The core objective here is to define the target platform and application architecture including cloud services, referenced across the technical and business functions, data requirements and business processes. The exercise will highlight the extent and nature of interoperability and integration, migration and operational concerns that need to be addressed. Cloud will not only consolidate resources and change the way the services are consumed and managed but also open new requirements and opportunities due to its properties and limitations.

In earlier chapters, we have covered technical aspects of cloud especially in relation to general technical architecture, data, infrastructure requirements and possible delivery models.

11.9.3 Technology for the Cloud

This aspect of to-be analysis is concerned with defining target cloud technology portfolio components. In this exercise, we map underlying technology and respective application components defined in the application architecture depending on the cloud model of choice. Depending on the business vision, and business architecture and business and technology maturity, the technology deployment may be a hybrid configuration which means that cloud will coexist within a modified current technology architecture. In this manner, we are making the technology platform cloud enabled to make necessary exchanges across a heterogeneous environment not only possible but optimised for business efficiency and effectiveness. In case of full migration to a new cloud platform again, we need to assess the technology and business readiness.

This element of the to-be analysis is concerned with physical realisation of the cloud provision; hence, there is an essential conduit for cloud transition planning and implementation.

11.10 Transition Plan

Transition plan consists of the activities that the organisation needs to maintain to close any strategic and delivery gaps identified in its implementation, utilisation and management of cloud as an IT resource. The key components of this aspect of the cloud roadmap primarily draw on the iterative assessment of fit-gap analysis in as-is and to-be analyses.

An important activity here involves assessment, validation and consolidation of business, functional and systems requirements through reviewing cloud technology requirements and gaps and solutions proposed. Once consolidated, it is important to identify functional integration points. As cloud services are delivered based on shared services and shared resources, it is important to assess the need and scope for reuse and interoperability. It is likely that business is not fully migrating to cloud and there is still need for utilising bespoke, COTS (commercial off the shelf) or third party services; hence, verifying service integration and interoperability is an important task. Any gaps and dependencies and appropriate solutions need to be identified, analysed and consolidated ensuring that any constraints on the implementation and migration plans are addressed.

The transition plan will be articulated as an overall cloud implementation strategy. The merits of different strategic approaches characterised by pace and scope of change/implementation need to be balanced against business constraints such as funding and resource concerns, technology maturity, existing business capabilities and opportunity costs. The organisation may opt for phased and incremental introduction of cloud or a big bang approach. Cloud computing requires a different strategy to the upgrade of existing IT infrastructure. Formulation of an appropriate strategic approach will rely on careful analysis of risks and change requirements.

11.10.1 Fit-Gap Analysis

Fit-gap analysis is widely used in many problem-solving-based methods and is concerned with validating the issues, solutions, plans, etc. The primary goal at this stage is to highlight any overlaps or shortfalls between the as-is and to-be states. It concentrates on evaluation of gaps, including further fine-tuning of priorities to consolidate, integrate and analyse the information to determine the best way to contribute to cloud implementation and transition plans.

The fit-gap analysis involves linking the as-is and to-be models for business, information systems and IT architectures, and compare, contrast and rationalise the trade-offs and interdependencies of the activities to validate the cloud requirement specification (within broader IS/IT portfolio) for organisation, business and technical perspectives. Logically grouping and organising activities into programme and project work packages will feed into the transition and implementation plans and requirements.

There are different categories of gaps to consider relating to business, systems, technologies and data.

Various techniques could be used in this exercise such as creating a simple gap matrix that lists as-is and to-be components in columns and rows with respective gaps in the intersection. Similarly, to consolidate gaps and assess potential solutions and dependencies, a gaps-solution-dependency table will be an easy technique to use. This can serve as a planning tool towards creating project work packages and initiatives.

11.10.2 Change Management

Change management is a structured approach to transitioning the organisation, teams, individuals and culture from the as-is state to the desired target (to-be) state. It aims to align the organisation and strategies with the target architecture through identifying, characterising and addressing issues relating to communications, process and system design, workforce management, performance management and overall governance features that can help to support the organisational and other changes as a result of adopting cloud.

Adopting cloud computing will inevitably require change that cuts across the organisation both in terms of understanding the cloud and its value proposition and opportunities and different ways it affects the business from to new ways to engage with the old and new business applications, possible changes to the current processes, new data related policies, the new operating model that uses 'services' as the key organisational construct, the new approach to accounting for cloud and management of IT resources, new roles, skills and competencies.

Change will be part of the business alignment exercise or 'organisational readiness' building block in the roadmap and important work package in the cloud programme or project management. The roadmap should outline the required change, goals and objectives and critical success factors, impact of change and strategies for implementation. The key activities involve change planning (change roadmap), change enablement, change management and embedding the change.

A change and capability maturity assessment early on will help determine readiness factors, qualified and quantified as well as potential constraints and risks, identified and planned. These form important deliverables of the change/transformation roadmap.

11.10.3 Risk Analysis

Risk-aware plans are crucial to success of projects. Cloud adoption comes with its bag of issues, risks and security concerns. It is important to perform risk assessment to identify and validate potential issues and consolidate appropriate mitigation strategies. This will form an integral part of the transition plans that will feed into the cloud project management. The business and technology drivers for cloud have to be assessed against the risk factors at the earlier stages of the process. The risks can be business, organisational, systems, data or people related. There are two broad categories of risk:

- 'Delivery' risk, which entails risk of not delivering the required or expected capabilities. For instance, unproven technology provision, reliance of vendors, lack of clarity of scope and deliverables, provider or technology compliance and standards issues, level of integration/interface required of cloud solution with existing systems, quality of project management, etc.
- 'Benefits' risk, which entails risk of not achieving expected business benefits such as lack of business–IT alignment, lack of alignment with technical standards and architectures, lack of appropriate security compliance, lack of credibility and measurability of business outcomes, change management requirements, senior management involvement, etc.

Risk mitigation strategy may leverage existing organisation's governance and capabilities or may require extending or developing capacity and competencies. As far as security of the cloud is concerned, there is a requirement to implement updated security strategies and governance framework needed to govern cloud operations and services to ensure their long-term stability. Some examples of technical consideration may include policies in relation to service availability, service scalability, performance management, service security policies, acceptable usage, auditing, data retention, etc.

Various parts of this text have addressed potential issues with cloud computing including the chapter on cloud security.

There are various tools and techniques to help with risk assessment. A risk classification matrix, followed by a tiered probability-impact matrix analysis, that is, identify risk elements in terms of their impact and probability being low, medium or high, serves as a useful technique. Similarly a risk scorecard and risk matrix can illustrate the risk, quantified impact, mitigation measures in a structured and traceable manner.

11.11 Realisation Plan

The main objective of realisation plan is supporting cloud business value delivery through creation of a viable implementation plan and recommendations. The key activities include assessing the dependencies, costs and benefits of the various transition projects. The prioritised list of projects will form the basis of the detailed realisation plan.

Some of the key deliverables of this phase include:

- Addressing/establishing management framework capability for cloud transformation aligned with organisation's strategic planning, operations management, performance management, programme and project management and governance frameworks.
- Value planning: Identifying business value drivers and assigning them to all relevant activities and projects. This will serve as a benchmark for performance management and monitoring. Analysis and assignment of strategic fit, critical success factors, business key performance indicators, cloud performance indicator, process performance indicators, return on investment, etc. will form a set of criteria and benchmarks to assess business value realisation of the cloud project.
- Cost–benefit analysis and validation using TCO, ROI and risk models assigned to each relevant project.
- Resource allocation, coordination and scheduling and capability planning to establish the resource requirements and operational delivery implications of the project.
- Aggregating, categorising and prioritising projects to establish projects sequence, time scales, timeline and key milestones in line with value delivery plans.
- Best practice recommendations for successful implementation.
- Roadmap governance process which entails the process of managing and evaluating the cloud roadmap and its implementation success.
- Integrating and documenting the roadmap.

11.12 Adapting the Roadmap

The method we have described above is a generic approach towards adoption of most systems including cloud and respective organisational requirements. In practice, it is of course necessary to modify or extend the roadmap to suit specific needs. One of the key tasks before applying the model is to produce an 'organisation-specific' roadmap. To do so, you need to review various steps and building blocks for relevance and fit and adapt them appropriately to the circumstances of the organisation.

Some of this adaptation exercise may, for example, involve changing the sequence of the phases. This is more so depending on the maturity of the organisation in terms of their business and enterprise architectures and alignment of current systems implementation processes with their business model. For example, organisations may opt for either an as-is or to-be first approach depending on their level of understanding of cloud and business and technology maturity. In as-is first, an assessment of the current state landscape informs the gaps and opportunities for cloud adoption, whereas, in the latter, a target solution is elaborated and mapped back to current state; gaps and change requirements are identified and assessed to inform the transition plans.

Cloud may be a natural evolution of system adoption in the organisation's IT portfolio, and the cloud business case may be already justified. In other cases, more work needs to be done to establish the vision for cloud followed by a detailed business architecture groundwork. In case of SMEs, it might be more appropriate to use a 'cut-down' model adjusted to their typically lower resource levels and system complexity. The roadmap adaptation is a function of practical assessment of resource and competency availability and the value that can realistically be delivered.

It is important to prioritise the cloud initiative and the adoption model according to business drivers and priorities. These may be affected by high-level strategic business objectives and the overall business model of the organisation.

In any case, articulating the organisation-specific guiding principles for the roadmap development at the planning stage will serve an important milestone towards successful implementation of the cloud initiative.

11.13 Review Questions

The answers to these questions can be found in the text of this chapter.
1. What should a cloud strategy and roadmap seek to achieve?
2. Why should a cloud strategy be aligned with overall IS/IT strategies?
3. Which aspect of the cloud strategy plans do you consider as most important? Explain why?
4. Should 'cost savings' be one of the strategic objectives? How about 'agility' and 'flexibility'? What roles do they play in the cloud roadmap and its implementation?
5. How can you get rid of all the IT-related activities that are not core to your business?

11.14 Group Exercise: Developing a Cloud Business Case

This activity is designed to enable you to consider and apply some of the models, tools and techniques introduced in this chapter and preceding chapters to develop a strategic cloud roadmap.

The idea is for you to consider the strategic context of cloud for a select industry sector or a company you are most familiar with and evaluate the as-is context of the business and systems in your cloud strategy and make recommendation on a suitable approach to cloud adoption or migration. The objective is to seek alignment between cloud provision and the strategic business objectives and business requirements.

The exercise builds on various parts of the textbook and requires additional research. You will need to revisit some of the concepts such as cloud types and business models, technical characteristics of the cloud economies of cloud and the investment appraisal, business benefits and value of cloud, IS/IT strategy, business–IT alignment and more. You are expected to research to build knowledge of some of the tools and techniques.

Use the templates to produce and deliver your results.

Task 1: Analysis of current systems and technology provision

    1a. Identify the current systems portfolio in the organisation.

    1b. Categorise each system according to the McFarlan IT portfolio grid.

    1c. Evaluate current systems using a simple SWOT analysis (five items for each section).

    1d. Evaluate the current technical enterprise architecture, applications, technical infrastructure, interfaces, metrics, data and information, governance, etc.

    1e. Assess the current technology landscape in light of business value versus technical quality grid.

    1f. Identify any areas of concern from the above evaluations and consider relevant actions or further analysis.

Task 2: Assess environmental pressures and opportunities to examine scope for innovative leverage of Cloud in the value/supply chain

    2a. Use Porter's five forces analysis to contextualise the business environment and potential cloud opportunities.

    2b. Analyse the impact of the cloud on the value chain and supply chains using Porter's value chain analysis.

Task 3: Assess cloud option

    3a. Assess the cloud in light of business value v technical quality grid.

    3b. Evaluate options using a simple SWOT analysis (five items for each section); create a matrix of various cloud service and deployment models and corresponding linkage to business.

    3c. Evaluate the to-be architecture, applications, technical infrastructure requirements, interfaces, metrics, data and information, governance, etc.

    3d. Determine the appropriate to-be cloud architecture including type and deployment model.

Task 4: Identify strategic gaps (alignment) that require further investigation in relation to investment in the cloud

    4a. Critically evaluate potential strategic gaps.

    4b. Critically evaluate potential business process gaps and opportunities for simplification, streamlining or redesign.

    4c. Critically evaluate potential technical gaps to support the business process and anticipated business benefits.

    4d. Prioritise potential cloud and other complimentary technology enhancements required.

    4e. Create an action plan to address the issues identified from the analysis; include a critical success factor analysis (CSF).

Task 5: Assess anticipated business value and business benefits

    5a. Identify and classify tangible and intangible value drivers for business in the cloud.

    5b. Identify and classify nonfinancial benefits in three categories of business, operational and technology capabilities.

    5c. Identify financial benefits and classify them in three categories of business, operational and technology capabilities. Create an incremental cash flow model and calculate some of the financial metrics (TCO, NPV, ROI and other tangible financial metrics) and critically evaluate in the context of the business.

5d   Create a cost–benefit model.

Task 6: Assess risk

6a. Identify potential risks and classify them in two categories of 'delivery' risk (risk of not delivering the required capabilities) and 'benefits' risk (risk of not achieving expected business benefits).

6b. For items in each category of risk, develop a tiered probability-impact matrix analysis, that is, identify (and ideally quantify) risk elements in terms of their impact and probability being low, medium or high.

6c. Develop a risk mitigation strategy/action plan.

Task 7: Develop the transition plan

7a. Identify the building blocks of transition plan by putting them into four categories of people (stakeholders, skills, training, communication, change management…), process (process modelling and analysis, business process change management…), organisation (decision-making, roles and tasks, budget and costs, SLAs, …), technology (infrastructure, architectures, service provision, monitoring tools, …) and methodology (programme and project management, governance, …).

7b. Elaborate on appropriate implementation priorities, scope and strategies.

Task 8: Develop the business case

8a. Develop the final business case comprising all the relevant deliverables from above.

8b. Include recommendations and roadmap for migration/adoption.

References

Robson, W.: Strategic Management and Information Systems. PITMAN Publications, London (2002)

Ward, J., Peppard, J.: Strategic Information Systems Planning. Wiley, Chichester (2002)

Cloud Computing Challenges and the Future

12

What the reader will learn:

- Cloud computing is a natural evolution of computing.
- The future of cloud computing brings inconceivable potential.
- Despite any unpredictability, many IT giants are investing heavily and see a future in cloud.
- There are drivers and barriers that can help anticipate emerging cloud trends.

12.1 Drivers and Barriers

In this book, we have examined a variety of reasons why cloud computing might succeed, and we have also seen some of its limitations. Table 12.1 summarises these:

Of course, we should be cautious when trying to foretell the future of cloud computing. IT has a long track record of being hard to accurately predict. On top of that, cloud is new. It is not a mature offering and things are moving very quickly (another familiar trait in IT developments). This volatility is part of the joy of working in the IT area. However, it does mean that, at least in part, this chapter will be out of date by the time it gets on to bookshelves. And for those trying to make strategic business decisions about their IT investments, the uncertainty is difficult to cope with.

One way to help bring some clarity is to apply some business diagnostic techniques, for example, SWOT analysis and various adaptations for IT of the five forces model of Porter.

As an example of using a SWOT to help understand the complex area of cloud, a recent expert group report commissioned by the European Commission called 'Opportunities for European Cloud Beyond 2010' has attempted to describe how

R. Hill et al., *Guide to Cloud Computing: Principles and Practice*, Computer
Communications and Networks, DOI 10.1007/978-1-4471-4603-2_12,
© Springer-Verlag London 2013

Table 12.1 Drivers and barriers

Drivers	Barriers
Cost savings, flexibility	Lack of standards
Being 'green', availability	Actual security issues
Revenue costs, rapid provisioning	Perceived security issues
Robustness, improved performance	Internet limitations

ready Europe is to meet the challenges of the cloud era. We summarise their findings as follows:

Strengths
- Knowledge background and expertise in related technological areas
- Significant expertise in building high-value industry specific applications
- Ongoing research projects and open source technologies
- Strong SOA and distributed systems research community
- Strong synergies between research and industry, technological platforms
- Concerted government effort (e.g. legislation)
- Selling products and telecommunications (as opposed to selling new technologies)
- Provisioning of complex processes as services, rather than of low-level infrastructures
- Strong telecommunication industry (research, consumer focus, investment capabilities)
- Commercial success stories

Weaknesses
- Few cloud resource infrastructures available in Europe
- Comparatively weak development of new (cloud) technologies in comparison to USA
- Primarily consumer; main cloud providers are not European
- Research timelines versus fast-moving markets
- No market ecosystem around European providers
- Subsidiaries and fragmentation of key industries
- No platform to find/select cloud providers

Opportunities
- Strong experience and involvement in standardisation efforts.
- European companies use (and need) their own clouds (private clouds) (cf. location).
- Growing interest from both industry and academia in cloud technologies (cf. 'readiness').
- Existing infrastructures with strong resources and in particular with strong communication networks (e.g. telecoms).
- Clouds provide an excellent backend for mobile phone applications (which have usually low-power local resources).

- Increase competiveness and productivity of service providers by adoption of local/hybrid/public computing platforms.
- Application provisioning instead of technology orientation.
- Support SMEs and start-ups with improved ROI (elasticity), reduced time to market and easy adoption.
- New business models for cloud improved products and cloud adopters.
- High awareness for the green agenda and new approaches to reduce the carbon footprint.
- Similar business incentives and infrastructure requirements between grid and cloud, facilitating the movement from grid to cloud provider.

Threats
- Better developed cloud infrastructures (mainly in the USA) already exist.
- High investment and funding required to build up infrastructure.
- Investment/economic benefit asymmetry (IPR, OSS, commercialisation).
- Lacking IaaS provider(s).
- Dependency on external (non-European) providers.
- Technological impact/development underestimated.
- Latencies (federation too inefficient).

As is typically the case with SWOT analysis, the *process* of collating the information required can be a great help in beginning to understand a complex environment, particularly in terms of having a clear, honest understanding of the current state. Their work has some other useful observations that can help us establish whether or not to take cloud computing seriously:

> [Cloud has been] ... a major commercial success over recent years and will play a large part in the ICT domain over the next 10 years or more.

Cloud technologies and models have not yet reached their full potential and many of the capabilities associated with clouds remain undeveloped and researched, to a degree that allows their full exploitation, thus meeting all requirements under all potential circumstances of usage.

Cloud would not be the first much-heralded technology to fail to deliver. IBM's OS/2, Cobalt Qube, and NeXT are examples of technologies that failed to fully exploit the market. Crucially, they did not deliver what was promised. Using expert reports like this can be a useful way of trying to establish the veracity of some of the overhyped claims made by vendors and service providers, which is why a good IT professional is not only technically skilled but also reads widely around and is knowledgeable about their field.

In a competitive environment, strategists will often refer to Porter's five forces model as a tool for reviewing the impact upon the business of the key drivers in decision-making (see Porter's seminal work (Porter 1980)). McFarlan (1984) builds on Porter's model in terms of IT/IS, and we can do the same in terms of cloud computing, giving rise to the following questions. Essentially, can cloud computing:
1. Build barriers to entry?
2. Generate new products or services?

3. Build in switching costs? (i.e. tie the customer in)?
4. Change the balance of power in supplier relationships?
5. Change the basis of the competition?

By the very shared resource nature of cloud, the first question is relatively easy to answer in the negative. In any case, it is the nature of ICT that any advantages gained are transient since, as history shows, it is relatively easy to copy what the competition has done. Look, for example, at the number of iPhone equivalents there are now on the market after Apple proved the concept to be a winner.

The second question, equally easily, has to be answered in the affirmative. Just look at the number of new services, such as those offered by Salesforce.com, or new software products available on the Google Apps platform. Costs, too, which used to be a big barrier to product creation, can be significantly lower for SaaS solutions, making innovation even more possible.

The third question is an interesting one. Cloud is new, and as we have seen, there are still no clearly defined standards in operation. This means that service providers, almost by default, are tying their customers in. Once you have taken the step to use, for example, a cloud-based CRM package and you begin to accrue useful data, you are in the hands of the service provider. If you become dissatisfied, how do you make sure you can get the data back, and in a format you can reuse in an alternative package?

From the perspective of an ordinary company which might use cloud services as part of their IS portfolio, switching costs are harder to envisage, although the use of a browser only interface to their outward-facing systems might prevent customers without high-performance computing available locally, from moving to a client/server-based solution offered by the competition.

Much research has already been carried out about how the web in general has changed the way that suppliers and customers interact. Cloud-based purchasing organisations may well be an obvious extension to the sorts of enterprises that have grown to help smaller businesses club together, to gain economies of scale and to change the power balance between themselves and suppliers.

e-Business is far from new, and we do understand some of the dynamics in this marketplace. One, as we saw with the advent of Web 2.0, was that the look and feel of the seller's site really is the equivalent of their shop front. A failure to adopt newer technologies when they come along is likely to, eventually, push customers away as they look for the easier search interface, or the instant chat facility that is missing from the older interface. There will, doubtless be some equivalent pressure for sellers to be seen to move with the times and have a presence in the cloud, even if that doesn't mean they actually have to change much technically.

As to the final question, there can be no doubt that the basis of competition will change with cloud. As we saw in Chap. 3 (Social, Political and Economic Aspects of the Cloud), low costs mean many more potential suppliers (described as the long tail) can get to market very easily.

Here we have answered these questions from a general perspective. All organisations will be different and will have to ask these questions for themselves, which will give rise to countless alternative possible answers. We now go on to examine in more detail some of the key factors that will affect where cloud computing goes from here.

12.2 Examining the Gartner Hype Curve

Gartner has a great way of describing the usual development path for ICT technologies called the hype curve. They are a firm of renowned consultants with the breadth of experience to enable them to recognise key technologies as they appear. The curve begins with a steep climb up to '*The Peak of Inflated Expectations*'. The suggestion is that someone has a good technological idea. It is seen by the press and PR professionals and is talked about as the next wonderful technology, even before it is fully developed, a process which, in itself, generates lots of positive spin as non-risk-averse IT professionals begin to fear being left behind. '*First-player advantage*' is also an oft used phrase at this time. If you adopt a new successful technology before the competition, then you will gain a period of competitive advantage, no matter how short.

The Peak's title indicates what normally happens here. Too much is read into the technology's advantages, and its disadvantages are forgotten, leading to highly inflated expectations from early adopters. As people begin to use the technology, they begin to see that all is not rosy. Usually there are downsides to new technologies. Perhaps costs are high for early adopters as economies of scale from mass production or adoption are not yet available. Or perhaps it just does not do all the things that people had said it would. And so it tumbles down to the '*Trough of Disillusionment*' where the hype is outweighed by the cold light of reality.

At this point, the technology is in danger of disappearing off the graph. If there are sufficient negative reactions from the market, it may just be quietly dropped (e.g. Microsoft Vista) or fail as a business idea (such as NeXT) or just become a niche product used by special interest groups (e.g. OS/2).

What investors in the technology are hoping for is that the uses and advantages will eventually be significant enough to halt the decline and allow the technology to become widely used, as it begins to be understood in the '*slope of enlightenment*' before ultimately entering the '*plateau of productivity*'.

Gartner has created a hype curve specifically for the subject of cloud computing (Fig. 12.1). We have looked at some of these elements throughout this book, but there are some interesting things to read from the graph itself (Fig. 12.1):

- Public cloud is ahead of private cloud in terms of heading towards general acceptability.
- Using cloud to store data is even further ahead.
- Virtualisation is on the *slope of enlightenment*, but of course it had a head start since we have seen virtualisation used in IT infrastructures for many years now.

Depending upon when you are reading this, you will be able to see which of these predictions comes (or came) true. Either way, the following are interesting observations from the graph.

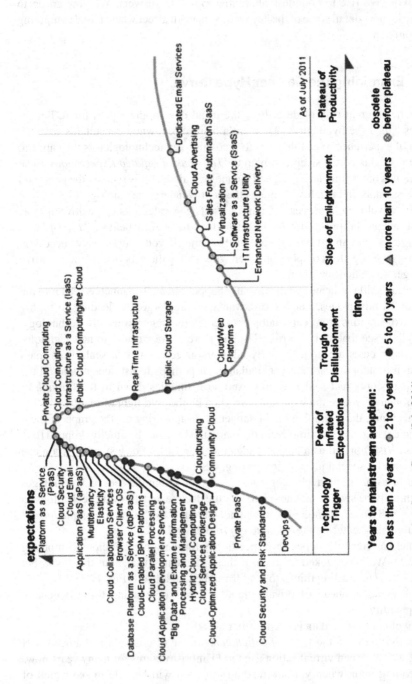

Fig. 12.1 Hype cycle for cloud computing. Source: Gartner (July 2011)
This figure does not represent Gartner's current view of the marketplace and should be viewed in historical context. This is a condition of approval by the copyright holder Gartner Inc

12.2.1 On the Way Up

- *Security and risk standards.* We have covered this in detail earlier. In short, until the domain matures sufficiently to allow for standards in the areas of security and data exchange, the entire cloud experiment is still somewhat uncertain.
- *Cloud-enabled BPM (or business process as a service).* Business process management (BPM) is not new. It is the activity of modelling processes, for example, the sales process, within a business with the intention of hoping to improve them. Some early adopters would argue that this is already on the plateau stage. Cordys (http://www.cordys.com/), for example, has customers worldwide using their cloud-based BPM system which boasts 'Google Apps Integration + Workflow and BPM'. They seem to be using the cloud as a way to improve the slightly tainted image that ERP systems have received in some quarters in the past, based on their Baan background. SAP too has a well-defined cloud strategy, though it sees cloud more as one approach, not wanting to move away from their already successful traditional platform delivery, and BPM is part of that cloud platform.
- *Big data.* Globally we collect unimaginably large amounts of data. This takes the form, for example, of business information, scientific readings and social interactions. IBM is one of the big players that have spotted the need that this brings. On their website, they say:

> Everyday, we create 2.5 quintillion bytes of data–so much that 90% of the data in the world today has been created in the last 2 years alone.

Big data consists of datasets that grow so large (beyond terabytes into exabytes and beyond) that they cannot be easily manipulated or analysed by standard RDBMSs or data warehousing and data mining techniques. A good insight of this area is available from a recent McKinsey report (Manyika et al. 2011)

However, the authors argue that this is placed incorrectly on the hype curve as this phenomenon is clearly very much here to stay. Companies must find ways of understanding the data they capture if they are to succeed and so there can be no doubt that, whatever happens with cloud computing, big data techniques will reach the plateau. Moreover, the benefits that cloud-based database technologies offer (see the data in the cloud chapter) will be a significant driver towards cloud being a requirement rather than a possibility.

12.2.2 Towards Disillusionment

IaaS. As part of research by CIO (http://www.cio.co.uk/), the head of IT at Oddbins, a UK-wide chain of wine and beverage retailers, is quoted as saying, in response to the question: Is there too much hype around cloud and IaaS?

No. The cloud and IaaS are a positive move towards reducing an organisation's capital outlay and providing a more structured and stable infrastructure.

Oddbins, though doubtless leaders in their field, with a turnover of $67 m are not in the big league, and yet they are looking to IaaS as a way to cut capital outlay.

This evidence of adoption by everyday businesses may demonstrate that IaaS is already on the plateau.

12.2.3 Upwards Again

Virtualisation. IBM rightly reminds us that the idea of virtualising the processes of a computer goes back 60 years to the days when mainframe was king. There is much useful information on their developer web pages that is about application virtualisation (Jones 2011).

What is important to note is that virtualisation is neither new nor the sole domain of the big providers: VMware and Microsoft Hyper-V. Optimising the utilisation of expensive computing resources makes virtualisation a winner, even without cloud.

12.3 Future Directions

It is clear that the best we can do is guess what the future holds for cloud computing. However, that does not mean we should avoid foretelling. Indeed, given the speed with which technologies change and develop, to do so is to run the risk of being left behind. This section, then, is a mixture of prophesies from a variety of sources, and it is for the reader to decide how realistic and how useful they will prove. One way to try and avoid random poor predictions is to ask lots of people for their views, especially knowledgeable people. In a recent survey of more than 800 Internet literate people, including industry experts, the Pew Internet & American Life Project were able to say:

> Technology experts and stakeholders say they expect they will 'live mostly in the cloud' in 2020 and not on the desktop, working mostly through cyberspace-based applications accessed through networked devices. (Anderson and Rainie 2010)

In the same report, 72% of experts said that most people will be using cloud technologies for everyday computing needs, rather than having a local PC. Even this high level of agreement does not guarantee that the prediction will come true. But it does give us a feeling for the way people in the domain are thinking. If you were a PC manufacturer, it would certainly be an appropriate time to review your long-term strategy.

Another indicator of the likely continued growth of cloud is the headlong rush that marketing and advertising departments are in, to include the word *cloud* in their copy. Functionality, previously described as web based, is now being regularly described as cloud based.

Relatively simple, everyday business tasks are being ported into the cloud environment. There are many examples of companies suddenly including pictures of clouds in their adverts. Some adverts try and cover all bases by saying their products are 'online cloud-based' or 'web-based cloud applications'. So we shall see cloud find its way into all aspects of life since it seems to attract customers!

The boundaries between PCs, tablets and smartphones are continuing to blur, and the increased appetite for mobile computing that this feeds will push more and more users into the clouds. On top of this blurring, the convergence of mobile technologies and cloud is already happening rapidly.

We can describe mobile cloud as the provision of an enabling infrastructure to mobile devices. After all, the smaller the device, the more appealing it will be for heavy processing and data storage to take place on some almighty server somewhere else. In a far-sighted, pre-cloud, Intel research report (Balan et al. 2002), the idea of cyber foraging is discussed:

> Meeting mobile users' ever-growing expectations requires computing and data storage ability beyond that of a tiny mobile computer with a small battery. How do we reconcile these contradictory demands?

We conjecture that cyber foraging, construed as 'living off the land', may be an effective way to solve this dilemma. The idea is to dynamically augment the computing resources of a wireless mobile computer by exploiting nearby compute and data staging servers.

In an environment where good broadband is widely available, mobile-to-cloud-to-mobile application combinations will enable this cyber foraging. A small mobile device, thoroughly incapable of processing millions of rows of data, for example, can initiate a link to a cloud-based resource and commission that resource to do the work on its behalf, managing the remote process as it happens. It is not really that different to today's standard client/server concepts, just that we now have very small and mobile clients!

The mobile device brings things to the party too. GPS and location information is creating a whole new set of location-aware applications. Already being developed are systems that combine patient health sensing devices with location information so that an alarm can be sent, to not only say that a patient is having a heart attack, but that it is on the corner of the high street, so the first responders know exactly where to attend.

Location-aware social networking is also already with us. But this too resurrects our old worry—security. Allowing systems to know our location so friends get more opportunities to meet us is one thing, but how do we prevent that information being monitored by others for evil purposes?

We should not forget that some of the changes will not be specifically about the technology, but that the technology allows new forms of business practice and social interaction to take place. As we have seen, there are several key driving factors that will significantly alter the way that IT is used in the future:

- The staggering volumes of data being stored
- The fact that this data is stored in many places
- The demand by consumers for easy (and cheap) access to applications

All of these factors play into the strengths of cloud. Indeed, it might be argued that they actually require the cloud as a prerequisite. And they will also doubtless trigger new business ideas and ways of conducting business and building software.

New combinations may happen to enable this. With components specifically written for Azure and Amazon EC2, for example, Zend has created the Zend PHP cloud application platform (http://www.zend.com/en/products/php-cloud/). This includes simple cloud API (http://simplecloud.org/), which allows the authoring of portable code, able to run across multiple cloud platforms (such as Microsoft, Amazon and Rackspace) and invoke their different services with one identical call. This is more than simply porting an IDE to the cloud and will have called for agreement from many organisations which traditionally keep themselves to themselves.

Not all of the future expansion of cloud will be business applications focused. In 2010 Microsoft launched Mediaroom 2.0 (Microsoft 2010) which:

> … can be deployed by operators as their entertainment cloud powering the delivery of a complete television service, including cloud digital video recording (DVR), on-demand features, interactive applications, and access to both operator-hosted content and externally hosted content such as Internet TV. The operators' service can be enjoyed by their subscribers on multiple screens including the TV (with Mediaroom set-top box), Windows Media Center, Web browsers (for Windows-based PCs and Macs), Xbox 360.

Apple's hitherto unassailable position as leaders of the cloud entertainment market will come under attack from many quarters as the market opens up. Already recently released is Amazon's cloud player which allows the user to play music on an Android device or kindle fire, or browser, streaming the binary data from the cloud. Its major advantage is that it does not require any local storage, thus freeing the user from disk size constraints.

Home security is another likely area for growth because of a cloud platform's ability to control remote devices and see outputs from them anywhere on a variety of devices. A new service from ADT (ADT 2012), for example, is called hosted video and is a:

> …cloud-based video storage and monitoring security service enabling you or your authorized employees the ability to access real-time or recorded surveillance video anytime, anywhere via any web-enabled device at an affordable cost.

In Chap. 7, we explored advances in the use of collective intelligence, for example, in constructing effective recommendation engines. We can only expect these to continue together with the further application of artificial intelligence to social network and user-generated multimedia data. Active, large-scale commercial and academic research in areas such as biologically inspired algorithms (e.g. genetic programming) is likely to increase the intelligence of these tools and give them seemingly 'human-like' abilities. The cloud is an ideal environment in which to operate. For example, I am currently editing this book in the cloud using Google Docs. Potentially, intelligent tools could be analysing my every key stroke and mouse click, 'reading' the text, 'viewing' any multimedia data and categorising my 'profile' via comparison with other users. This analysis could lead to personalisation of the tool to improve my experience, to general future enhancements of the tool and, of course, to commercially advantageous strategies such as targeted ads.

The concept of cloud bringing IT as a utility has been discussed in this book and was introduced in Chap. 1. When this concept becomes reality, it will allow whole new business models to evolve. Think of the way we regard electricity, one of our core utilities, and we see how significantly different it is to the way we think of other products and services a business has to purchase. Very few organisations think twice about 'outsourcing' their electricity supply. In-house electricity production, where it happens, is often as a backup from a diesel-powered generator.

How big a leap would it be to think of data storage the same way? To an extent that is already happening, of course, with the elastic nature of public cloud allowing ad hoc storage to cope with processing peaks.

In these 'greener' days, some companies and individuals are using solar and wind generation to supply their electrical needs. If they generate more than they can use, in the UK, the Electricity Board will purchase that electricity and supply it elsewhere, reducing their own need to generate.

What if the same model were to be used on server farms? What if one company's spare space could become another company's response to a spike in demand? The technology is already available, but of course there are many hurdles to overcome such as security. But in 10 years time, who knows, this could happen.

The point here is that, with technologies changing so rapidly, almost anything is possible. A sensible business will monitor and review opportunities as they occur. Some may be less risk averse and try some new ideas out. Some of those will fail. But some, maybe even ones as initially implausible as the one above, may just catch on. After all, the guy from Lotus 1-2-3 who famously said: *'We don't see Windows as a long-term graphical interface for the masses'* was somewhat adrift with his prediction.

12.4   What Do Other People Think About the Future of Cloud?

There can be little doubt that cloud computing helps to bring us closer to an era of ubiquitous computer access. For many, the benefits this brings in terms of being able to do business or communicate from anywhere at any time, so great that they think nothing should get in the way.

And yet there are potential dangers in having computing at the centre of everything. Research by Lorenz M. Hilty et al. (2004), for example, suggests that:

> [Based on the research] it turned out that Pervasive Computing bears potential risks to health, society, and/or the environment in the following fields: Non-ionizing radiation, stress imposed on the user, restriction of consumers' and patients' freedom of choice, threats to ecological sustainability, and dissipation of responsibility in computer-controlled environments.

If you are reading this, you are quite likely to be an enthusiast for technology. As professionals in the field, we do need to be cautious and always check our natural assumption that all advances are for the greater good. To quote Isaac Asimov:

> I do not fear computers. I fear lack of them.

And to quote comedian Emo Philips:

> A computer once beat me at chess, but it was no match for me at kick boxing.

Many factors will actually effect whether or not cloud is successfully adopted. In their research paper, Low et al. (2011) found:

> … that relative advantage, top management support, firm size, competitive pressure, and trading partner pressure characteristics have a significant effect on the adoption of cloud computing.

None of these factors are purely technological. In other words, decisions about technology adoption are not exclusively in the hands of the specialists.

12.5 Views from the Industry

We asked a few leading sources in the trade what they thought would happen with cloud in the future. What follows is a digest of some of their thoughts. They are presented in no particular order.

> "Today, cloud Computing has matured operationally to delivery the strategically and tactical value expected. Companies not willing to learn from the hyper-cycle history will not reap the benefits and will eventually struggle to thrive and survive. On the other hand, companies that are able to adopt and innovate their business model will create and deliver value in new ways, thrive and gain a competitive advantage."
>
> Henrik von Scheel, Director at NEO 7EVEN and ethority GmbH
>
> "For those tasked with engaging cloud services, they will recognize that the value of the service. But soon the shift in thinking will be around the cloud ecosystem. Here is my definition of a cloud ecosystem:
>
> "A Cloud Ecosystem is the organisation of cloud services to facilitate the execution of business processes. Service-level agreements for those relationships will be oriented around the process and not the individual services. In turn, Enterprise operations can be mapped and executed with quality standards within the ecosystems.
>
> "This evolution of thinking will demand more from the cloud providers. In the end only a few cloud ecosystem providers will prevail. Companies like Salesforce, SAP, and NetSuite have already made great headway to become Cloud Ecosystem providers. The importance of this move will have a profound effect on the industry and for businesses in general. All other cloud providers will have to find a way to participate with Cloud Ecosystem provider's environments."
>
> IT Executive and consultant, Sina Moatamed (http://www.manufacturing-executive. com/people/sinam)

One factor in the successful adoption of cloud will be that of geography. When asked, Jie Song, Associate Professor at the Software College, Northeastern University, in China observed:

> "The network speed is important for cloud computing user experience. But the network speed in China is very slow, so something must be done in the next few years to improve the speed, or it will become a big obstacle. Standardisation is a key factor in the development of cloud computing. A standard unified interface for different vendors' access provided by cloud platform is needed. Cloud is just started to develop in China, and is getting more and more attention. In universities and large corporations, cloud is a hot topic now."

Ajaz Ahmed, founder of Legal365.com and board member at Yorkshire Forward, says:

"I believe that cloud technologies are only just starting to take off and as we see more and more smart phones and tablet devices with apps instead of software and browser based solution we won't even think of the cloud, we'll just take it for granted. I use Evernote and every time I see a webpage I like I just press the Evernote button and clip the webpage, I can then view it from all my devices, I don't even think about the cloud.

"A lot more software will be moving to SaaS and Apps, mobile and tablets will have the cloud at their heart by default and people will expect to have access to their data from whatever device they are using, the days of being tied to one device are slowing dying."

For Agrawal et al. (2011), one of the key areas of importance for cloud will be with scalable databases:

"Scalable database management systems (DBMS)—both for update intensive application workloads as well as decision support systems for descriptive and deep analytics—are a critical part of the cloud infrastructure and play an important role in ensuring the smooth transition of applications from the traditional enterprise infrastructures to next generation cloud infrastructures."

This serves to remind us that cloud actually encompasses many functionalities, and some of them may succeed where others fail, and yet cloud itself may be seen as a success because some of it succeeds.

Of course there are already some areas of cloud which are already successful. As we saw in the social and political chapter, SNS and other, more person-focused elements of cloud are here to stay and seeing tremendous growth.

Storage of music is one such area. It's not unusual for wealthy Western families to have several devices which can play music. Removing the need to store the music locally by having a cloud account opens up whole new possibilities in terms of using your music. End users have proved very willing to pay for flexibility.

12.6   Summing Up

Cloud computing is here to stay! There will be limitations to overcome and trade-offs and interdependencies to manage. Though, the cloud technology, standards and business models are maturing fast to offer benefits to users and vendors alike. For businesses, the real advantage/benefit of the cloud will emerge from innovation and differentiation. Cost advantage will not have a long-term impact as IT resources will be more accessible and affordable. So the competitive threshold will be lowed as a result. The long-term impact will emerge as a result of careful, smart and strategic and innovative planning, design, orchestration and deployment or IT resources via cloud to add business value. The core of this will be business process innovation and IT portfolio management and their alignment.

Moving to utility model computing will change the competition landscape as a result of corrosion of technology-based competitive advantage that comes from technology investment in unique and expensive infrastructure. This is not to say that these will disappear, but the dynamics of competition in this space will change, and much smaller players will be able to raise the bar for competition as advanced tech-

nological capabilities are quickly commoditized. The shift of resources and responsibilities in a cloud model results in shifting the management of technical complexity
to cloud providers; hence, there will be less steep learning curve in being able to
engage and tap into innovation which in turn results in reducing the risk of adoption
and increasing the quick leverage factor.

Cloud computing is perhaps only the natural evolution of how we do IT and is
going to be part and parcel of future computing. It will continue to influence practice in many areas of IT in the way we plan, strategise and operationalise IT
resources. Cloud will continue to have a defining role in business models, standards,
value chains, SOA and enterprise architectures and ecosystems to better serve the
business and the users.

12.7   Review Questions

The answers to these questions can be found in the text of this chapter.
1. What are some of the future challenges of cloud computing adoption? Research
   and identify top five trends in cloud computing enabling technologies and business models.
2. How do you envisage the cloud computing mature in different industries? Give
   some examples.
3. Discuss some of the business and technology opportunities that cloud computing
   can offer in the future?
4. What do you consider to be the key drivers for cloud computing flight path into
   the future? Give some examples of business and technology.
5. What is your interpretation of Gartner hype curve? Critically discuss your point
   of view.

12.8   Extended Study Activities

These activities require you to research beyond the contents of this book and can be
approached individually for the purposes of self-study or used as the basis of group
work.
1. Based on some of the views in this chapter and your own research, develop a
   roadmap for adopting emerging technologies for business advantage. What factors would you consider and why?
2. Discuss the relationship between emerging technologies and business innovation? What would be the impact of IT commoditisation on future business
   models?
3. Visit the website of Skills Framework for the Information Age (SFIA: www.sfia.
   org.uk/). Access the SFIA framework. In light of future developments in IT, for
   example, cloud computing, and future skills requirements, map your competencies

to appropriate statements from the framework and create a professional development plan. How do you think the cloud maturity over the years will change the IT competencies and skills needs?

References

ADT: Video Security Goes to the Cloud. ADT Whitepaper. http://www.adt.com/commercial-security/products/hosted-video (2012)

Agrawal, D., Das, S. Abbadi, A.E.: Big Data and Cloud Computing: Current State and Future Opportunities. Department of Computer Science University of California, Santa Barbara EDBT 2011, March 22–24, 2011, Uppsala, Sweden (2011)

Anderson, J., Rainie, L.: The Future of Cloud Computing. Pew Research Center's Internet & American Life Project, Washington, DC, 11 June 2010

Balan, R., Flinn, J., Satyanarayanan, M., Sinnamohideen, S., Yang, H.: The case for cyber foraging. 10th ACM SIGOPS European Workshop, St. Emilion, France, September 2002

Hilty, L.M., Som, C., Köhler, A.: Assessing the human, social, and environmental risks of pervasive computing, human and ecological risk assessment. Int. J. **10**(5), 853–874 (2004)

Jones, M.T.: Application virtualisation, past and future, An introduction to application virtualisation. IBM Developer Works, ibm.com/developerWorks, IBM (2011)

Low, C., Chen, Y., Wu, M.: Understanding the determinants of cloud computing adoption. Indus. Manag. Data Syst. **111**(7), 1006–1023 (2011)

Manyika, J., et al.: Big Data: The Next Frontier for Innovation, Competition, and Productivity. McKinsey Global Institute, McKinsey & Company (May 2011)

Microsoft: Microsoft Unites Software and Cloud Services to Power New TV Experiences. Press Release, 06 Jan 2010

Index